Beyond the Sunshine

A Timeline of Florida's Past

Rick Baker

Pineapple Press, Inc.
Sarasota, Florida

Inquiries should be addressed to:
Pineapple Press, Inc.
P.O. Box 3889
Sarasota, Florida 34230

www.pineapplepress.com

Unless otherwise credited, all images are from the Florida Photographic Collection of the State Library and Archives of Florida.

Library of Congress Cataloging-in-Publication Data

Names: Baker, Rick (Richard Murray), 1956- author.
Title: Beyond the sunshine : a timeline of Florida's past / Rick Baker.
Description: Sarasota, Florida : Pineapple Press, Inc., [2017] | Includes
  bibliographical references and index.
Identifiers: LCCN 2017014354 (print) | LCCN 2017016685 (ebook) | ISBN
  9781683340157 (ebook) | ISBN 9781683340133 (hardback) | ISBN 9781683340140
  (pbk.)
Subjects: LCSH: Florida–History–Chronology.
Classification: LCC F311 (ebook) | LCC F311 .B33 2017 (print) | DDC
  975.9–dc23
LC record available at https://lccn.loc.gov/2017014354

First Edition
10 9 8 7 6 5 4 3 2 1

Design by Modern Alchemy LLC
Printed and bound in the USA

This book is dedicated to all Floridians, past and present, whose struggles, talents, toils and successes have brought us to this point in the journey.

The further backward you can look . . .
the further forward you can see.

Winston Churchill

Contents

Pensacola

Fort
Walton
Beach

Panama City

Tallahassee

Jacksonville

St. Augustine

Gainesville

Ocala

Daytona Beach

Orlando

Lakeland

Clearwater

Tampa

St. Petersburg

Bradenton

Sarasota

West
Palm
Beach

Fort Myers

Ft. Lauderdale

Naples

Hialeah

Miami

Key West

Key Largo

Santa Rosa
Escambia
Okaloosa
Holmes
Jackson
Walton
Washington
Bay
Calhoun
Liberty
Gulf
Franklin
Gadsden
Leon
Jefferson
Wakulla
Taylor
Madison
Hamilton
Suwannee
Lafayette
Columbia
Baker
Nassau
Duval
Union
Bradford
Clay
Alachua
Putnam
Flagler
Dixie
Gilchrist
Levy
Marion
Volusia
Citrus
Sumter
Lake
Seminole
Hernando
Orange
Pasco
Osceola
Hillsborough
Polk
Brevard
Pinellas
Hardee
Indian
River
Manatee
Highlands
Okeechobee
Sarasota
St Lucie
DeSoto
Martin
Charlotte
Glades
Lee
Hendry
Palm Beach
Collier
Broward
Monroe
Miami-Dade

Suwannee River
St. Johns River
Kissimmee River
Peace River
Caloosahatchee River
Lake
Okeechobee

N
W E
S

Informing the Future

Beyond the Sunshine is written for all Floridians. It is especially intended for those who make decisions impacting the future of our cities, regions, and state. Leaders who are informed by our past have a foundation to better guide us forward. It is in the hope of providing that foundation that I have written the chapters that follow.

This book is a timeline history. The format enables even casual readers to gain a thorough understanding of Florida's past quickly and in an approachable form.

As the reader walks through these pages describing the individuals and natural events that have brought Florida to where we stand today, it becomes apparent that there are certain characteristics that make our state unique and that draw the world here like a magnet.

First, Florida is a free spirit. It has always attracted risk takers, entrepreneurs, and dreamers. Hamilton Disston bets his family inheritance on 4 million acres of swampland. Flagler and Plant invest fortunes in railroads and magnificent hotels in the hope that people will come. Governor Napoleon Bonaparte Broward—his name itself is a statement—gambles mightily on a plan to completely overhaul the state's ecosystem with dreams of an agricultural empire. Periodic real estate booms and busts create and crater fortunes. Citrus growers fight back freezes and disease. With Florida as a launching pad, a modern generation of explorers races beyond the pull of Earth, while Walt Disney quietly assembles land in central Florida and creates a kingdom that attracts a global audience of those who still believe in magic.

From the world's first passenger airline and air conditioner to the nation's most contentious presidential election recount, Florida's entrepreneurial, self-confident, and independent spirit has produced a state on the cutting edge of the human drama.

Second, the prosperity of Florida is inseparably tied to the health of its land. Our tourism and retirement businesses will only thrive if our beaches, waterways, and air are clean and only if there is enough water for both people and our natural places. Modern industries of all types are attracted to states that place a premium on quality of life. Floridians and visitors alike want to dive in the reefs along the Keys, surf on South Beach, tube the Ichetucknee River, canoe down the Suwannee, enjoy the Panhandle beaches, and fish in the Atlantic, Gulf, and our many lakes. They want to know that the snowy egret and great blue heron will always be around and that the Everglades' "River of Grass," one of the nation's most important ecosystems, will be returned to its prior health.

This is our watch. We are now the Floridians who are charged with keeping the free spirit of the Sunshine State alive and passing on a natural environment that is better than the one we received. As we make decisions going forward, let us ask questions that reflect our understanding of the past. Will the paths we choose encourage the entrepreneurial spirit that has driven our predecessors to build this remarkable place? And will the directions we select enhance the natural environment that defines the character and heart of our state? With wise choices, we will advance boldly into Florida's next chapter of adventure and progress.

As someone who has spent most of his life living in north, central, and south Florida, I feel blessed to have had the opportunity to live in the best state in the best nation on Earth. I hope you enjoy reading our collective history as much as I have enjoyed learning it, living it, and sharing it with you.

Rick Baker

> *"The miracle of the light pours over the green and brown expanse of saw grass and of water, shining and slow-moving below, the grass and water that is the meaning and the central fact of the Everglades of Florida. It is a river of grass."*
>
> **Marjory Stoneman Douglas**
> *The Everglades: River of Grass*

Overview of Florida's Past
Beyond the Sunshine

Florida will always be about sunny days and ocean breezes. But there is a Florida story beyond the sunshine: the story of an exotic and beautiful place, with dreamers, explorers, scoundrels, and saints. It is a tale that begins with a mangrove wilderness in America's Southeast, inhabited for thousands of years by evolving native cultures until the Spanish arrive after the discovery of the New World in 1492. A couple of decades later, a Spanish explorer arrives on the coast of today's Sunshine State and names his discovery *La Florida*, Spanish for "land of flowers." Another arrives on Florida's west coast and leads the first European expedition that crosses North America from the Atlantic to the American West, eventually arriving in today's Mexico City.

A gator warms itself in the sun in the Florida Everglades.

The Florida native cultures succumb to European conquest and disease. Creek natives migrate from Alabama and Georgia, becoming the Seminoles. They expand throughout the peninsula until a future American president prosecutes the first of three wars that will result in the Indian nation being almost eradicated from the state, but not conquered.

Settlers populate St. Augustine and Pensacola, then spread to other parts of the peninsula. The sons of Florida take sides in the nation's Civil War, and railroads make their way through the state. At the dawn of the twentieth century, cities throughout Florida obtain roads, telegraphs, telephones, electricity, schools, and trolleys. Tourism develops as a core industry, in addition to cattle, agriculture, citrus, and fishing.

A massive effort is undertaken to drain the land around Lake Okeechobee, including portions of the Everglades, in order to expand the state's agricultural industry and control flooding. The effort is remarkably successful at achieving its purpose, but it also has a dramatic and negative impact on the ecosystem of the Florida Everglades and the plants and animals that depend on it for their existence. Striking the balance between the water needs of south Florida, the preservation of the Everglades, and the need to control flooding will test the political will of Florida politicians into the twenty-first century.

The emerging state supports the nation in the Great War, booms during the 1920s, suffers during the Great Depression, and hosts military training bases during World War II.

Florida prospers with the nation during the post-war years. Military industries arrive. In the 1960s, the divisions within the state reflect those of a nation struggling through the Cold War, Watergate, the Vietnam War, and the Civil Rights movement. The state expands its tourism industry with the growth of beach hotels, while Walt Disney announces that a magic kingdom is coming soon to Orlando. A space industry grows, and for the first time in the planet's history, a man steps off Florida soil and then onto the moon.

During the first decade of the twenty-first century, Florida sets out on an aggressive path to expand its technology sector and improve its education system. The nation's urban centers prosper, a trend reflected in many of Florida's major cities. As the period covered by this book closes, the nation is at war with terrorism and is struggling through the Great Recession, but the hope and confidence in Florida's future is unshakable.

It is an American story. It is a Florida story. A story flavored with sunshine, sandy beaches, and swampland. And ultimately it is a story about a beautiful and exotic corner of America that, in a short slice of mankind's journey, transforms beyond its roots into a special place where those who believe can still come to pursue their dreams.

The next day the governor raised standards in behalf of Your Majesty and took possession of the country in Your Royal name . . . the Indians of that village arrived . . . they made many gestures and threats, and it seemed as if they were telling us to leave the country.

Alvar Núñez Cabeza de Vaca, treasurer of the Narváez expedition, describing the 1528 landfall on Florida's west coast. He is seemingly perplexed that the natives don't welcome them.

Chapter 1

Florida's Early Years: Prehistory Through 1815

Humans crossing the Bering Straits into Alaska traverse the North American continent, eventually making their way to the Florida peninsula. For thousands of years, the peninsula is inhabited by aboriginal cultures who leave temple and burial mounds, along with mounds called middens, which are primarily shellfish trash piles, on the coast. Some of these mounds can still be seen today. The natives develop civilizations harvesting shellfish, hunting, using primitive tools, growing corn, and developing religious and social structures.

1513: First European Explorers land
1564: French Fort Caroline
1565: Spanish St. Augustine
1763: British Rule
1783: Britain cedes Florida to Spain

A series of Spanish explorers—Juan Ponce de León, Pánfilo de Narváez, Hernando de Soto, and others—come with the authority of the Spanish crown in search of gold but will never leave the Western Hemisphere alive. They will die without riches but will leave behind angry natives and disease for which the natives have no immunity. By the end of the era, most of the original native tribes vanish; however, the Creek, who enter Florida in the mid-1700s and become known as Seminoles, expand their tribes in the northern and central parts of the peninsula.

The Florida territory is occupied by France, claimed by Spain, and ceded to Britain. Toward the end of this era, a revolution creates a new United States of America, and Florida is again transferred to Spanish rule.

Throughout this book events in Florida are set in Roman (non-italics), and events outside Florida are set in *italics*.

A 13-foot-tall skeleton of a giant ground sloth, excavated in 1975 in the Daytona Bone Bed fossil site. The skeleton is on display at the Museum of Arts and Sciences in Daytona Beach.

Timeline

20,000 B.C.

Some historians estimate that this is the time of the greatest expanse of the intercontinental land bridge between today's Alaska and Russia. The bridge crosses today's Bering Strait and is sometimes referred to as "Beringia" or the "Bering Land Bridge." This is also believed to be the coldest period of the Pleistocene Ice Age, the planet's most recent Ice Age, estimated to have occurred between 70,000 B.C. and 8000 B.C. From 20,000 B.C. forward, the earth will begin to slowly warm, with a corresponding melting of ice and rise of sea level. By the end of the Ice Age the land bridge between the great continents will be gone.

11,500 B.C.

Historians believe that either before or during this era, humans enter North America through the Bering Land Bridge.

10,000 B.C.

Mammoths and mastodons were so abundant in Florida that their teeth are the most commonly found fossil remains in the state.

Historians estimate that nomads reach the Florida peninsula sometime before or during this era. The nomads are classified as "Paleo-Indians," the word *paleo* coming from the Greek adjective for "old." They hunt mastodons, giant bison, ground sloths, saber-toothed tigers, and other mammals. Sea level is much lower than today's level, and Florida's west coast is about one hundred miles west of where it is today.

8000 B.C.

Historians estimate that Florida's prehistoric animals become extinct as the last great Ice Age comes to an end. Temperature rise will accelerate, with a corresponding rise of the sea level as the planet's ice melts. Eventually, the Florida peninsula will narrow to its present width. As the sea rises and the Florida peninsula narrows to today's width, many of the early native sites found along Florida's earlier coast will be under water.

7500 B.C.

As the Florida Paleo-Indians develop and respond to environmental changes, they eventually evolve into a distinct Florida culture that archaeologists will label Archaic. The Archaic people live near wetlands and sources of water. They gather food and hunt. Shark and wolf teeth are attached to wood to create tools. They weave fabric using fibers from saw palmettos and sable palms. By 3000 B.C., the Archaic culture populations will expand to most parts of today's Florida. By 2000 B.C., they will learn to make multiple types of fired clay pottery. The Archaic period will end around 500 B.C. as cultures with regional distinctions emerge.

4000 B.C.
Settlements form along the St. Johns River.

3300 B.C.
Historians estimate that this is roughly the beginning of the Bronze Age in the Near East, an era when bronze will be used to make tools and weapons. Bronze is a mixture of tin and copper, creating a metal stronger than copper alone. The

period will begin at different times in different parts of the world and continue until about 500 B.C. The period before the Bronze Age, when stone was used to make tools and implements, is known as the Stone Age. The Bronze Age will be followed by the Iron Age.

3100 B.C.
Pharaoh Menes unites Upper and Lower Egypt, beginning the dynastic period of Egypt. The kingdom will develop quarrying, surveying, and construction techniques that enable it to create temples, obelisks, and the great pyramids.

3000 B.C.
Pottery begins in the Americas, in today's Colombia and Ecuador. In the southern portion of today's Florida peninsula, saw-grass begins to grow in what will become the Everglades ecosystem. The Seminoles will call the area *Pa-Hay-Okee* or "grassy water." By the twentieth century, the flow of the ecosystem will begin in central

A 1956 rendering of the Florida saber-toothed tiger and Pleistocene horses. The remains of saber-tooth tigers have turned up in several locations on both coasts of central Florida, the most famous coming from a sinkhole cave in Citrus County, known as Saber-Tooth Cave.

Florida's Lake Tohopekaliga and Lake Kissimmee, move down the Kissimmee River to Lake Okeechobee (a Seminole Indian term meaning "big water"), then south as a shallow river of grass to Florida Bay.

1800 B.C.

During this period the Mayan culture will develop, located in the tropical lowlands of today's Guatemala. It will grow into a great civilization and last for centuries until it abandons the remainder of its great stone cities in A.D. 900. During the sixth century A.D., the Maya Empire will be at its height of influence and power. The culture will reach a peak population of up to two million people, have about forty cities with populations up to 50,000, and be advanced in agriculture, pottery, writing, mathematics, and calendar-making. It will achieve great accomplishments in architecture and construction, including plazas, palace temples, and pyramids.

1200 B.C.

Historians estimate that this is roughly the beginning of the Iron Age in Mesopotamia, an era when iron is used to make cutting tools and weapons. Iron is produced when mined ore is heated in a stove and reduced.

500 B.C.

Regional Florida cultures emerge from the Archaic people and will often be later named for modern geographic landmarks that are near where they are identified. The cultures are generally contained within environmental and landform regions. They are defined by the types of tools they use (such as shell, bone, and stone), the mounds where they bury their dead or dispose of garbage, the design of their pottery, the food they grow and eat (e.g. corn, fish, and shellfish along coast), and other characteristics. They include:

- the *St. Johns* culture in the northeast and Atlantic coast (early post 500 B.C.);
- the *Deptford* culture around the coastal bend of Florida and inland (early post 500 B.C.);
- the *Swift Creek* culture in today's panhandle counties of Gadsden, Leon, and Jefferson (A.D. 100);
- the *Santa Rosa-Swift Creek* culture in the western panhandle (A.D. 100); and
- the *Belle Glade* culture, which develops in the large savanna around Lake Okeechobee, called Lake Mayaimi by the natives.

336 B.C.

Alexander the Great, at the age of twenty, succeeds his father, Philip II of Macedon. Beginning in 334 B.C., Alexander will lead his armies through Asia Minor and Egypt and east to the Indus River of India, creating one of the world's great empires. He is a student of Aristotle.

221 B.C.

Shih Huang-ti of the Chin Dynasty unifies China under his control.

6 B.C.–0

Historians' estimates of the probable date of birth of Jesus Christ at Bethlehem. The world will mark its calendar based on the life of Jesus, separating B.C. ("before Christ") from A.D. (Anno Domini, "in the year of the Lord").

A.D. 117

This year the Roman Empire controls the largest territory it will hold, stretching through much of Europe, Asia Minor, and North Africa.

300

The *Weeden Island* culture, which will continue until about A.D. 1000, emerges from the *Deptford, Swift Creek, Santa Rosa-Swift Creek,* and related cultures. It stretches from today's Sarasota County north through Florida and to Alabama. It is named for Weedon Island in today's St. Petersburg, where the Smithsonian Institution will conduct an extensive study and issue a report on October 14, 1924, although the different spelling of "Weeden" was adopted. Subcultures of Weeden Island include the *Cades Pond* culture in today's Alachua and Putnam Counties; the *Manasota* culture in the St. Petersburg-Tampa area; and the *North Peninsular Coast* culture around the Florida bend. Weeden Island villages gather shellfish along the coast, hunt, build burial and other mounds, and manufacture ornate ceramics. They have complex trading networks and social structures. The northern Weeden Island cultures will begin to grow corn around A.D. 800.

542

The bubonic plague devastates Europe.

600

Florida native cultures begin to develop into more complex societies with villages, village chiefs, village officials, and surrounding agricultural homesteads, justifying a departure from the Weeden Island culture classification:

- The *Alachua* culture in today's Alachua and Marion Counties (A.D. 600).
- The *Suwannee Valley* culture in northern peninsular Florida (A.D. 750).
- The *Safety Harbor* culture in today's St. Petersburg-Tampa region (A.D. 900).
- The *Fort Walton* culture in the panhandle (A.D. 1000).
- In southern Florida, late pre-Columbian cultures include the *Glades* culture in the large region stretching from southeast Florida to southwest Florida; and the *Caloosahatchee* culture along today's river with the same name.

1000

A February 9, 1915, photo of Turtle Mound near New Smyrna Beach on the Canaveral National Seashore. The turtle-shaped mound is an estimated 50 feet high and more than 600 feet long, and contains more than 35,000 cubic yards of shells, mostly oyster. It is the largest shell midden on the Florida coast, and was built by people of the Timucuan culture.

The Tocobagan thrive in today's Safety Harbor. They are called the *Safety Harbor* culture by some historians, and are part of the *Mississippian* Indian culture. Their area extends from Charlotte Harbor to Crystal Bay, near today's Crystal River. Tocobagans live in small villages with shell middens paralleling the shore, and they maintain separate temple and burial mounds. Their villages have ten to twenty houses and are presided over by a chief. The Tocobagans have a complex social structure with ceramics, jewelry, and extended trade. Shell midden, temple, and burial mounds from this era remain.

1100

During this century, a tribe begins in the Cusco region of today's Peru. In 1438, under the leadership of Sapa Inca ("paramount leader") Pachacuti, the tribe will develop a strong military and expand significantly to create the Inca Empire. Among other achievements, the people will build pyramids and a magnificent walled estate high in the Andes Mountains for the emperor Pachacuti. It is today's Machu Picchu.

Also during this century, a tribe who call themselves "Mexica" leave the region north of today's Mexico and travel south to a region in today's central Mexico. They will build pyramids and, in the early to mid-1300s, develop an extraordinary city at today's Mexico City that they call Tenochtitlán. The settlement becomes the center of the Aztec Empire.

1492

On August 3, Spanish Admiral Christopher Columbus leaves Palos, Spain, commanding three ships: the Nina, *the* Pinta, *and the* Santa Maria. *After a stop in the Canary Islands and a five-week journey across the Atlantic, he arrives in the Bahamas, landing on an island he names San Salvador. In December he will establish a small settlement in nearby Hispaniola. He had been searching for a western passage to the Indies but, instead, arrives in today's Americas.*

1493

In September, Columbus sets out with seventeen ships on his second voyage to the Americas. In November he arrives in Hispaniola, the settlement he established in 1492. After finding that the crew he left behind is dead and the settlement destroyed, he sails east in search of a better port location and settles La Isabella in today's Dominican Republic.

1507

On April 25, German geography professor Martin Waldseemüller publishes the first map displaying the New World as a continent separate from Asia. He names the continent "America" after Amerigo Vespucci, an explorer who has sailed for both Spain and Portugal. Vespucci claims to have discovered the continent in 1497, but historians mark his arrival on the mainland at 1499. Columbus first sighted the mainland coast of South America in early August 1498.

1513

On March 3, having received a royal charter from King Charles V of Spain for Puerto Rico and exploration to the north, Spaniard Juan Ponce de León's three ships leave Anasco Bay on the coast of Puerto Rico. He sails north through the Bahamas, then west toward the Atlantic Coast of today's Florida.

Juan Ponce de Leon, who arrives in Florida in 1513

On March 27, Ponce de León's expedition sights the Florida coast. He will come ashore in early April during the time of Holy Week's *Pascua Florida,* the "Feast of Flowers." Because of the time of the year and the beauty of the land, Ponce de León names his discovery "La Florida." His initial landing is likely north of today's Cape Canaveral, and he proceeds south to explore the coast. He sails around today's Miami and Florida Keys and up the Gulf coast. He lands again in a harbor that is believed to be today's Charlotte Harbor.

While ashore, the expedition engages in both trade and combat with the Calusa, the latter bringing casualties on both sides.

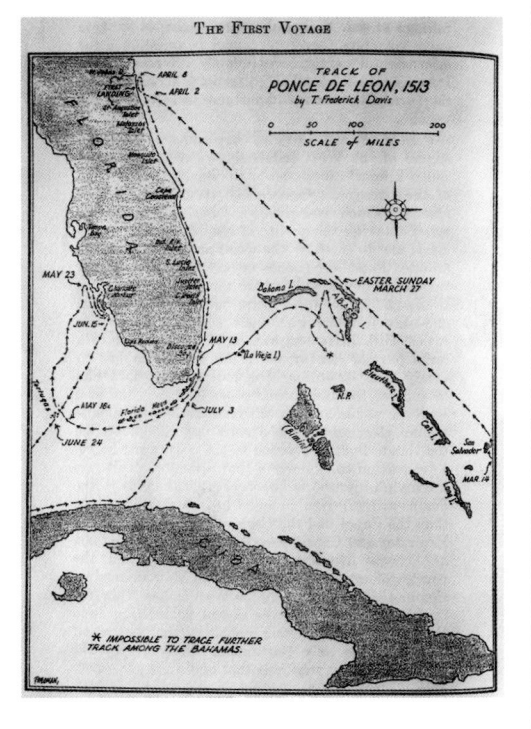

Map of Juan Ponce de Leon's first expedition to Florida

At the time the Spaniards arrive, the native population of today's Florida is estimated by some to be about 350,000. Among the Florida tribes present who have evolved from the early native cultures are:
- the *Matecumbe* in the Keys;
- the *Tequesta, Jeaga,* and *Ais* on the east coast;
- the highly populated *Calusa* in the southwest;
- the *Tocobaga* in the St. Petersburg-Tampa region;
- the *Ocale* near today's Ocala;
- the highly populated *Timucua* in the northeast;
- the *Apalachee* in the east panhandle; and
- the *Pensacola* in the west panhandle.

On May 14, Ponce de León departs the Gulf Coast for the journey back to Puerto Rico.

On September 25, Spanish conquistador and explorer Vasco Nuñez de Balboa first sights what the Spaniards call Mar de Sur, *the "South Sea." He is the first European to explore the eastern shore of today's Pacific Ocean. He arrives at the body of water after crossing the jungles of today's Panama. He claims the shores for Spain, opening the way for Spanish exploration and conquest along the western coast of South America. In November of 1520, the Portuguese explorer Magellan will later name the ocean* Pacifica, *meaning "peaceful."*

1519
On September 6, Ferdinand Magellan and his crew set sail from Spain with five ships to circumnavigate the globe for the first time. Magellan will be killed in today's Philippines during the trip, but his crew will complete the journey in 1522.

1520
Spaniard Juan Bono Quexo becomes the first European explorer to see the St. Johns River in northeast Florida. The natives call it "River of Lakes" and the Spaniards first call it "River of Currents." It will eventually be named after the Mission of St. Juan, located along the river.

1521
In late February, Ponce de León sails two ships with two hundred expedition members from Puerto Rico en route to La Florida. Although it is believed he lands near today's Port Charlotte in southwest Florida, his exact location is unclear. Upon landing the expedition becomes engaged in a major battle with natives, and many die on both sides. Ponce de León retreats to Cuba and will die in Havana of wounds suffered in the battle. As the Spaniards flee,

they leave behind a herd of Andalusian cattle that had been brought to feed the expedition. The cattle, from the Andalusia coastal region of Spain, are believed to be the first domesticated cattle in North America. Their presence is the starting point for a future industry that will be critical to Florida and the nation.

On August 13, the Aztec capital of Tenotchitlan, today's Mexico City, falls to Spanish conqueror Hernando Córtez. Aztec ruler Montezuma dies in the conquest.

1525

In the summer, Spanish explorer Lucas Vásquez de Ayllón assembles his ships in order to act on the royal letter he has received from King Charles V of Spain to explore New Andalusia, an area along North America's southern Atlantic coast, including today's Carolinas and Georgia. In 1526, Ayllón will set sail with a fleet of six ships and nearly six hundred Spanish, Caribbean, and African colonists, landing that year on the Atlantic coast in today's Georgia. He brings the first group of African slaves to the New World.

1526

In late September, Vásquez de Ayllón's expedition establishes the settlement of San Miguel de Gualdape, near today's Sapelo Sound, Georgia. Many colonists suffer from disease, lack of food, and cold. Vásquez de Ayllón dies on October 18 and, in mid-November, the expedition abandons the settlement and returns to the Antilles. Only about 150 of the original 600 make it back to Spanish settlements.

Pánfilo de Narváez, leader of the first European expedition to travel across the American continent. His journey starts in today's St. Petersburg and ends on the Pacific Coast of Mexico.

On December 11, King Charles V of Spain gives Pánfilo de Narváez a license to conquer and divide all the territory between the Rio de la Palmas in New Spain, today's Mexico, and New Andalusia. Narváez will search for gold and riches of the type taken by Cortéz in Mexico. Narváez's expedition will ultimately pass through today's Florida, Mississippi, Louisiana, Texas, Northern Mexico, and southwest United States, and will reach Mexico in 1536. They will be the first European expedition to cross from the Atlantic to the American West in the New World.

1527

On June 17, Narváez departs Spain, bound for Florida with five ships carrying almost 600 people, including sailors, officers, troops, and slaves (likely the second group of slaves brought to the New World), along with some family members. Their first stop, after about a week, will be the Canary Islands, where they will regroup before crossing today's Atlantic Ocean. By mid-September they will reach Hispaniola at the port of Santo Domingo in today's Dominican Republic. Narváez will add one ship in Santiago, Cuba. He will lose two ships and sixty men in a storm off Trinidad, Cuba. After taking time to acquire two replacement ships and waiting out the winter, the expedition will set sail on February 22, 1528. After storms and currents drive them into the Gulf of Mexico they will decide to proceed directly to Florida.

1528

On April 7, Narváez's expedition sights land on the west coast of Florida. When they reach the coast, they turn south and sail along the shore in order to determine the primary orientation of the land and to search for a harbor. The expedition's master pilot, Diego Miruelo, had advised of a large bay, today's Tampa Bay, which would make an ideal harbor. Narváez decides to stop looking for a harbor and, instead, sails his ships through an inlet, likely into today's Boca Ciega Bay, in order to prepare to come ashore near signs of a native village, which are seen from the ships. Historic evidence supports that his landing site is in the Jungle area of today's St. Petersburg, although the exact location of the landing is not certain. It is believed

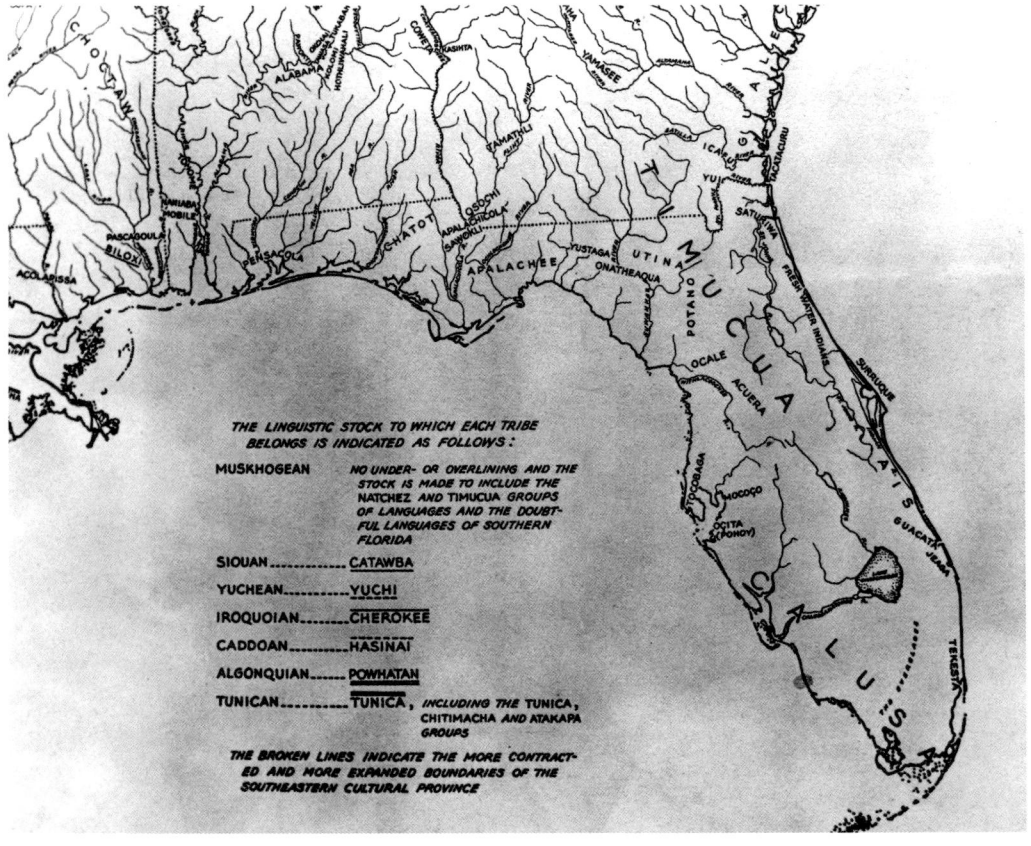

An early map showing native cultures in Florida at the time of Spanish exploration

that one thousand to two thousand natives live in the area around today's St. Petersburg at the time that the Spanish arrive.

On April 14, Narváez sends ashore a group led by Alonso Enríquez to meet with the natives. Enríquez is greeted by men dressed only in breechclouts and women in skirts woven from Spanish moss. The natives are heavily tattooed, some with ears and other body parts pierced, and decorated with pearls, bone and shell beads, and copper. The natives trade fish and venison to the Spanish for glass beads and other items. Enríquez reports back to Narváez that he saw no signs of gold or great wealth from the natives.

On April 15, Good Friday, Narváez and his landing party come ashore. Upon arriving, Narváez discovers that the natives encountered by Enríquez had fled overnight. A search of the village reveals small round houses made of tree trunks

and palmetto leaves, a large meeting house, fishing nets, and a single piece of gold—a rattle. Tomorrow, Narváez will declare himself royal governor of La Florida. He begins a march that will be chronicled in the 1542 memoirs of the expedition's treasurer, Álvar Núñez Cabeza de Vaca. Cabeza de Vaca will be one of the few to survive. After crossing the Pinellas Peninsula, the Spanish discover a large body of water and Narváez names it *La Bahia de la Cruz* ("Bay of the Cross"), today's Tampa Bay. They terrorize the local Tocobagan village of Ucita, killing many and pillaging the community while searching for gold. The force of three hundred who were brought ashore now march north in search of the "Apalachen," having been told by the Tocobagans that its people have gold.

On June 25, Narváez arrives in the land of the Apalachee. To reach the Apalachee region, Narváez travels north

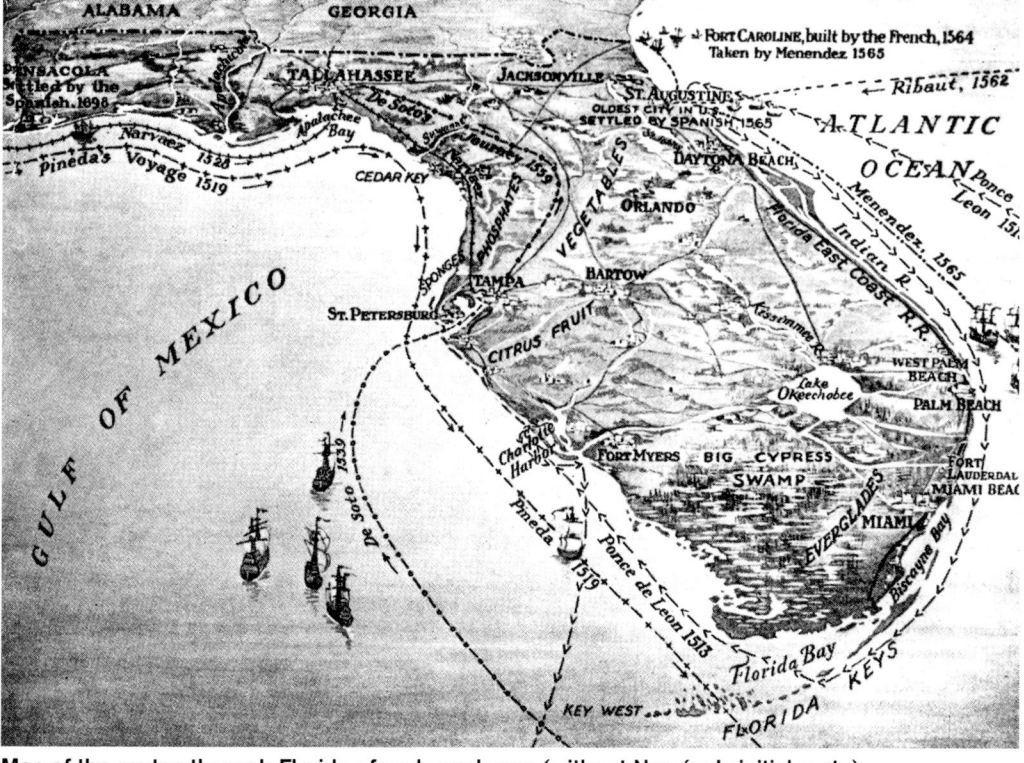

Map of the routes through Florida of early explorers (without Narváez's initial route)

from the Tocobagan Safety Harbor village, crosses today's Withlacoochee River into Alachua territory, moves north until crossing today's Suwannee River into Timucua territory, then north until crossing today's Aucilla River into Apalachee territory. The expedition encounters both friendly exchanges with the natives and fatal confrontations on the way. They also have lost all contact with their ships and remaining expedition members, and have no sure way of returning home.

The Apalachee are part of the Mississippian culture. They fish, grow corn, are skilled archers, live in villages with many large houses, and play games—both lacrosse and "the ball game," a rugbylike game that can go on for hours or even days. Narváez does not find gold there. During their stay Narváez's troops are under constant attack from the Apalachee until the Spaniards finally flee to the south toward Aute, a coastal town where they are told they can find food. Aute is a series of villages on today's Wakulla River, south of today's Tallahassee.

On September 20, Narváez's group completes construction of five 40-foot raftlike boats in order to attempt to sail along the coast. Of the original expedition, 242 people are left as they shove off south of today's Tallahassee into the Gulf of Mexico along the Florida Panhandle. They head west in search of Pánuco, a Spanish settlement in today's coastal Mexico.

In November, somewhere off the coast of today's Texas, Narváez and two of his crew are lost at sea and presumed dead. The rest of his expedition continues west in search of Pánuco. Along the journey, they face starvation, cold, and attacks from natives. At times the starvation will be so severe that survivors will eat their dead. By the spring of 1529, only fourteen remain of the three hundred expedition members who came ashore in April 1528. By summer of 1535, four expedition members are still alive and are enslaved by native tribes along the southern coast of today's Texas. Among them are the expedition's treasurer Cabeza de Vaca and an African Moroccan slave named Esteban. They escape, but abandon their search for Pánuco, instead heading west through inland Mexico and today's southwest United States toward the Pacific Coast. They are embraced by native tribes along the way after demonstrating an ability to perform medical miracles.

1533

On August 29, Spanish Governor Francisco Pizarro executes Inca Chief Atahualpa as part of Spain's conquest of Peru. The Spanish conquer the native civilization and return home with great quantities of Inca gold and silver.

1536

On July 23, four remaining members of Narváez's expedition arrive in Tenochtitlán, today's Mexico City, and are greeted by Cortéz. In April, they had reunited with the Spanish in San Miguel de Culiacán, today's Sinaloa, on Mexico's Pacific Coast. Of the three hundred expedition members who came to shore on Florida's west coast in 1528, only two will return to Spain—Cabeza de Vaca and Andrés Dorantez.

1539

On May 18, Hernando de Soto sails from Cuba bound for La Florida with a fleet of five large and four small ships, along with an expedition force of more than seven hundred people. De Soto had received a royal contract in November 1536 to establish a Spanish colony. The contract supersedes the claims of Ayllón and Narváez, both of whom are now dead. While in Seville, Hernando de Soto had met with Narváez's treasurer Cabeza de Vaca to learn of Narváez's expedition and to seek Cabeza de Vaca's enlistment in the upcoming expedition to La Florida. Cabeza de Vaca refused. De Soto had left Spain in April, 1538, ultimately bound for today's Tampa Bay.

Hernando de Soto sets sail from Spain to conquer Florida in April 1538.

In late May, about a week after leaving Cuba, Hernando de Soto's expedition arrives on Florida west coast, near today's Tampa Bay, probably at today's Longboat Key near Sarasota. After settling in a camp near the mouth of today's Little Manatee River, de Soto's expedition marches north in search of the Apalachee territory. De Soto's expedition will encounter Juan Ortiz, a Spaniard who had been deployed from one of Narváez's ships in 1528 to search for the lost expedition, but had been captured by the Tocobagans. Ortiz relates to the Spaniards that Tocobagan Chief Uzita ordered that he be burned to death but that the chief's daughter pleaded for his life and he was spared. Ortiz will serve as translator for the new expedition.

In October, Hernando de Soto's expedition reaches Iniahica, the main town of the Apalachee nation, and establishes a winter camp. They had traveled up west central Florida encountering, and at times fighting, many native tribes. They had

intended to camp at the village of Ocale, near today's Ocala, but there was insufficient food for the army. The expedition feeds its army on the food stored by the natives and at times captures natives for service as guides and bearers. In 1987, an archaeological identification of de Soto's Iniahica winter camp will establish its location in today's Tallahassee.

1540

A 1541 map of North and South America

In the spring, Hernando de Soto's expedition leaves today's Florida to explore north and west. They will travel through today's Georgia, Carolinas, Tennessee, Alabama, Mississippi, and to the Mississippi River, where de Soto dies of disease on June 20, 1542. The expedition builds boats to travel down the Mississippi River to the Gulf of Mexico and then to a Spanish settlement near today's Tampico, Mexico, where the 311 survivors arrive in 1543.

1559

An artist's sketch of Tristan de Luna y Arellano, who established a Spanish settlement on today's Pensacola Bay in 1559

On August 14, an expedition led by Spanish Colonel don Tristán de Luna y Arellano arrives in today's Pensacola Bay to establish a Spanish settlement. He names the bay *Bahía Filipina del Puerto Santa María*. The bay will later be named after the Choctaw word *Panzacola,* which means "long-haired people." Luna had left a Mexican (New Spain) port in June with thirteen ships and an expedition of five hundred soldiers, cavalry, and craftsmen under orders to occupy and defend the area.

1562

Jean Ribault, commander of the French who arrived on the St. Johns River near today's Jacksonville on April 30, 1562

On April 30, three French ships with 150 people, under the command of Jean Ribault, arrive on the Florida Peninsula at today's St. Johns River near today's Jacksonville. He enters the river on May 1 and names it "River of May." The French attempt to settle in an area north of the river, but after a fire destroys their supplies and food becomes scarce, they return to France.

1564

On June 22, French Huguenots (French reformed Protestants) come to east Florida in three ships with three hundred men led by René Goulaine de Laudonnière, Ribault's second in command. They choose a site five miles from the mouth of the St. Johns River and construct a settlement named Fort Caroline. They find the native Timucuan to be friendly.

1565

On March 15, Spanish Admiral Pédro Menéndez de Avilés receives a royal charter from King Philip II of Spain to explore and serve as governor of La Florida and to remove the French settlement there. His contract follows those given to Ayllón, Narváez, and de Soto, all of whom are now dead. Menéndez, who has served as captain-general of New Spain (Mexico), will depart Spain on June 20 with nineteen ships and one thousand people on board.

A 1565 drawing of Spanish Admiral Pédro Menéndez de Avilés, founder of St. Augustine

Drawing of the Great House of the Selby tribe of the Timucuan Nation in St. Augustine. The chief of the Selby invited Pédro Menéndez de Avilés to occupy the Great House.

On September 8, Menéndez de Avilés comes ashore off a harbor on the east coast of Florida and names it St. Augustine, because he has reached Florida on the day of the festival of San *Agustín*. The Spanish will establish a colonial settlement there. The Spanish bring cattle from Spain to the St. Augustine settlement and maintain herds there in order to feed the Spanish garrison and surrounding community. It is also believed that the Spanish planted Florida's first orange trees in St. Augustine sometime around this period. By the 1800s, there will be wild citrus trees growing in many of Florida's forests and cultivated orange groves will grow along the St. Johns River.

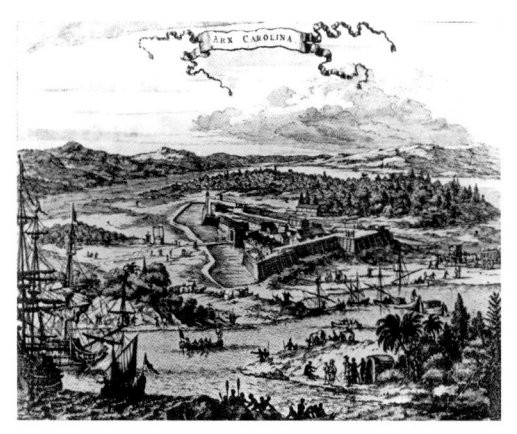

A 1670 lithograph of Fort Caroline, the French settlement near the St. Johns River that is conquered by Menéndez in 1565

An artist's rendering of Menendez and natives in Florida

On September 20, Menéndez de Avilés attacks French-held Fort Caroline, near St. Augustine, capturing the fort and killing most of its inhabitants. Days later, Menendez will locate 208 French men who had been shipwrecked. He takes them prisoner and then orders all of them, except the ten who are Catholic, to be slain. The sight of the massacre has become known as Matanzas, or "Place of Slaughter."

1566

In February, Menéndez de Avilés sails south, eventually to southwest Florida, Calusa territory, establishing the settlement of San Antonio. He writes about a large Calusa town with a mullet fishery called "Tanpa," on the mouth of today's Charlotte Harbor, which is then called Bay of Tanpa. The name will later be applied by Spaniards to today's Tampa Bay, presumably thinking they were in the body of water identified by Menéndez de Avilés.

1567

In March, Menéndez de Avilés arrives in today's Tampa Bay. After he leaves his soldiers in December, they will all be killed by Tocobagans at their village in today's Safety Harbor, north of today's St. Petersburg. There will be no further European exploration in the area for decades.

1574

The inscription reads: "Headboard and Coffin of Pédro Menéndez, Founder of our Nation's First City, Nombre de Dios Mission, St. Augustine, Fla."

This year, Menéndez de Avilés, Spanish governor of La Florida, dies. The Spanish influence south of St. Augustine will become gradually diminished as settlements are abandoned.

1586

A drawing of Englishman Sir Francis Drake, who attacks St. Augustine in 1586, looting and burning the outpost

On June 7, Englishman Sir Francis Drake arrives at St. Augustine with twenty-three warships, nineteen other ships, and two thousand men. The small number of Spanish defenders flee in advance of the English fleet. Drake enters St. Augustine and destroys much of the city before he departs. In order to better defend the city from both French and English threats, the Spanish will return and build Castillo de San Marcos to defend the city. The large fortress made of coquina stone takes thirty years to complete.

An early sketch of the construction of the east wall of the Castillo de San Marcos in St. Augustine

A 1947 view of the Castillo de San Marcos, which can be visited today in St. Augustine

1588

The British defeat the Spanish Armada, an event that begins the decline of the Spanish empire.

1603

Spanish explorer Fernando Valdes surveys the lower Florida Gulf coast and finds no traces of European colonization.

1607

On April 26, English Captain Christopher Newport and his crew of 105 men arrive and land on today's Virginia coast where they establish a colony called Jamestown. Thirty-nine members of the crew died en route from England.

1620

On December 11, an advance crew from the ship Mayflower *lands on the coast of today's Massachusetts and names their settlement New Plymouth. The group of religious dissenters, led by Captain Miles Standish, had set sail from Plymouth, England, on September 16 in pursuit of religious freedom. Earlier, on November 21, the "Mayflower Compact" was signed on ship by representatives of all aboard to establish a political organizing structure for the settlers.*

1622

*On September 6, a Spanish Plate Fleet (*plata *is Spanish for "silver") sets sail from Havana heading for Spain. Generally, the Plate Fleet*

leaves from Spain with settlers, troops, and manufactured goods headed to the New World. Upon arriving in the Caribbean, the fleet divides into three fleets. The Tierra Firme fleet goes to Porto Bello in Panama to unload cargo and pick up gold and Peruvian silver (which traveled across land after sailing up the Pacific coast on Spain's South Seas fleet), then gathers emeralds in Colombia and pearls in Venezuela; the New Spain fleet sails to Veracruz, taking on gold and silver from Mexico, as well as silks, porcelain, and spices from China (which cross Mexico overland after arriving on the Pacific coast in Spain's Manila fleet); and the Honduras fleet collects goods from that country. The three fleets then rejoin in Havana, along with armed escorts to make the trip back to Spain.

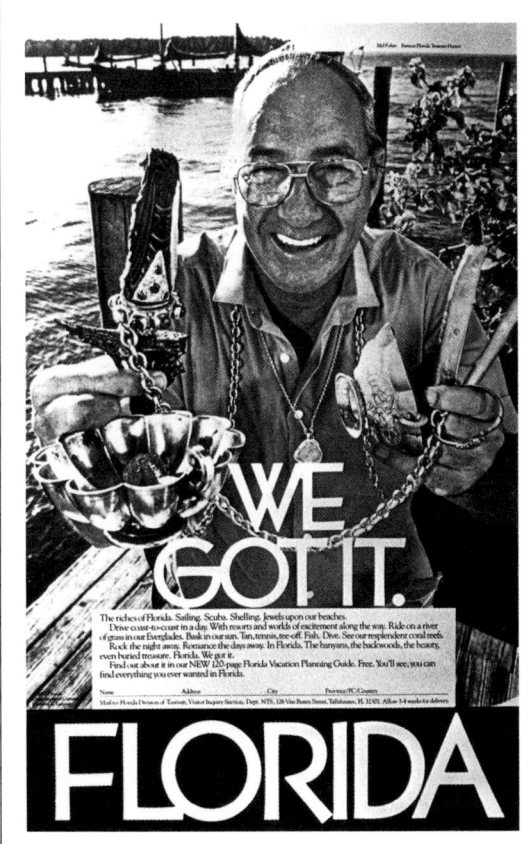

The Spanish ship *Atocha* sank off the Florida Keys in 1622. Treasure hunter Mel Fisher, shown here in a Florida tourism ad, discovered it more than 350 years later.

A 1680 Map of the Caribbean, including Florida

During the night, the Spanish Plate Fleet's twenty-eight ships encounter a hurricane. The fleet runs to the open waters of the Gulf of Mexico, but eight of the ships fail to get by the reefs along the Florida Keys, including two ships heavily laden with treasure. The *Nuestra Senora de Atocha* sinks after striking the reefs. The *Santa Margarita* strikes a sandbank and eventually is buried by the sand and currents. The ships will be located more than 350 years later and artifacts and treasures from the ships will be displayed at the Mel Fisher Maritime Museum in Key West. The value of the *Atocha* treasure, located on July 20, 1985, will be $450 million in contemporary dollars, and will include more than forty tons of silver and gold, including more

than one hundred thousand Spanish silver coins, gold coins, emeralds, and more than one thousand silver bars.

1658

This year, the English settle in South Carolina. They will raid St. Augustine in 1665 and 1668.

1672

On September 27, the Royal African Company receives monopoly slave rights under the English flag. In the next two centuries almost twelve million Africans will be kidnapped and shipped to the New World as slaves. The British develop a "triangular trade system" where ships leave England with goods to be traded for slaves along the West African coast; then transport the slaves across the Atlantic to be sold at auction in the Americas; then acquire cotton, tobacco, rum, and other items to bring back to sell in England. It is estimated that about 15 percent of the Africans die on board the slave ships in brutal captivity.

1698

In November, Spanish Admiral Andrés de Arriola lands at the *barrancas*, Spanish for "bluffs," near Pensacola to establish a settlement and fort. The fort will be called Presidio Santa María de Galve, and will be later renamed Fort San Carlos de Austria. The French will burn the fort in 1719, and the Spanish and French will exchange possession four times. In 1723, the Spanish will build a fort on Santa Rosa Island called Presidio Isla de Santa Rosa.

1702

In September, British South Carolina Governor James Moore occupies St. Augustine, having entered Florida with 1200 men—half native and half white. Spanish Governor Zúñiga moves the city's population of 1445 into the Castillo de San Marcos, along with the 323 men under his command. Moore lays siege to the fort and a two-month battle ensues. After British reinforcements from Jamaica fail to arrive, and Spanish help from Cuba arrives in December, Moore ends the siege and retreats back to South Carolina, but not until after he destroys the city.

1715

On July 24, a Spanish Plate Fleet sets sail from Havana loaded with treasure from the New World, heading for Spain.

Days after leaving Cuba, the Plate Fleet is caught in a hurricane off Florida's east coast. Eleven of the fleet's twelve ships sink near today's Vero Beach and more than a thousand sailors are lost. Spanish crews will give up their search for the ships

after three years, but treasure from the ships will be searched for and salvaged by treasure hunters for the next three centuries, from Ft. Pierce north to Sebastian, twenty-eight miles up the Atlantic shore, along what will become known as Florida's "Treasure Coast."

An 1886 drawing of a Spanish galleon, similar to those that sailed with the Spanish Plate Fleet of 1715

1718

A drawing of Captain Edward Teach, the infamous pirate known as Blackbeard, who terrorizes the Atlantic and Caribbean from 1716 until he is killed in 1718. The period from the late 1600s through the early 1700s is referred to as the "Golden Age of Piracy."

On November 22, Edward Teach is killed by Lieutenant Robert Maynard, commander of two

Royal Navy sloops off the coast of North Carolina, a British colony. Teach is better known as "Blackbeard," perhaps the most famous pirate of his day. He is a brutal pirate who braids his beard and reportedly puts burning rope under his hat in order to look fierce. Blackbeard and his crew of fellow pirates had been ambushing ships and terrorizing the Atlantic and Caribbean since 1716. The period of about 1650 to 1730, along with the later period of about 1775 to 1821, will become known as the "Golden Age of Piracy" as pirates attack and hijack ships, kill and capture crew and passengers, and seize gold, silver and, more often, cargo such as grain, molasses, rum, rope, tools, and ammunition. The attack on Blackbeard's band is one example of the British Royal Navy's increasing efforts to stop the pirates. Notorious pirates of the first "Golden Age" include "Black Bart" Roberts (attacks hundreds of ships from 1719 to 1722), Captain William Kidd (began as a pirate hunter in 1696 and switched), Captain Henry Morgan (Caribbean privateer, pirate, and buccaneer who becomes Lieutenant Governor of Jamaica and is the Captain Morgan of today's rum fame), Jack Rackham (the fabric in his colorful clothes earns the name "Calico Jack"), and many others.

1733

On July 13, the New Spain Fleet leaves Havana harbor to return to Spain, filled with treasures. It is escorted by four armed vessels (to protect from pirates), sixteen merchant ships, and two smaller ships carrying supplies. The day after the fleet sails, the wind shifts and intensifies from the east, signaling an approaching hurricane. Lieutenant-General Rodrigo de Torres, commander of the fleet, senses the storm and turns the fleet back toward Havana, but not in time.

By nightfall on July 13, much of the New Spain Fleet will be scattered, sunk, or swamped along eighty miles of the Florida Keys. Four ships will make it back to Havana and one will sail on to Spain. Although the Spaniards recover most of the treasure shortly after the disaster, thirteen of the sunken ships along the Keys can be explored today. In 1990, the United States Congress will designate 2,900 square miles off the Florida Keys to be the Florida Keys National Marine Sanctuary, triggering federal regulations that prohibit the removal or disturbance of cultural resources in sanctuary waters, including shipwrecks. By

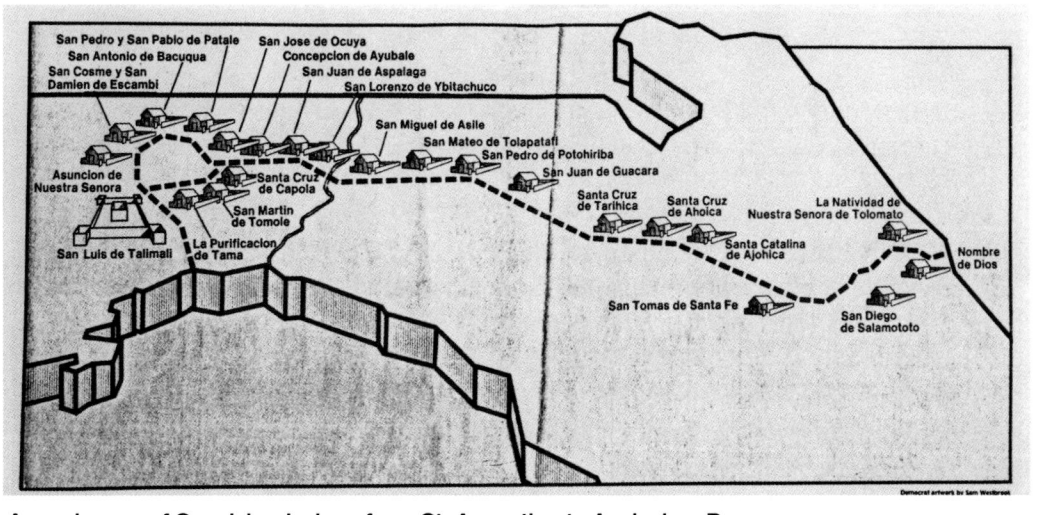

An early map of Spanish missions from St. Augustine to Apalachee Bay

2010, the shipwrecks will be among the oldest artificial reefs in North America.

Also this year, the British establish a colony in Georgia.

Militia under Georgia Governor James Oglethorpe will attack St. Augustine in 1740 and 1742.

1740

From this year through 1812, bands of Creek from Alabama and Georgia move to at least six villages in north Florida. More will follow. They will be called Seminoles, from the Spanish term *cimarrón* meaning "runaway" or "wild one." Some speak Muskogee and some speak Mikasuki. By 1760 the largest Seminole camps will be in Alachua (county of today's Gainesville), Leon (county of today's Tallahassee), and Levy (county of today's Cedar Key). By the time the Seminoles arrive, most of the native Timucuans, Apalachee, Calusa, Yamasee, Tocobagan, and other native cultures are gone—to conquest or European disease, such as smallpox, measles, and typhoid fever. The Florida population will not again reach the level of the pre-Columbian native population (350,000) until the 1880s.

1750

This drawing is based on information received during the excavation of the Spanish mission San Francisco de Oconee in today's Jefferson County, east of Tallahassee.

To convert the natives to Christianity, the Spanish have established forty missions in Florida, with seventy friars and housing 26,000 Native Americans.

1754

On April 2, Lieutenant Colonel George Washington sets out with 160 men to attack French forces in the Ohio River Valley who had taken over a British fort and named it Fort Duquesne. It is the first engagement in the French and Indian War.

1757

In mid-April, Don Francisco Maria Celi, pilot of the Royal Spanish Fleet, sets sale for Florida's west coast. Upon arriving he names the southern point of today's St. Petersburg *Punta del Pinal* ("Pine Point"), later anglicized to Point Pinellas. He renames the bay *La Bahia de San Fernando* in honor of Spanish King Ferdinand VI. It is today's Tampa Bay. He also surveys today's Egmont Key, which he names *Isla de San Bias y Barreda*. The island will later be renamed by the British in honor of the Second Earl of Egmont, a member of the Irish House of Commons.

1763

On February 10, after a series of British military victories, the Treaty of Paris is signed, ending the Seven Year War between the English and French, including the American theater known as the French and Indian War. French influence in North America is significantly reduced. As part of the treaty, Florida is given by Spain, France's war ally, to Britain. England receives Canada from France. Spain receives Cuba, whose capital, Havana, had been captured by the British.

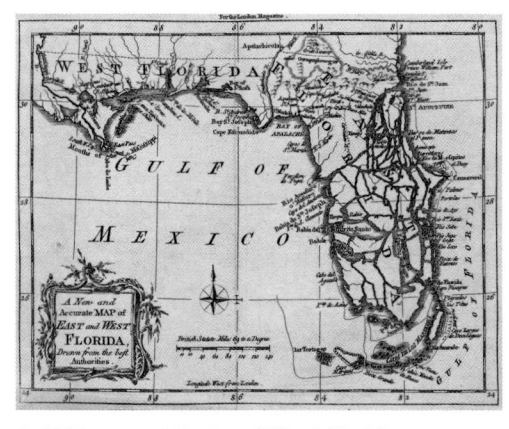

A 1760 map of East and West Florida

The Florida territory will remain British until 1783. The British divide the Florida territory into two: West Florida, comprising most of the Panhandle west to the Mississippi River, and East Florida, including everything east of the Apalachicola River.

On July 20, the British take control of St. Augustine, capital of East Florida, and will move into Pensacola, the capital of West Florida, in August. Under a British land grant program the London Board of Trade offers 100 acres to those who agree to settle on Florida land. The British will deed more than 2.8 million acres in East Florida and 380,000 acres in West Florida. In advance of the British rule, 3,500 residents of East Florida evacuate from St. Augustine to Havana and Vera Cruz, Mexico, and 800 in West Florida evacuate from Pensacola. Very few Spanish remain.

1770

On March 5, British soldiers fire on a mob of patriots in Boston, killing three. The Boston Massacre will become a rallying cry for independence.

1774

On September 5, the First Continental Congress meets at Carpenters' Hall in Philadelphia to discuss American resistance to the rule and policies of the British.

1776

On July 4, the Declaration of Independence is signed in Philadelphia and the American Revolutionary War begins. The war will continue until 1783.

Four colonies in America will remain loyal to the British during the Revolutionary War, including East and West Florida and Upper and Lower Canada.

1777

On October 17, British General Burgoyne surrenders to American General Gates at Saratoga, New York. Six thousand British soldiers surrender and 1,400 are killed in the battle. It is a major setback for the British in the northern campaign.

On December 25, General George Washington's troops at Valley Forge, Pennsylvania, suffer through a cold and bleak Christmas. Washington sends Congress a letter warning that new supplies are urgently needed or the army will "starve, dissolve or disperse."

1780

On March 1, Pennsylvania becomes the first colony to pass legislation banning slavery.

On May 12, American forces suffer a major defeat at Charleston, South Carolina, losing four ships and surrendering five thousand troops under General Benjamin Lincoln. The loss has a strong and negative impact on American morale.

1781

On May 10, British Major General John Campbell surrenders Pensacola to the Spanish, ending British control of West Florida.

On October 19, troops under the command of British General Cornwallis march through columns of American and French soldiers and surrender to officers under command of George Washington at Yorktown, Virginia. Cornwallis had abandoned his outer defenses on September 30 after French warships blocked escape and American and French cannons bombarded the British fortifications. It is the final battle of the Revolutionary War.

1783

The front page of the May 10 to May 17, 1783, edition of the *East Florida Gazette*, Florida's first newspaper, which is based in St. Augustine. Among other items on the front page is a $10 reward for anyone returning James Seymour's eight-year-old, 14-hands-high horse that was stolen or strayed out of his yard.

On September 3, the Treaty of Paris is signed by representatives of the United States, England, Spain, France, and the Netherlands, and the Revolutionary War ends, resulting in the independence of the United States of America. Britain cedes Florida back to Spain in exchange for the Bahamas. Florida's first newspaper,

the East Florida Gazette in St. Augustine, proclaims the British defeat.

1788

On July 2, Congress confirms that the Constitution of the United States has been ratified.

1789

On February 4, George Washington becomes the first president of the United States of America. John Adams is vice president.

1790

The King of Spain offers homestead grants to "foreigners" agreeing to settle in East Florida. In a Spanish Land Grant, each household head receives one hundred acres and each additional family member or slave qualifies for an additional fifty acres. Homesteaders must settle for ten years to acquire title.

1803

On December 20, the Louisiana Territory is officially conveyed from France to the United States in exchange for $15 million. The transaction, negotiated by James Monroe on behalf of President Thomas Jefferson, doubles the size of the United States. The annexed property encompasses almost 828,000 square miles and includes the future states of Arkansas, Missouri, Iowa, and Nebraska, as well as portions of Montana, Wyoming, Colorado, Oklahoma, Kansas, Louisiana, North Dakota, South Dakota, and Minnesota.

1804

On May 14, an expedition commissioned by President Thomas Jefferson to explore the Louisiana Purchase region leaves St. Louis, heading up the Missouri River. The expedition, led by Captain Meriwether Lewis and Lieutenant William Clark, has a crew of thirty-three men. After eighteen months and a journey of almost four thousand miles they will reach the Pacific Ocean. The Lewis and Clark Expedition is *joined by a Shoshone squaw guide, Sacajawea. On September 23, 1805, the expedition will return to St. Louis after completing a 7,000-mile, 28-month journey. They will bring back valuable maps of the new American land along with journals, drawings, and descriptions of the plants, natives, animal life, and geography that they encounter. It will form the basis of trade, further exploration, and American western expansion.*

1806

On February 10, the Boston Globe *reports about Frederick Tudor, a wealthy Bostonian who ships eighty tons of ice out of Boston Harbor bound for Martinique in the Caribbean. Tudor is the first to ship ice in this manner. He harvests the ice in frozen Massachusetts ponds and ships it to southern ports. By 1847, an estimated 52,000 tons of ice will be sent by railroad or ships to twenty-eight cities around America. The ice is packed with sawdust and wood shavings during shipment, but much of it melts along the way. After John Gorrie receives a patent for the first mechanical ice machine in 1851, manufactured "artificial ice" will become possible (see 1851).*

1808

An 1894 or 1895 photograph of Fort Dallas at the mouth of the Miami River

On February 27, the Spanish give a land grant of one hundred acres to John Egan for a settlement along the Miami River. After Florida becomes part of the United States, the federal government will establish Fort Dallas on the river. The population in the area will grow after the Second Seminole War begins in 1835. Natives originally named the lake we call Okeechobee Lake *Mayaimi*, meaning "sweet water." It is the source for today's Miami name.

1812

On June 18, the United States declares war on Britain in response to Britain's impressment of seamen, disregard of trading relationships, and encouragement of Indians to warlike acts. The War of 1812 begins. It will continue until 1814.

1814

On August 24, the British army, led by Major General Robert Ross, enters Washington, D.C. Before leaving, the British will burn the Presidential Mansion (today's White House), the Capitol, and other federal buildings. President James Madison escapes and his wife, Dolley, rescues a life-size portrait of George Washington and the original Declaration of Independence.

On September 13, British warships pound Fort McHenry in Baltimore Harbor with shells and rockets in an effort to take the city and advance the war effort. Francis Scott Key, a 35-year-old American lawyer, watches the bombardment from Chesapeake Bay eight miles away while under British guard. As fires burn at the fort through the night, Key fears that the Battle of Baltimore is lost. But the dawn's early light on September 14 reveals to Key that the American flag still flies over the fort. Inspired by the moment, Key writes an anthem about the flag and puts it to the tune of a popular English song. The song is distributed under the title "Defense of Fort McHenry." Today, the song is known as "The Star Spangled Banner," America's national anthem.

An 1810 print depicting the battle for Pensacola fought between the British and Spanish. The British occupy Spanish Pensacola during the War of 1812 to provide a base in the war against the Americans, but are forced out by Andrew Jackson in 1814.

On November 7, United States General Andrew Jackson arrives in Pensacola Bay, part of Spanish Florida, to engage the British, who had occupied Pensacola to provide a base of operations against the Americans during the War of 1812. After a short skirmish the British surrender and the British fleet abandons the port. Jackson will later return the port to the Spanish.

On December 24, the Treaty of Ghent is signed ending the War of 1812. Because of communication delays, the war will continue into January 1815 at the Battle of New Orleans and at sea as late as March 1815.

1815

An 1815 engraving depicting General Andrew Jackson leading American troops to victory over the British at the Battle of New Orleans

On January 8, the British attack entrenched American positions in New Orleans, the first of three attempts, all of which will fail. The Americans and British have been engaged here since late December. During the third British assault, the British commander will be killed. British casualties total more than two thousand and American casualties total seventy. After the British return to their ships on January 27 and set sail, American commander General Andrew Jackson's reputation as a war hero is cemented. Jackson will play a significant role in Florida history during the next era.

On June 18, Napoleon Bonaparte of France is defeated at Waterloo by Britain's Arthur Wellesley, Duke of Wellington. It is the end of the reign of the French emperor, who had taken power in 1799 and had conquered much of Europe. He will be sent in exile to St. Helena and will die there in 1821.

> **"**Let it be signified to me through any channel that the possession of Florida would be desirable . . . and in sixty days it will be accomplished . . . [and with additional provisions and men] I will assure you that Cuba will be ours in a few days.**"**
>
> **General Andrew Jackson, to the secretary of defense, anxious to take on the Spanish**

Chapter 2
American Territory and State: 1816–1859

The era begins with United States General Andrew Jackson making incursions into Florida, conquering Spanish settlements and their allied runaway slaves. His actions will spark what will be the first of three wars with the Seminoles of Florida, wars that will result in most of the Seminole population being killed or relocated to the western United States. Those who refuse to surrender and refuse to be relocated prove elusive

First Seminole War: 1817–1818
Second Seminole War: 1835–1842
Third Seminole War: 1855–1858

to the pursuing American government. Eventually the fighting simply stops and a small group of unconquered Seminoles remains.

General Jackson's aggressive actions also influence the Spanish decision to cede Florida to the new United States of America. Florida becomes the twenty-seventh state. The first roads and railroads are built. In Apalachicola, an ice-making machine is developed – an invention that will lead to air conditioning and change the fate of the state in the next century. As the era moves to a close, the nation appears headed for Civil War.

Timeline

1816

A drawing of a Creek Indian village on the Apalachicola River in the early 1800s

On July 27, a United States boat traveling up the Apalachicola River through Spanish West Florida is challenged by former slaves at the "Negro Fort" along the river. During the ensuing firefight gunpowder magazines at the fort explode, killing 270 of the fort's occupants and injuring many others. Earlier this year United States Fort Scott was organized north of the Negro Fort in southwest Georgia near Spanish West Florida to provide the military with an outpost from which to pursue runaway slaves into the Spanish territory. Some of the former slaves are living among the Seminoles.

On December 4, United States Secretary of State and Democratic-Republican candidate James Monroe of Virginia defeats Federalist Rufus King of New York in the campaign for the presidency. Virginia is the home of four of America's first five presidents.

1817

On November 21, soldiers from Fort Scott under the command of Colonel Edmund Gaines cross the Flint River and attack the Mikasuki village of Fowltown, in southwest Georgia.

Mikasuki Chief Neamathla had warned Gaines not to cross the river and Gaines took it as a provocation. Five Mikasuki are killed.

In retaliation, a week later the Mikasuki attack a supply boat on the Apalachicola River and kill thirty-seven soldiers in addition to six women and four children. In response, United States Secretary of War John C. Calhoun orders Major General Andrew Jackson to Fort Scott, with power to wage war. Jackson will take command on December 26 and head south into Spanish West Florida territory in pursuit of the Seminoles and their runaway-slave allies. General Jackson's pursuit marks the beginning of the First Seminole War, which will end in 1818 with Jackson's consolidation of control over West Florida. It is the first of what will be three Seminole Wars that ultimately result in the displacement of the Seminoles and the opening of Seminole territory for resettlement.

1818

An 1818 print depicting two Seminole chiefs captured at St. Marks by troops under General Andrew Jackson's command

Throughout this book events in Florida are set in Roman (non-italics), and events outside Florida are set in *italics*.

Jackson hangs two Scottish men, British subjects, for cavorting with the Seminoles and Spanish against the United States. Robert Ambrister is shown here at his trial.

On March 9, Andrew Jackson, with a force of 4,800 men, including 1,500 Creek, marches against 1,000 Seminoles, destroying settlements and crops. He hangs British subjects Robert Ambrister and Alexander Arbuthnot for supporting the Seminoles and Spanish in crimes against the United States. In addition to the Indian villages, Jackson conquers the Spanish town of St. Marks and occupies Spanish Pensacola in May, leaving St. Augustine the only major Florida city under Spanish control. Jackson offers to continue his conquest, promising Secretary Calhoun to take possession of Florida in sixty days and, if given the authority and troops, to continue on to take Cuba. Jackson's success brings the United States to the verge of occupying all of East and West Florida and provides the Spanish with few options but to negotiate withdrawal. Jackson will later describe his encroachments against the Seminoles and blacks in West Florida as necessary "to chastise a savage foe, combined with a lawless band of Negro brigands."

1819

On February 22, the United States and Spain sign the Adams-Onís Treaty, providing for the United States to receive East Florida and West Florida from Spain in exchange for the United States assuming $5 million in claims against Spain. As part of the treaty, the United States agrees to recognize Spanish Land Grant titles. At this time there is only one significant road in the entire territory: King's Road from St. Augustine to the St. Marys River. Today, the St. Marys constitutes the border between Florida and Georgia in the northeastern corner of the state. The Adams-Onís Treaty will go into effect in 1821 after it is ratified by the United States Senate.

1821

Portrait of Andrew Jackson, governor of the territories of East and West Florida from July 17, 1821, to October 5, 1821

On April 15, President Monroe names Andrew Jackson governor of East and

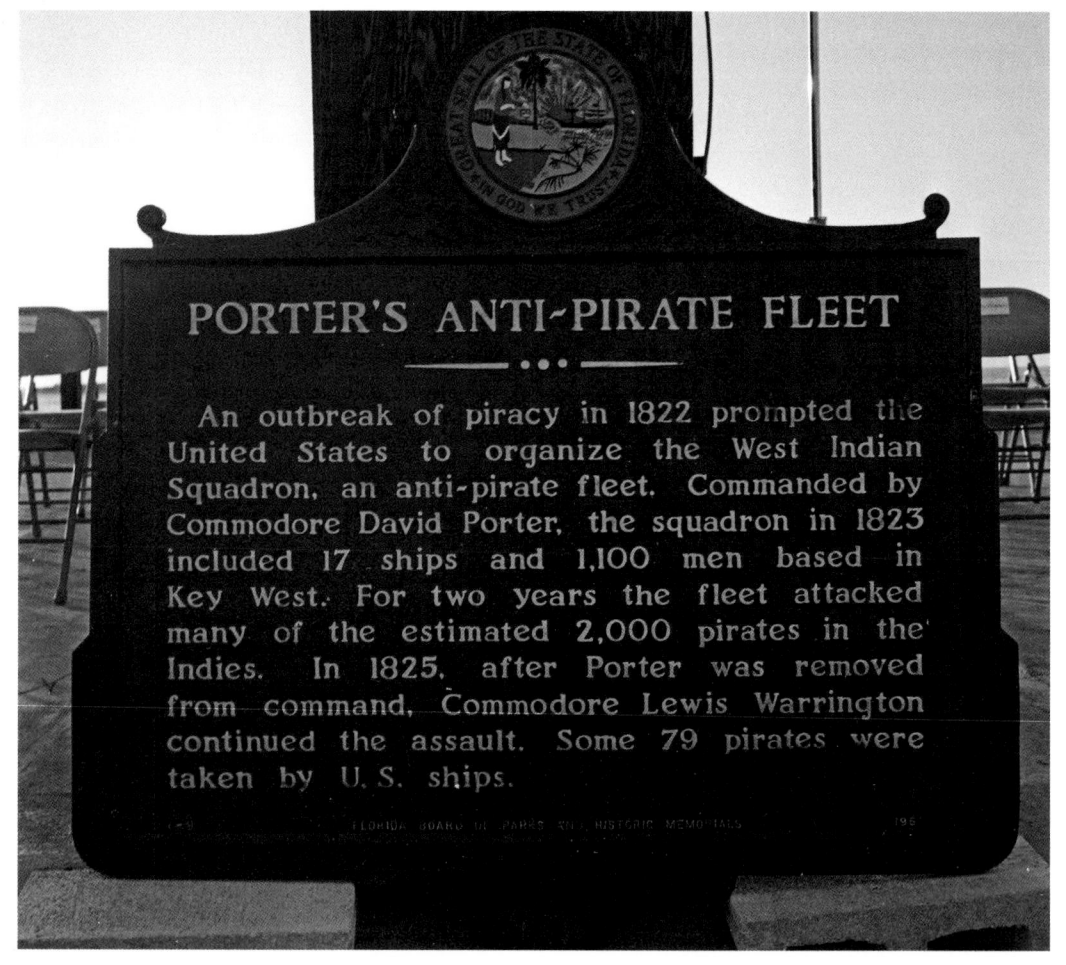

PORTER'S ANTI-PIRATE FLEET

• • •

An outbreak of piracy in 1822 prompted the United States to organize the West Indian Squadron, an anti-pirate fleet. Commanded by Commodore David Porter, the squadron in 1823 included 17 ships and 1,100 men based in Key West. For two years the fleet attacked many of the estimated 2,000 pirates in the Indies. In 1825, after Porter was removed from command, Commodore Lewis Warrington continued the assault. Some 79 pirates were taken by U. S. ships.

FLORIDA BOARD OF PARKS AND HISTORIC MEMORIALS

A historical marker in Key Largo describing Commodore David Porter's squadron of the "Anti-Pirate Fleet." The maker notes that in 1823 Porter led 17 ships and 1,100 men based in Key West, attacking an estimated 2,000 pirates.

West Florida, which the United States officially receives on July 17, 1821. Jackson will remain in Florida until October 5, 1821, when he notifies the president that he has accomplished his mission and is returning to Tennessee. President Monroe will appoint William P. Duval as the state's territorial governor to succeed Jackson. Duval is a Virginian who grew up in Kentucky and is now a United States judge at Pensacola. Duval will become the name of both the county in northeast Florida where Jacksonville is located and the street in Tallahassee that runs between the state

Capitol Building and the Florida Supreme Court.

In September, three American merchant ships are captured by pirates near the entrance to Matanzas Harbor in Cuba. Most of the crew members are killed or tortured. In response to this and other pirate activities, President James Monroe, in a December 6, 1822, message to Congress, writes of "multiplied outrages and depredations which have been committed on our seamen and commerce by the Pirates in the West Indies and Gulf of Mexico . . ." He urges Congress to organize a force capable of pursuing them. Congress responds by establishing the West Indies Squadron to commence a campaign against pirates around Florida and the Caribbean. Many ships and crews prosecute the "pirate wars." Among them are the USS *Sea Gull* and the USS *Enterprise*. The latter has many successes, including the capture of Charles Gibbs, a ruthless pirate who admits to murdering four hundred people.

1822

On March 30, President Monroe signs the congressional act passed on March 20, creating and organizing the United States Territory of Florida as a single territory, uniting the former East and West Florida. Among other items, Congress provides that sessions of the Florida Legislative Council will alternate between St. Augustine and Pensacola. The street that today lies in front of Tallahassee's Florida Capitol Building will be named after the current United States president, James Monroe. Presidential appointments to Florida's Territory Governor position will include William P. Duval (1822 to 1834); John Eaton (1834 to 1836); Richard Call (1836 to 1839); Robert Reid (1839 to 1841); Richard Call (1841 to 1844); and John Branch (1844 to 1845).

A circa 1920s view of a horse and buggy in front of the post office and custom house in Key West

On May 7, Congress establishes a United States customs district at Key West, in addition to districts in St. Augustine and Pensacola. Among other jobs, customs officers are responsible for the development, maintenance, and operations of lighthouses in their districts.

On June 10, Florida Governor William P. Duval intends to hold the first Legislative Council in St. Augustine; however, a shipwreck of delegates traveling from Pensacola delays the session. One council member will die in another shipwreck. When similar experiences delay the 1823 Pensacola session, Governor Duval will call for a study to recommend a central location for the territory's capital.

In November, the USS *Alligator* wrecks on a reef off Islamorada that will later be named "Alligator Reef." The ship, part of America's West Indies Squadron, had just captured three pirate ships.

1823

An 1858 or 1859 engraving of wreckers at work off the Florida coast

The sculpture *Wreckers* by Miami sculptor James Mastin, on display in Key West. Wrecking was a significant part of the early Key West economy.

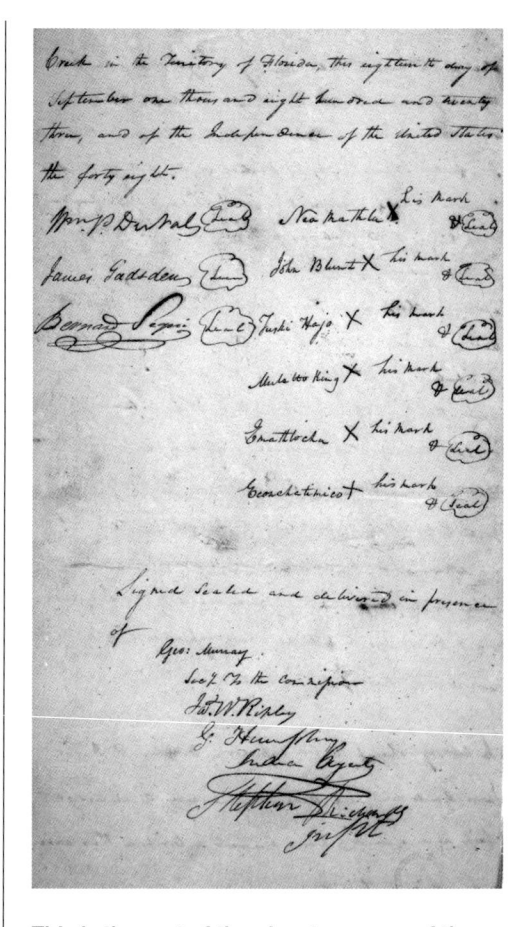

This is the part of the signature page of the Treaty of Moultrie, identifying the locations where the Seminoles would be permitted to live. Among others, signatures are those of: Florida Territorial Governor William P. Duval, James Gadsden, Bernard Segui, Neamathla, John Blunt, Tuski Hajo, Mulatto King, Emathlocha, and Econchictimico.

This year, the territorial government enacts the Florida Wrecking Act. "Wreckers," common in the Florida Keys, are people who go to the site of a sinking or run-aground ship, save the passengers, and salvage the cargo for profit. The law provides a process for reporting the salvaged cargo and compensating the wreckers. It also makes it a crime to hold "false lights, signal devices, or anything with the intent to mislead . . . any vessel on the high seas." The latter provision is enacted in response to devious wreckers who constructed lights intended to draw ships into hazard so the wreckers can salvage the cargo after the resulting shipwreck. As more lighthouses are built around the state and steamships provide ships with more control, the number of coastal shipwrecks will diminish.

On September 18, the Treaty of Moultrie Creek is entered into between the United States and thirty-two Seminole chiefs. The Seminoles agree to give up their rights to occupy twenty-four million acres of Florida land in exchange for four million acres between the Withlacoochee River (enters the Gulf at today's Yankeetown, north of Crystal River) and Peace River (enters the Gulf at today's Port Charlotte), along with specified financial compensation.

1824

In January, the United States Army erects Fort Brooke, named after Colonel George Mercer Brooke, at the mouth of the Hillsborough River. It is a military outpost and frontier trading center and the beginnings of what will become the city of Tampa.

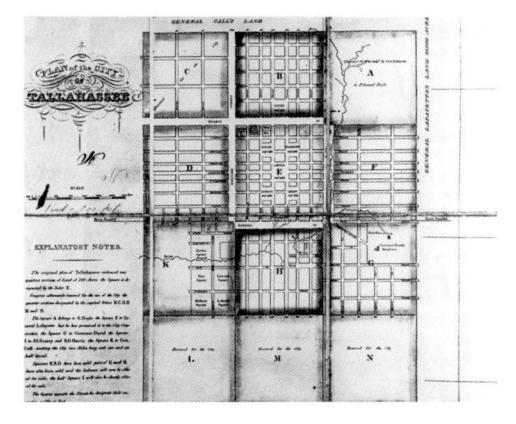

An 1829 plat of Tallahassee, the capital of the Florida territory

On March 4, after receiving the study he ordered in 1823 to identify the best location for a capital, Florida Territorial Governor William P. Duval issues a proclamation naming Tallahassee the capital of the new U.S. possession. The site is selected as a compromise because it is geographically midway between St. Augustine and Pensacola, the territory's major cities. At this time travel by water around Florida is time consuming and can be dangerous. Land travel is still long and challenging because no rail links the two cities.

A map of Florida's 1830s era roads

A circa 1910 view down the Bellamy Road that runs from St. Augustine through Tallahassee to Pensacola. It became Old St. Augustine Road and is still a paved street in Tallahassee.

On December 21, John Bellamy, a wealthy South Carolina planter, begins construction of the Bellamy Road. The Florida Territorial Council, with an appropriation from Congress, authorized the construction of the road from the St. Johns River, which runs south-north to the west of St. Augustine, to the Ochlockonee River, which runs south from Georgia to the Gulf of Mexico, west of Tallahassee. Eventually the road will extend from the west bank of the St. Johns River, through Tallahassee, to Pensacola. In present-day Tallahassee and Jacksonville it is still called the Old St. Augustine Road. The sixteen-foot-wide road, which runs along an old Spanish trail is called the Military Road west of Tallahassee since that leg will be built by Bellamy's son-in-law, Captain Daniel E. Burch of the Army Quartermaster Corps. The $20,000 project, which is the first federally funded road construction in Florida, will be completed in 1826.

On December 29, Mosquito County, Florida's eleventh county, is established. In recognition of the orange groves in central Florida, the county will be renamed Orange County in 1845. It is the home of today's Orlando.

This year, a lighthouse will be built in St. Augustine as the United States begins a significant effort to construct lighthouses along the coast of the newly acquired Florida territory. In 1789, the United States Congress had passed an act giving the Treasury authority over aids to navigation, including lighthouses. In 1825, lighthouses will be built at Key West, Cape Florida (on Key Biscayne), Carysfort Reef (six nautical miles east of Key Largo), Sombrero Key (about eight nautical miles south of Marathon in the Florida Keys), Garden Key (Dry Tortugas), and Pensacola (the first U.S. lighthouse on Florida's Gulf coast). From 1824 to 1890, the United States will construct at least thirty lighthouses along Florida's east and west coasts, along the keys, and at the entrances to rivers, bays, and inlets. The lighthouses guide ship navigation and warn of reefs, sandbars, mudflats, and other dangers below. At times, light keepers also keep a lookout to announce ships coming to port. "Wreckers," who make a living salvaging shipwrecks along the coasts, are angered by the lighthouse development (see 1823).

Also this year, Congress grants the Marquis de Lafayette, French supporter of the American Revolution, $200,000 and an allotment of land. He selects land near Tallahassee, but never visits the city.

1825

On February 9, after almost two months of uncertainty, John Quincy Adams is named president of the United States by the United States House of Representatives. He is the son of the second president, John Adams. No candidate received a majority of the electors after the December 1824 election, so under the Constitution the decision is made by the House.

An 1885 photograph of the St. Augustine lighthouse, originally constructed in 1824

Losing candidate Andrew Jackson believes that a deal was cast to deliver the votes to Adams and make Henry Clay the Secretary of State. Jackson lashes out at the "corrupt bargain." Jackson will take Adams on again in 1828.

In October, a location is chosen for a navy yard near Pensacola. The yard will be the base of the Gulf Squadron, with a mission of suppressing slave trade and piracy in the Gulf of Mexico and Caribbean. Later, beginning in 1829, Fort Pickens, Fort McRee, and Fort Barrancas will be built to protect the yard. The Pensacola Navy Yard will be decommissioned in 1911 and in 1914 will be re-commissioned as the Pensacola Naval Air Station, which is still in operation today.

Also this year, Thomas Dummett and his son Douglas establish an orange plantation on Merritt Island, west of Cape Canaveral. They develop a new grafting technique for oranges that will be adopted by many growers in Florida. They graft sweet orange trees onto sour orange trees, creating trees called "frost-resistant trees" because the budding begins several feet above the ground. The Dummetts stay on Merritt Island during the Second Seminole War and Thomas serves as captain in the Mosquito Roarers militia.

1826

In March, the United States Congress authorizes a survey to evaluate the feasibility of building a canal connecting the St. Marys River (north of Jacksonville) and the Suwannee River in order to allow shipping to cross the state from the Atlantic to the Gulf of Mexico without having to navigate the Florida Straits, with its distance, reefs, pirates, storms, and barrier islands. The survey report will be completed in 1829 and will reject the proposed route but will suggest an alternative route

from the St. Johns River to the town of St. Marks. The canal is not constructed at this time, but the push for a cross-Florida waterway will gain steam again in the 1930s, 1942, and the 1960s.

1828

On December 3, Andrew Jackson and his new Democratic Party win the presidency, soundly defeating President John Quincy Adams.

On December 22, the Baltimore and Ohio Railroad begins carrying passengers along a thirteen-mile stretch of rail from Baltimore west to Ellicott City, with passenger cars being pulled by horses.

On August 28, 1830, inventor Peter Cooper tests the experimental steam locomotive Tom Thumb on the rail line by carrying the B&O directors in a passenger car.

1831

John James Audubon's watercolor of an American flamingo. Audubon first sees a flock of flamingoes in Florida on May 7, 1832, near Indian Key. He writes: "I thought I had now reached the height of all my expectations, for my voyage to the Floridas was undertaken in great measure . . . to study these lovely birds in their own beautiful islands."

On November 20, John James Audubon arrives in St. Augustine. He has come to Florida to collect waterbirds for the third volume of his illustrated book, *Birds of America*. He will spend six months exploring Florida's east coast and the Florida Keys. While in Florida, he will discover 52 types of birds that he had not seen before. While in the Keys, he writes to his wife: "The air was darkened with whistling wings," noting that his "heart swelled with uncontrollable delight."

1832

On May 9, fifteen Seminole leaders agree to the Treaty of Payne's Landing. Seminole leaders will also sign the Treaty of Fort Gibson on March 28, 1833. The Seminole and United States representatives will have ongoing disagreement as to whether the Seminoles, under the treaties, agreed to be relocated to the western United States on land controlled by the Creeks.

1834

Tallahassee Railroad Company's mule-drawn car traveling between Pensacola and Jefferson streets in Tallahassee in 1894

On February 10, the Tallahassee Railroad Company is incorporated by act of the Florida Legislature. When its track construction is completed in 1836 it will be Florida's first railroad, running twenty-two miles from Tallahassee to Port Leon. The train consists of small wooden cars pulled by mules and a passenger coach, which is a box with two bench seats holding eight people. The rail will carry cotton from the plantations in northern Florida and southern Georgia to the Gulf of Mexico for transport to the mills.

A depiction of the battlefield near today's Bushnell, where Major Francis Dade and 108 American soldiers are massacred by the Seminoles under Chief Osceola

1835

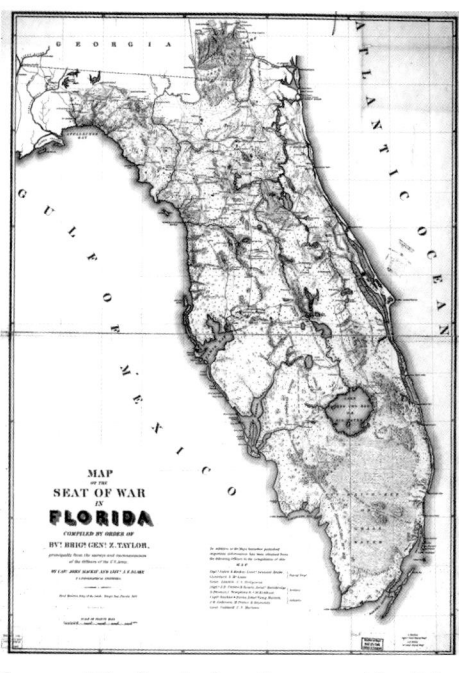

A map of the "seat of war" prepared for Brig. General Zachary Taylor during the Second Seminole War

On December 28, Major Francis L. Dade and 108 soldiers are massacred by the Seminoles near Bushnell, which is about twenty miles north of today's Dade City. Chief Osceola is leading the Seminoles in their effort to resist both white encroachment into the territory granted to them under the 1823 Treaty of Moultrie Creek and forced Indian relocation to the western United States. Seminole warriors hide their families in the Everglades and fight. The attack on Major Dade's company begins the Second Seminole War, which will continue until 1842. Chief Micanopy will serve as chief of the Seminole Nation during the war. His capital village during the war is Cuscowilla, at the intersection of two Indian trails south of today's Gainesville. It is today's Micanopy.

1836

On February 26, Mexican General Santa Ana leads approximately five thousand troops into San Antonio to put down a Texas rebellion.

An 1800s portrait of Seminole Chief Micanopy, who unites the Seminoles as a people and serves as chief of the Seminole Nation during the Second Seminole War

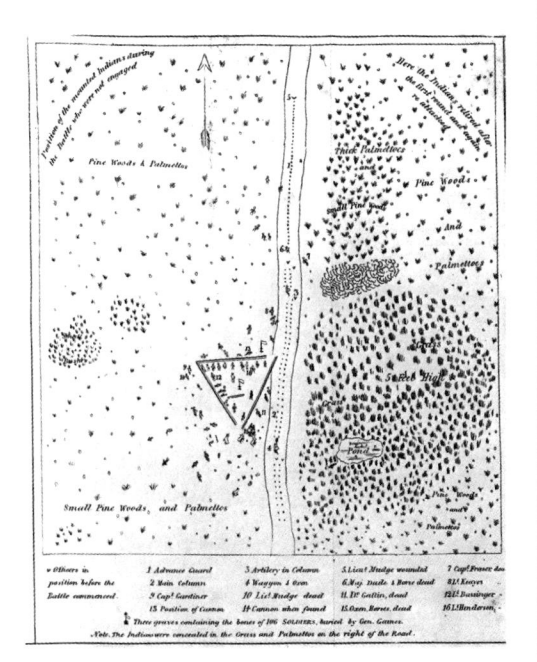

Map of the battleground and site of the massacre of Major Dade and his soldiers

Colonels William Travis and James Bowie retreat with their force of approximately two hundred defenders into the Spanish Mission Alamo where, on March 6, the last defenders will be overtaken and killed. By April, Santa Ana and his forces will be conquered by General Sam Houston and Mexico will acknowledge the independence of Texas.

A replica of the first steam engine to operate in Florida, in 1836, on the Lake Wimico & St. Joseph railroad line in Florida's Panhandle

On September 5, Florida's first steam locomotive runs along the Lake Wimico & St. Joseph railroad line, about one hundred miles southwest of Tallahassee, near Apalachicola. The rail line runs from a wharf off St. Joseph (today's Port St. Joe) on St. Joseph Bay to Lake Wimico, a navigable portion of the Apalachicola River. Effectively the new railroad allows cotton and other products on steamboats from the river waterways to connect to ships on the Gulf of Mexico.

1837

On October 27, U.S. Brevet Major General Thomas Jesup seizes the Seminole leader Osceola, later widely referred to as Chief Osceola, while during a council held under a white flag truce. Osceola is imprisoned at the Castillo de San Marcos in St. Augustine, which has been renamed Fort Marion since 1821 (until 1942 when

Congress will restore the original name). The Seminole leader will die at Fort Moultrie, South Carolina, on January 31, 1838. While the Second Seminole War will continue for four more years, the loss of Osceola is a major setback to the Seminoles. Years from now, representatives of the same government that went to war with Chief Osceola will name a Florida county and a national forest in his honor.

On December 25, Colonel Zachary Taylor, a future American president, at-

An 1800s view of Castillo San Marcos (Fort Marion) in St. Augustine, where Seminole Chief Osceola is imprisoned in 1837

Chief Osceola of the Seminoles

tacks the Seminoles at their prepared positions near Lake Okeechobee, forcing them to flee. Taylor will be commissioned a brigadier general and, on May 15, 1838, will assume command of the war.

Also in December, U.S. Army Fort Ann is built in the North Merritt Island area in order to protect troops during the Second Seminole War.

1838

On December 3, fifty-six elected members of Florida's first Constitutional Convention meet in St. Joseph (today's Port St. Joe) to draft a charter to become a state. At this time the port city, one hundred miles southwest of Tallahassee, is a bustling port town of twelve thousand people. On January 11, the elected Florida Territory delegates will approve a constitution, anticipating statehood. The following May, voters will ratify the constitution. Florida congressional delegate David Levy Yulee will lead Florida's statehood effort.

David Levy Yulee, Florida Congressional delegate, who leads Florida's statehood effort

Photograph of the January 1956 dedication of the Constitution Museum in Port St. Joe commemorating the 1839 Florida Constitution Convention in St. Joseph (today's Port St. Joe), where state delegates would sign the first state constitution. Governor LeRoy Collins is seated to the speaker's right.

This monument to Florida statehood was erected in St. Joseph in 1922 and cites the year 1838, when the delegates first convened. It bears the names of the convention delegates.

1839

In October Fort Gatlin is established southeast of today's downtown Orlando. The fort is named after Dr. John Slade Gatlin, a soldier who was killed during the Dade Massacre. At this time forts are being constructed throughout the settlement areas of the state in order to protect both settlers and travelers from attacks by Indians.

1840

On January 12, the first Internal Improvement Act for Florida is passed, establishing a board calling for the construction of railroads.

An 1870s photoprint of the garrison at Fort Brooke

In October, federal gunboats from Tampa's Fort Brooke destroy William Bunce's fish "rancho" at Palm Island. U.S. Army Brigadier General W.K. Armstead, who ordered the attack, will later assert that the rancho had been a hiding place for Spaniards who were dealing with Indians hostile to the U.S. troops. On March 3, 1847, Bunce's estate will be awarded $1,000 to compensate for the Army's actions.

1841

On March 4, President William Henry Harrison is inaugurated president of the United States, but he will die of pneumonia in one month on April 4 at the age of 68. He had given a lengthy inaugural address on a cold and wet day. Vice President John Tyler becomes the tenth president of the United States. He is the first vice president to ascend to the presidency

An 1837 lithograph showing barracks and tents at Fort Brooke in what is now Tampa

upon the chief executive's death and will be labeled "His Accidency" by detractors.

On April 2, the Fort Harrison military outpost opens in today's Clearwater as a convalescent post for soldiers from other Florida forts who are suffering from malaria and other diseases. Fort Harrison will be abandoned on October 26, 1841. The fort is named after President Harrison, who dies two days after its opening.

During the summer, a cargo ship from Cuba carries a passenger with yellow fever into Port St. Joseph in the Florida Panhandle, one hundred miles southwest of today's Tallahassee. Within a few weeks, three-fourths of the town dies from the disease and the remaining residents flee. For three years the town remains deserted. A September 1844 hurricane will destroy most of the buildings in the city, leaving the town a ghost of its former life.

1842

A photograph of Billy Bowlegs, who becomes chief of the Seminoles at the end of the Second Seminole War

By April, only 300 Seminoles remain in Florida, 112 of whom are warriors. All other Seminoles have been killed or relocated west of the Mississippi River, to Oklahoma and Arkansas. Colonel William Jenkins Worth, now in command of U.S. forces in Florida, is based at Cedar Key. Worth proposes to the War Department that the remaining three hundred Seminoles be allowed to stay in a 6,700-square-mile section of southwestern Florida, about half of today's Big Cypress Swamp. On May 10, President Tyler orders a halt to the continued military action, ending the Second Seminole War. Seminole Nation Chief Micanopy has been captured and relocated to the Oklahoma Territory, where he will die in January 1849. Billy Bowlegs becomes the chief for the Seminoles.

On August 10, the United States Armed Occupation Act, which follows the Second Seminole War, is signed into law. The act opens up prior Seminole lands south of Gainesville and north of the Peace River by granting 160 acres to settlers if they agree to build a house, clear five acres, plant crops, and live on the property for at least five years. Cattlemen from Georgia, Alabama, and the Carolinas will homestead 200,000 acres in Florida under the homestead provisions of the act, bringing large numbers of cattle from overstocked herds in those states. Florida's cattle industry will grow dramatically this decade.

1843

On June 13, Spaniards Antonio Máximo Hernández, Joe Silva, and Juan Levique receive permits, granted under the 1842 Armed Occupation Act, to settle on Florida's west coast. Hernández, who had served in the United States military during the Second Seminole War, settles in south St. Petersburg, today's Maximo Point, supplying fish to Cuba and acting as fishing guide to Fort Brooke soldiers in Tampa. Silva and Levique are fishermen who settle on the eastern shore of Boca Ciega Bay. Levique will sell his 157 acres after the Civil War in order to settle a forty-six-dollar grocery debt. Hernández's widow will sell his 136.25 acres in 1886 for one hundred dollars.

Other settlers taking advantage of the 1842 Act are Aaron and Mary Jernigan, who move from Tallahassee to Mosquito County (to be renamed Orange County in 1845). They bring seven hundred head of cattle and establish a homestead on the shore of today's Lake Holden. Aaron Jernigan will be Orange County's first representative to the Florida legislature after Florida becomes a state in 1845.

1844

On May 24, Samuel Morse sends the message "What hath God wrought" from Washington, D.C., to Baltimore, marking the first telegraph message sent between two cities.

On December 7, Democrat James Polk of Tennessee is elected president of the United States over Whig candidate, Henry Clay of Kentucky. During the next four years, President Polk will lead the admission of new states and a massive expansion of United States territory, including the annexation and admission of Texas as a state on December 29, 1845 (more than 389,000 square miles), the acquisition of the Oregon Territory by treaty with Great Britain on June 15, 1846 (almost 287,000 square miles), the admission of Iowa as a state, the admission of Wisconsin as a state and, after prosecuting a war with Mexico, the acquisition of the "Mexican Cession" under the Treaty of Guadalupe Hídalgo signed effective July 4, 1848 (more than 529,000 square miles). U.S. territorial acquisitions under President Polk include today's states of Texas, California, Arizona, Nevada, New Mexico, Utah, Oregon, Idaho, and Washington, along with parts of Montana, Wyoming, Kansas, Oklahoma, Colorado, and New Mexico. Collectively, it will be the greatest territorial expansion by any single president in United States history.

1845

On March 3, the last day of President John Tyler's term, he signs into law the act admitting Florida as the twenty-seventh state in the Union, with a constitution permitting slavery. At this time Florida's population is estimated between 60,000 and 70,000. Florida's admission is paired with the free state (slavery not permitted) of Iowa, which will be admitted in 1846.

A 1976 view of the Old Capitol, originally built in 1845, along with the almost-complete new capitol behind it

On June 25, William D. Moseley, a Democratic lawyer from Jefferson County, is sworn into office as the first governor of the State of Florida. His inaugural address contains a lengthy discussion of the rights of the states versus the federal government, which he refers to as "a government of strictly limited powers, a government formed and established through the agency and by the express authority and assent of the States, as independent sovereignties." He declares the establishment of the National Bank and Internal Improvement Fund to be "infractions of the Constitution, as usurpations of the rights of the States . . . unwise, inexpedient and impolitic." Governor Moseley will serve until 1849 under the terms of the Florida Constitution of 1838, passed in 1839, which provides that the governor is elected for four years, and "shall not be eligible to re-election until the expiration of four years thereafter." The new governor is sworn in beneath the newly built state capitol's east portico. Today, Governor Moseley's capitol, now called Florida's "Old Capitol," stands in front of the more modern high-rise capitol building and, since 1982, has been used as a museum and Florida historical education center.

1846

On May 13, President Polk signs a Declaration of War against Mexico. War is triggered after the Mexican army crosses the Rio Grande, attacking United States forces.

1848

On January 23, U.S. Army General William Harney writes to Buckingham Smith, a lawyer appointed by President Polk to investigate the Everglades, that Florida may be made "susceptible of cultivation and instead of being, as now, a waste of waters fit only for the resort of reptiles." At this time Lake Okeechobee does not have a natural river outflow. The Caloosahatchee River begins three miles west and flows to the Gulf of Mexico, and the St. Lucie River begins twenty miles to the east and flows to the Atlantic Ocean. During the rainy season the lake overflows to the south, moving slowly as the Everglades "river of grass" to Florida Bay. Smith concludes in his 1848 report that the area should be drained by (1) deepening Lake Okeechobee; (2) building a canal east from the lake to the St. Lucie River; and (3) building a canal west to the Caloosahatchee River. The cost is estimated to be under $500,000, and the expected benefits include expansive agricultural land, an Atlantic-to-Gulf waterway for shipping, and new industries for south Florida, such as timber and fishing.

On September 25, a hurricane and tidal surge known as the Great Gale of '48 strikes the St. Petersburg-Tampa area from the southwest, forming two new inlets along the barrier islands off St. Petersburg. Several sand keys between Mullet Key and Pass-a-Grille are washed away. Most of today's Pinellas is under water and ships are washed ashore and wrecked. During the hurricane, Egmont Key lighthouse keeper Marvel Edwards places his wife and five children in a small boat and ties the boat to a cabbage palm in the center of the island, as the island is covered by six feet of water. The family survives the fierce storm, but Edwards retires from the lighthouse-keeping business, presumably for good.

An 1880s photograph of the lighthouse at Cape Canaveral. The original 1848 lighthouse was rebuilt in 1868 and was painted with black bands in 1873.

The Cape Canaveral Lighthouse is one of the first man-made structures built on the cape. It will be rebuilt in 1868 and painted with black and white bands in 1873. Due to enemy submarines in the Atlantic, the beacon light at Cape Canaveral will be extinguished during the World War II years.

1849

On March 23, an Executive Order is issued reserving Mullet Key, in the waters off the southwest coast of today's St. Petersburg, for military purposes. The order follows a survey of Mullet Key and Egmont Key by four U.S. Army engineers aboard the schooner *Phoenix* and is issued in response to a report by recording officer Brevet Colonel Robert E. Lee. Lee, the future commander of the Confederate Army, had recommended to his superior officer that fortifications be constructed at

Egmont Key and that the surrounding keys be preserved.

On October 1, Thomas Brown, a Whig legislator and hotel operator from Tallahassee, is sworn into office as Florida's second governor. Governor Brown, a veteran of the War of 1812, delivers an inaugural address discussing the importance of internal improvements, specifically railroads, and education for the state's youth. He strikes a conciliatory tone with the North, pledging in "the discharge of duty, my humble efforts shall be directed to a firm and unyielding support of the rights of the South, and the cultivation of a good understanding with our Northern brethren."

1850

On July 9, President Zachary Taylor dies from an attack of cholera. Vice President Millard Fillmore assumes the presidency.

On September 18, President Fillmore signs into law the Fugitive Slave Bill, providing for federal jurisdiction over runaway slaves and for their return to their owners. It is part a package of laws proposed by Senator Henry Clay of Kentucky in January of this year, known as the "1850 Compromise," designed to ease tensions between the North and South; however, the Fugitive Slave Bill will infuriate anti-slavery factions in the North.

On September 28, Congress passes the Swamp Land Act of 1850 giving every state title to all swamp and overflowed land within its borders, for drainage and reclamation.

In Florida, by the end of Governor William S. Jennings' administration in 1905, there will be 20,133,837 acres of swamp and overflowed lands patented to the state. This land becomes available for railroads, agriculture, and development. The "swamp" land will be held in the Florida Internal Improvement Fund and distributed to railroad companies and settlers.

1851

John Gorrie, inventor of the first ice-making machine—predecessor to ice plants, refrigerators, and air conditioning. These are all inventions that will transform Florida forever.

Among other advancements brought about by Gorrie's invention, plants producing ice will be built throughout Florida and the United States. Here is a 1926 photograph of Florida Power and Light Company's ice plant in Miami, offering both wholesale and retail sales.

On May 6, John Gorrie, an Apalachicola physician, receives a patent on the first ice-making machine, developed to cool the rooms of patients with fever. The machine utilizes a steam-driven compressor to cool air.

Using Gorrie's technology, ice plants will be built in cities throughout America to manufacture "artificial ice" for delivery to the iceboxes of homes and businesses. America's first ice plant will open in New Orleans in 1868. The industry will grow until, by the end of the nineteenth century, homes across the country will use their iceboxes to keep milk, meats, and other fresh food cold. The technology from Gorrie's invention is also used in the development of air conditioning, although the first air-conditioning system will not be developed until 1902. By the middle of the twentieth century, the air conditioner will have a major impact on Florida living. Today Gorrie is one of two Floridians honored with a statue at the Capitol in Washington, D.C.

Women dancing in front of the Wescott Building at the Florida State College for Women in 1915

Also this year, the Florida Legislature provides for the establishment of two state colleges, located east and west of the Suwannee River. The West Florida Seminary will open in Tallahassee in February 1857. It will become Florida State College, then, in 1905, it will become an all-women's school, the Florida State College for Women. On May 15, 1947, Florida's

governor will sign a bill making the school coeducational again, and renaming it Florida State University. The East Florida Seminary is chartered in Ocala in 1853. It will be renamed University of Florida in 1905. UF will be relocated to Lake City in 1905 and to Gainesville in 1906.

On the Banks of The Suwanee River, Fla

A scenic view of canoers paddling "way down upon the Suwannee River," made famous by Stephen Foster's 1851 song

Also this year, Stephen Foster writes the song "Old Folks at Home" while in Pittsburgh. The song will become known as "Way down upon the Suwannee River" and will be adopted as the Florida official song in 1935, although Foster will never visit the state.

1853

On October 3, Democrat James E. Broome, a judge, planter, and store operator from Leon County, is sworn into office as Florida's third governor. His inaugural address focuses on three needs. The first need is to raise funds for the "common schools [sufficient] to place a plain English education within the reach of every child in the State." The second need is to complete the removal of the Seminoles from Florida, referring to their presence as "a blight to our prosperity, in violation of their treaty obligations, and in open defiance of the power, authority and importity of the Federal Government." The third need is the internal improvements of the state with a focus on "connecting with bands of iron our western, eastern and southern section." Governor Broome expresses confidence that "the triumphant election of General [Franklin] Pierce to the Presidency" will result in a strict construction of the Constitution to limit the exercise of the powers of the Federal Government as applied to the "Sovereign States."

1854

On March 20, in Ripon, Wisconsin, an organizing meeting is held which will lead to the formation of the Republican Party. The new party, which takes its name from Thomas Jefferson's party, is committed to opposing slavery.

On April 3, U.S. Navy surveyor Lt. C.H. Berryman anchors in Tampa Bay and begins to take more than thirty thousand soundings, looking for a site for a deep-draft seaside railroad depot. The effort is in response to plans revealed by Florida Senator David Levy Yulee to build a railroad line from Fernandina to the Gulf coast. Berryman chooses today's downtown St. Petersburg as the optimum railroad port site and issues a report, published in 1855, praising the area. He constructs a small hamlet with temporary barracks, a short

pier, and a smokehouse on today's Fifth Avenue North where today's Vinoy Hotel is located. In August, Berryman's hamlet is abandoned by the Navy. Yulee will elect to extend the railroad to Cedar Key and will complete his line in 1861. Berryman's report will not be forgotten and will eventually be read by Peter Demens, who brings the railroad to St. Petersburg in 1888.

On December 18, in the Big Cypress area near Ft. Myers, thirty Seminole warriors open fire on a United States military detachment led by Lieutenant George L. Hartsuff, vandalizing their camp, wounding four, and killing four. The attack marks the beginning of the Third Seminole War. The Seminoles have only one hundred warriors in Florida, but the war will continue until 1858.

1855

On January 6, Governor James Broome signs into law the Internal Improvement Fund Act of 1855. It grants railroad builders a 200-foot-wide right-of-way across land owned by the state in order to build railroads. The act also provides that the state will guarantee interest on bonds, for up to thirty-five years, for approved railroad companies building lines. In 1856, Congress will grant more land to Florida for railroads. The act will spark the development of the Florida Railroad from Fernandina to Cedar Key, completed in 1861, but will put the state in financial peril when the railroad defaults on the bonds. Florida's inability to pay the interest in the face of massive interest defaults after the Civil War will lead to a bailout by Hamilton Disston in 1881.

1857

On October 5, Democrat Madison Stark Perry, a planter and legislator from Alachua

County and a native of South Carolina, is sworn into office as the fourth governor of Florida. His inaugural address includes a discussion of his support of education, the expansion of the railroads, the support of agriculture, and the prospect of "compelling the Indians to emigrate thus relieving the State from a curse which has so long retarded the settlement of a very extensive and interesting portion of our territory." Governor Perry saves the longest part of his speech to press the case for slavery in Kansas and to issue a warning regarding the need to protect "the safety of our institution" from the efforts of anti-slavery men in the North.

Covered wagons in Leon County. Covered wagons and stagecoaches provide land-based transportation in the state for many years before railroads and automobiles.

Also this year, United States Army Captain Abner Doubleday builds a wagon trail road linking the New River in today's Ft. Lauderdale to Fort Dallas—today's Miami.

1858

On May 8, the Third Seminole War ends with 164 Seminoles being removed to the western United States. Captured and surrendering Seminoles are held at Egmont Key before being sent west. Two hundred Seminoles remain in Florida, mostly in the Everglades and Big Cypress regions. Seminole leader Billy Bowlegs and more than one hundred of his followers will relocate to the American West; but the small remaining number of the Seminole Tribe will be known as "unconquered." By the end of the Third Seminole War, 98 percent of Florida's native population who have not died from disease or conquest have been relocated west of the Mississippi River.

1859

In August, Edwin Drake taps an underground supply of oil in Titusville, Pennsylvania, opening the possibility of obtaining oil in large quantities. The substance is touted as a lubricant and an illuminant. New wells in western Pennsylvania will follow. By 1865, Cleveland, Ohio, will have thirty refineries.

On December 2, John Brown is hanged in Charleston, Virginia, today's West Virginia, after being found guilty of treason, murder, and conspiring with slaves to lead an insurrection at Harper's Ferry. The hanging of John Brown captures the nation's attention and serves as a prelude to the brewing national conflict that will erupt in the coming era. Ominously, future presidential assassin John Wilkes Booth attends Brown's hanging.

> **"It is said that some of the inhabitants of the key were required to sign an oath not to take up arms against the Government of the (so called) United States during the present war."**
>
> **Confederate Brigadier-General J.H. Trapier, revealing a Southern attitude about the "so called" United States in his report to headquarters on the Union occupation of Cedar Key**

Chapter 3

Civil War and Reconstruction: 1860–1877

As this era begins, much of southern Florida remains a subtropical wilderness with few settlers and scattered Seminoles. Major cities include Key West, Jacksonville, Tallahassee, Pensacola, Fernandina, and Cedar Key. As the winds of war grow stronger, both Northern and Southern interests begin to position themselves around Florida's ports.

When the nation enters the Civil War, Florida joins the other states in rebellion. Florida's young men enter the fight and the state is significant to the Confederate effort as a supplier of beef, salt, turpentine, and other products.

The Union will control Florida's significant ports during the war and make an effort to destroy salt works and capture or destroy supplies intended for the Confederate forces to the north, especially cattle. In the coastal areas, local activity involves skirmishes between the federal blockade ships and the "runners" who attempt to elude the federal ships and provide supplies for the Confederacy. Some locals join the Union forces and the blockade.

A photograph of a painting of the CSS *Florida*, a Rebel blockade runner. The Confederate States steamer is propelled by steam engine and a sail rig. It will be captured by the USS *Wachusset* on October 7, 1864, and sunk off Norfolk in a collision with a U.S. Army transport the following month.

During and after the war railroads begin to develop to connect Florida to the rest of the country, but the large railroad development will wait for the next era. After the

Union victory, Florida, like other Southern states, resists the reforms mandated by the victorious Union government, but eventually changes its constitutional structure to a point sufficient to allow removal of Reconstruction troops.

Timeline

1860

In May, the United States Navy rescues 1,432 Africans from three American-owned ships, the *Wildfire,* the *William,* and the *Bogota,* which are engaged in the illegal slave trade. U.S. steamships *Mohawk, Wyandotte,* and *Crusader* bring the freed Africans to Key West, where they receive clothing, shelter, and medical treatment. By August, more than one thousand survivors will be shipped to Liberia, West Africa, a country founded for former American slaves. Hundreds will die on the ships before reaching Liberia.

An 1860 drawing showing captives on the deck of the slave ship *Wildfire.* The captives are rescued by the U.S. Navy and brought into Key West.

Throughout this book events in Florida are set in Roman (non-italics), and events outside Florida are set in *italics.*

This sign marks the African cemetery at Higgs Beach in Key West, where the remains of 294 African men, women, and children are buried. The enslaved Africans were rescued by the U.S. Navy but succumbed to various diseases due to the conditions of their confinement on the illegal slave ships.

An 1890s view of the lighthouse and keeper's house at Jupiter Inlet

On July 10, a 108-foot lighthouse is lighted in Jupiter, nineteen miles north of West Palm Beach. The lighthouse sits at the junction of the Indian River and Jupiter Inlet. Confederate sympathizers will disable the light during the Civil War. The lighthouse will be relighted in 1866.

In the fall, a group including John Bethell, Abel Miranda, and James Hay decide to "wage a war of extermination" against the bears, panthers, wildcats, and alligators in Point Pinellas, today's St. Petersburg, because the animals are killing hogs. In November and December they kill ten bears, thirty-seven wildcats, three panthers, and countless alligators. At this time the area also abounds with deer, turkey, geese, quail, blue and white cranes, raccoons, opossums, squirrels, and rabbits. John Bethell will later bemoan the "brainless pothunters" who slaughter tens of thousands of plume and songbirds "of every description" for plumes, feathers, and skins (*see also* 1886, 1900, 1903, 1905).

On November 6, Abraham Lincoln is elected President of the United States carrying 180 of the 303 electoral votes. Lincoln is not on the Florida ballot and the state is carried by John C. Breckenridge of Tennessee.

On December 20, South Carolina unanimously votes to dissolve the union between South Carolina and the United States. Mississippi will secede on January 8, 1861, joined by Florida on January 10, Alabama on January 11, Georgia on January 19, Louisiana on January 26, Texas on February 1, Virginia on April 17, Arkansas on May 6, North Carolina on May 20, and Tennessee on June 8.

A drawing of slaves who were on the slave ship *William*, which was captured by the USS *Wyandotte* and brought to Key West

Florida forces seize U.S. Fort Clinch at Fernandina Beach in advance of the Civil War. Today it is a state park, shown in this 1954 photograph.

1861

On January 7, three days *before* Florida votes to secede from the Union, state militiamen are ordered to seize St. Augustine's Fort Marion, today's Castillo de San Marcos. As 125 Confederate troops approach the fort, a U.S. sergeant surrenders the fort without a fight. Rebel forces remove the fort's cannons and send them to Fernandina. On January 8, Florida troops seize Fort Clinch on Amelia Island. Federal forces also hold Fort Taylor in Key West and Fort Jefferson in the Dry Tortugas.

On January 9, United States Lieutenant Adam Slemmer is given orders to take whatever measures are needed to protect the Union forts at Pensacola. Slemmer abandons Pensacola-area Forts Barrancas and McRee and consolidates his forces at Fort Pickens on Santa Rosa Island. Fort Pickens' location allows Union forces to control the harbor. Fort Pickens was named for Revolutionary War General Andrew Pickens. Along with Forts Barrancas and McRee, it was built between 1829 and 1834 to guard the Pensacola Navy Yard and the entrance to the harbor at Pensacola Bay. Fort Pickens will remain in Union control throughout the war.

On January 10, Florida adopts an Ordinance of Secession by a vote of sixty-two to seven in an open convention, withdrawing from the United States union. The ordinance provides that: "The State of Florida is hereby declared a sovereign and independent Nation." At the time Florida leaves the Union, slaves outnumber whites two to one in the northern Florida cotton-producing counties of Jackson, Gadsden, Leon, Jefferson, and Madison.

A Confederate battery at Pensacola Bay. The Confederacy seizes batteries at Fort Barrancas and Fort McRee on Pensacola Bay on January 12, 1861, two days after Florida votes to leave the Union. Fort Pickens on Santa Rosa Island remains in Union control and has a strategic advantage for traffic through the bay.

INSIDE THE BATTERY NORTH OF FORT McREE AT PENSACOLA

The Confederate battery at Fort McRee at Pensacola, shown here, will bombard Union-controlled Fort Pickens. The lack of uniforms suggests this photograph was likely in the early days of the war.

On January 12, hundreds of Confederate troops from Florida and Alabama take over the Pensacola Navy Yard. Confederate troops will also occupy abandoned Forts Barrancas and McRee, leaving Fort Pickens in Union control.

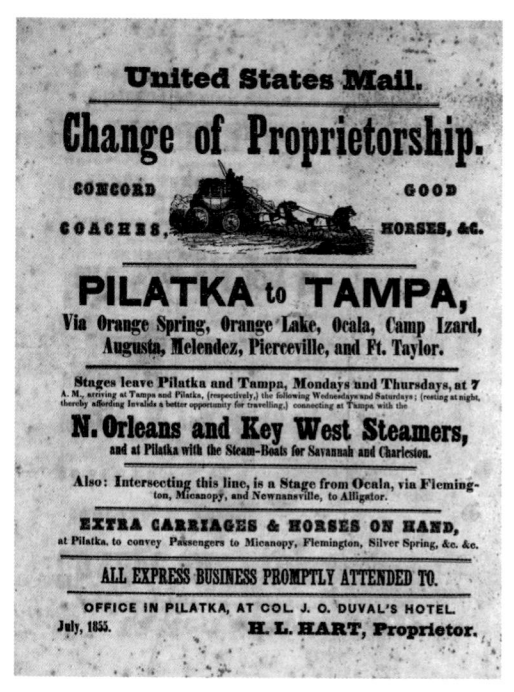

A July 1855 flyer describing the stagecoach route from Tampa to Palatka (spelled "Pilatka" in the flyer)

On January 13, news of Florida's separation from the Union arrives in Tampa via a stagecoach that traveled from Gainesville. Before the railroads arrive, internal transportation within Florida is along a few roads via horseback, foot, covered wagon, or stagecoach. As shown in the July 1855 flyer above, stagecoaches are deployed in Florida to deliver the United States mail and they solicit passengers. In the case of this flyer, it describes a route from Palatka (spelled Pilatka) on the St. Johns River waterway to Orange Spring, Orange Lake, Ocala, Camp Izard, Augusta, Pierceville, Fort Taylor, and ending in

Tampa. Stages leave Palatka and Tampa at 7 A.M. Mondays (arriving Wednesdays) and Thursdays (arriving Saturdays). Tampa has connections to steamboats to New Orleans and Key West. At Palatka, the coach connects to steamboats that take the St. Johns River to the Atlantic and then to Savannah and Charleston. Presumably, guests rest overnight at inns during the two nights of the trip.

On February 4, Florida representatives join other Southern states to form the Confederate States of America. As of the 1860 census, Florida's population is 140,424. Roughly 62,000 (44 percent) are black slaves, and 78,000 (55 percent) are white, with a small number of free black Floridians. Slave owners number 5,125 or about 3.7 percent of the population. If you draw a line between St. Augustine and Cedar Key, most of Florida south of that line has a population of less than two inhabitants per square mile. The state's largest population concentration is in the seven-county slave-based plantation belt around Tallahassee. This area also has a disproportionate elective representation because of the constitutional requirement to count slaves as three-fifths of a person for voting purposes. At about 2,900 residents each, Pensacola and Key West are the largest cities, followed in order by Jacksonville, Tallahassee, St. Augustine, Apalachicola, Milton, Monticello, and Fernandina. Of the eleven Confederate states, Florida has the smallest number of people. Its population is only 30 percent of the population of Arkansas, the next lowest populous state in the Confederacy.

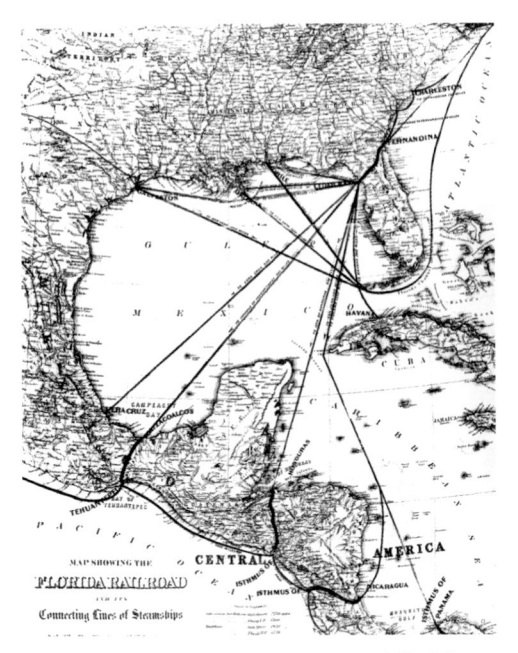

An 1870 map showing the routes of Florida Railroad connecting with steamship routes from Cedar Key and Fernandina

A circa 1800s photograph of the St. Johns Railway running from Tocoi on the St. Johns River to St. Augustine

On March 1, the Florida Railroad Company, led by David Levy Yulee, completes the first cross-state railroad, 156 miles from Fernandina on the Atlantic to Cedar Key on the Gulf of Mexico. The railroad is intended to connect New York, Havana, and New Orleans with steamers coming to and departing from each end of the new line, thus avoiding the long trip around the peninsula and through the Florida Straits. Steamers already travel the Atlantic from New York through Charleston and Savannah to Fernandina. On the Gulf side, steamers running from New Orleans to Havana already stop at Cedar Key. Fernandina on the Atlantic coast lies along the mouth of the St. Marys River. Among the attractions of Cedar Key is its port on the Gulf of Mexico and access to nearby lumber forests and sawmills processing cedar. Pine and cypress from the surrounding area will also be sold. By the late 1800s much of the forests will be depleted and the city's development retarded.

The railroad depot at Fernandina, the end point for Florida's first cross-state railroad, the Florida Railroad, which goes to Cedar Key

After completion of the Florida Railroad to Cedar Key, there are 414 miles of railroad in Florida, including the Florida Railroad—156 miles from Fernandina to Cedar Key, with a stopover in Gainesville; the Pensacola and Georgia Railroad—114 miles from Alligator (now called Lake City) to Tallahassee; the Florida, Atlantic, and Gulf Central—60 miles from Jacksonville to Lake City; the St. Johns Railway—15 miles from Tocoi along the St. Johns River to St. Augustine; and the Tallahassee Railroad—23 miles from Tallahassee to St. Marks on the Gulf of Mexico. By 1880, only 63 more miles of railroad will have been added.

On April 1, Confederate General Braxton Bragg is in command of five thousand men poised to attack Fort Pickens on Santa Rosa Island off Pensacola. Pensacola has strategic transportation importance as a rail hub and port for shipping. Florida Senator David Yulee advises the Tallahassee secession convention that all Pensacola forts should be seized. It appears that Fort Pickens may become the scene of the first shots fired in the war to come.

Confederate war steamer heading to the Pensacola Navy Yard on July 20, 1861

The Union's second reinforcement of Ft. Pickens, Pensacola, on April 16, 1861

On the night of April 11, under orders from President Lincoln to protect federal property, two hundred troops reinforce Fort Pickens in Pensacola. The Union's Civil War strategy as it pertains to Florida will be to: (1) occupy the major coastal ports in order to disrupt Confederate shipping and supplies and to maintain bases of operations from which to launch attacks on salt-producing facilities along the coastal areas; (2) maintain a naval blockade around the state to prevent supplies being im-

ported into the Confederacy and revenue coming in from the export of raw materials, such as cotton; and (3) launch attacks inland from the Union's coastal-controlled areas in order to seize beef and slaves and to prevent salt, beef, and other supplies from reaching Confederate forces to the north.

On April 12, Confederate guns fire on Fort Sumter, South Carolina, marking the beginning of the Civil War. The war will continue until 1865.

Of the 77,746 whites in Florida as of the 1860 census, some 15,000 will serve in the Confederate military services and about 5,000 will be killed. An additional number of white and black Floridians will serve in the Union military.

On April 14, Confederate forces at Pensacola attack Union forces but are repulsed. In May, Confederates will sink vessels to block the channel between the Gulf of Mexico and Pensacola Bay in an

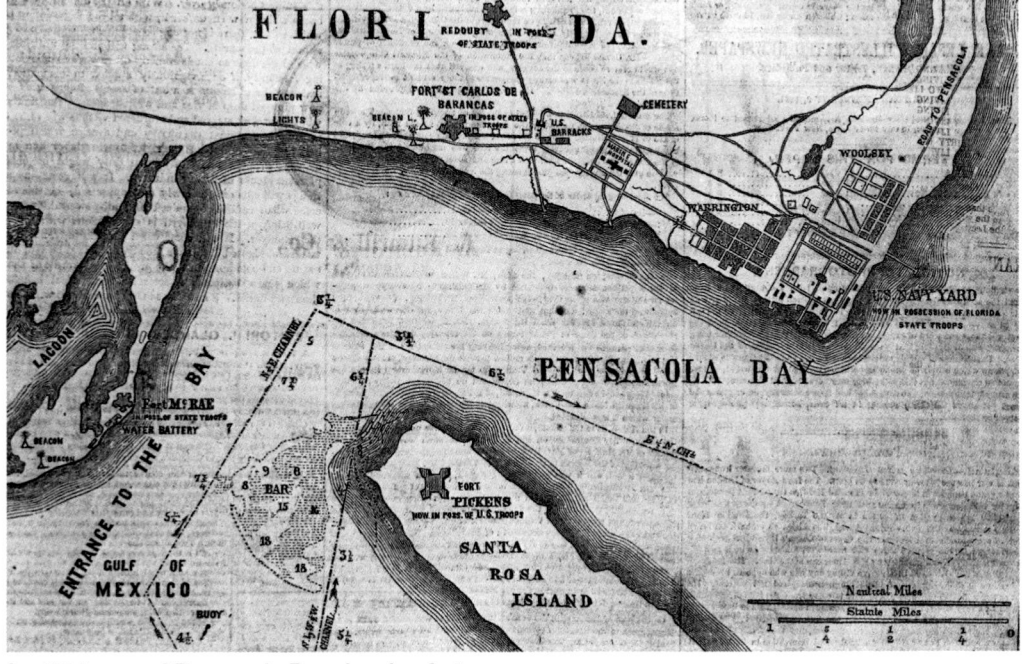

An 1861 map of Pensacola Bay showing forts

attempt to isolate the Union forces at Fort Pickens.

An 1864 image of the USS *Tahoma*, part of the East Gulf Blockading Squadron, ordered by President Lincoln to seal off the west coast of Florida from trade

On April 19, President Lincoln orders a naval blockade of the Confederate states, including Florida.

The waters around Florida are patrolled by U.S. Navy ships. In 1862, the Florida U.S. blockade units will be divided into four squadrons. As an example, the territory of the East Gulf Blockading Squadron will be the coast from Cape Florida, near today's Miami, to St. Andrew's Bay, near today's Panama City. The other three squadrons cover the west Gulf (from St. Andrew's Bay to the Rio Grande) and the north and south Atlantic coasts of the Confederacy (north of Miami). The mission of the squadrons is to close the shores and bring the war to Confederate Florida.

On April 27, Florida adopts a new constitution that, among other items, provides that the state's General Assembly "shall have no power to pass laws for the emancipation of slaves" but "shall have power to pass laws to prevent free Negroes . . . from immigrating to the State."

On May 10, Major French, the Union commander at Key West, places the island under martial law. He will shut down the local pro-Confederate newspaper and sever civil control from the state of Florida. Key West, one of Florida's largest cities, with 2,900 residents, will be the only city south of the Mason-Dixon Line that remains in Union control for the entire war.

On July 21, the first major battle of the Civil War takes place in Prince William County, Virginia, near the city of Manassas. The battle, known alternatively as the First Battle of Bull Run or the Battle of First Manassas, ends with a retreat by the Union troops led by General Irvin McDowell. The heroic efforts of Confederate General Thomas Jackson in the engagement earn him the nickname "Stonewall." This battle result effectively dashes Union hopes for a swift end to the rebellion.

Also in July, Union forces occupy Egmont Key, off today's St. Petersburg, ending its use as a base for Confederate blockade runners. The key becomes a base for the East Gulf Blockading Squadron and a haven for Northern sympathizers and runaway slaves, called contrabands. Confederate Navy prisoners are held on Egmont Key. James Hay, a Union supporter, sells his lower Pinellas Clam Bayou property to William Coons and joins the blockaders at Egmont Key. He receives a purchase price of twenty-five dollars and a silver watch and permanently leaves the peninsula.

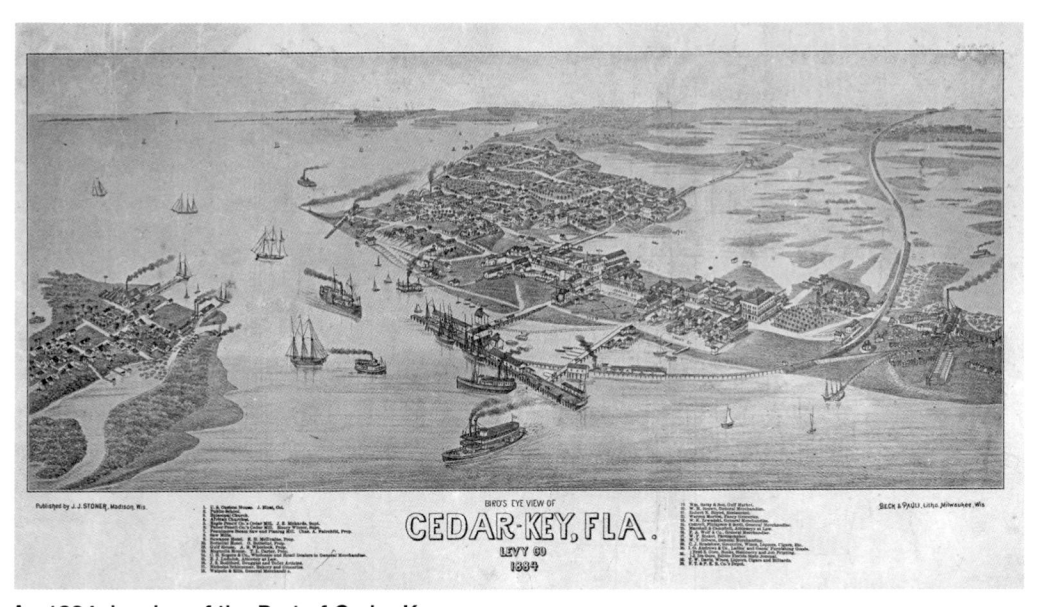

An 1884 drawing of the Port of Cedar Key

On August 5, in order to provide funding for the Civil War, President Lincoln signs the Revenue Act of 1861, creating the nation's first national income tax. The tax is a flat tax of 3 percent on income above $800.

A Confederate Florida five-dollar bill signed by Governor John Milton

On October 7, Democrat John Milton, a native of South Carolina and a Jackson County lawyer and planter, becomes Florida's fifth governor. Governor Milton has been a strong secessionist and advocate for the seizure of United States military forts and installations in Florida.

On October 24, the first cross-country telegraph message is sent by the chief justice of the California Supreme Court in Sacramento to President Lincoln in Washington, D.C.

On November 22, at 10 A.M., Union forces at Fort Pickens in Pensacola Bay and the USS *Niagara* and *Richmond* begin a barrage of cannon fire on Confederate forces at Fort McRee and the city of Pensacola. Damage is inflicted, but no ground changes hands. The stalemate between Union forces at Fort Pickens, who control entrance to the bay, and Confederate forces at Pensacola's two other forts and the Navy Yard, will continue. After an extended siege, on February 27, 1862, Confederate General Bragg will announce the abandonment of Pensacola, and Union forces will occupy the Navy Yard, other forts, and town on May 12, 1862.

Also in November, Confederate General Robert E. Lee determines that the only Atlantic Confederate coastal defenses to be protected are Charleston, Savannah, and Brunswick, a decision that leaves Jacksonville and St. Augustine in peril.

An 1862 artist's rendering of Union troops marching down Second Street in Fernandina

1862

On January 16, Union gunboats approach Cedar Key, a Florida Gulf coast port city and southern terminus of the Florida Railroad. The Union's *Hatteras* begins to fire, destroying several boats in the harbor and setting the Florida Railroad wharf on fire. Union troops come ashore and capture the Confederate commander along with most of the small force protecting the port. The Union will control Cedar Key for the remainder of the war. Union forces will use the coastal city as a staging place for attacks on Confederate salt works and supply depots.

On February 22, Jefferson Davis, former United States Senator from Mississippi, is sworn into office as President of the Confederate States of America.

On February 24, Confederate General James Trapier receives permission from General Robert E. Lee to evacuate Florida's Amelia Island and Georgia's Cumberland Island and to abandon defenses at Fernandina, located about thirty miles north of Jacksonville.

On February 28, federal troops sail from Port Royal, South Carolina, en route to occupy Fernandina on Florida's east coast. The town evacuates in advance of the federal occupation.

Also in February, federal troops from Egmont Key on Florida's Gulf coast attack the Point Pinellas Big Bayou home of Abel Miranda, an ardent secessionist, and burn it down. They destroy Miranda's orange grove and kill his cattle. The raid may be in retaliation for the ambush of Unionist brothers Scott and John Whitehurst in which Scott Whitehurst was killed.

On March 3, Union ships arrive at Fernandina and fire shots while the Confederates are abandoning Fernandina's Fort Clinch. The Confederate steamboat *Ottawa*, a blockade runner, is captured by Union forces, who take the city and will control Fernandina for the duration of the war.

An 1864 photo of the U.S. barracks at St. Augustine

On March 11, Union gunboats arrive off the coast of St. Augustine threatening the city. The night before, all Confederate troops had evacuated the city, leaving it defenseless. With no options, St. Augustine Mayor Bravo raises the white flag at Fort Marion and then surrenders the city to Union Commander Rogers. St. Augustine will remain in Union control for the remainder of the war. It will become a convalescent camp for wounded Union soldiers.

Also on March 11, Union forces capture a deserted Jacksonville and abandon the town a week later. Union forces will reenter and abandon the town again in October 1862 and March 1863, before taking the city for good on February 7, 1864.

On March 22, Union warships *Penguin* and *Henry Andrew* are at the inlet off Smyrna (today's New Smyrna), about fifteen miles south of Daytona Beach. They are in search of blockade runners. Since the Union has occupied Florida's three major ports—Jacksonville, Pensacola, and St. Augustine—the South now trades using smaller ports along the state's coast. European ships bring military and other supplies to the Bahamas, where the cargo is transferred to smaller blockade-running ships. The cargo is then delivered by the blockade runners and exchanged for cotton or tobacco, which the South exports.

A Union raiding party from the *Henry Andrew* and *Penguin* goes ashore off today's Indian River and burns the Confederate blockade runner *Katie*, but the force is ambushed by Confederate forces on the way back to their ship, leaving seven killed and thirty wounded.

By the end of April, Lieutenant William Eaton of the East Gulf Blockading Squadron has twenty-five Florida Unionists and their families under his protection and support at Egmont Key. The Florida Unionists will assist federal forces in the capture and destruction of several Confederate vessels.

On May 9, with Rebel troops needed in other regions and after failing to oust the Union forces at Fort Pickens, the Confederate forces evacuate Pensacola. The city and its harbor will remain in Union control for the remainder of the war.

On May 20, the U.S. Homestead Act of 1862 is passed, giving homesteaders 160 free

An 1875 Florida map showing railroads

acres if they occupy and improve land in the public domain for five continuous years.

On September 17, forces under the command of Union General George McClellan attack those under the command of Confederate General Robert E. Lee near Sharpsburg, Maryland, and Antietam Creek. After both sides incur large numbers of casualties, Lee's forces will be forced to withdraw back into Virginia, ending his invasion of Maryland. Lincoln will use momentum from the victory to announce his intention, in five days, on September 22, to free all slaves in the South; however, his frustration with General McClellan's failure to pursue Lee following the victory, along with ongoing unhappiness with his general, will cause Lincoln to remove McClellan as commander of the Potomac on November 5. McClellan will run against Lincoln in the 1864 presidential election.

A 1984 aerial view of Fort Jefferson in the Dry Tortugas, which suffered an outbreak of typhoid and yellow fever in 1862

Also in September, typhoid and yellow fever first appear in Key West and spread quickly through the island. Hundreds of Union soldiers will die from the diseases in Key West and at Fort Jefferson at the Dry Tortugas, seventy miles west of Key West.

On December 15, Union Major General Ambrose Burnside withdraws the Army of the Potomac, ending the Union attack against General Robert E. Lee's Confederate Army of Northern Virginia in and around Freder-

icksburg, Virginia. There are more than twelve thousand Union and five thousand Confederate casualties in the battle.

1863

On New Year's Day, President Abraham Lincoln signs the Emancipation Proclamation freeing all slaves in the Confederate states, including Florida.

A circa 1864 portrait of Confederate Captain John Jackson Dickison, captain of Company H of the Second Florida Cavalry. He and his 200 men are charged with defending the stretch from Palatka up the St. Johns River to Volusia County. He serves in the Florida legislature after the war.

On March 27, a Union force of five hundred infantry, while heading south on the St. Johns River aboard the transport *Mary Benton*, is attacked by Confederate Captain John Dickison's two hundred mounted men in Company H of the 2nd Florida Cavalry. The attack near Palatka, about fifty miles south of Jacksonville, leaves many Union men killed or wounded, including the commanding officer, Lt. Colonel Liberty Billings. The Union troops retreat to Jacksonville.

On May 3, Robert E. Lee's Army of Northern Virginia repulses an offensive by Union Major General Joseph Hooker's Army of the Potomac near the village of Chancellorsville, Virginia. In the multiple-day engagement resulting in a Union defeat, there will be more than seventeen thousand Union and more than thirteen thousand Confederate causalities. Confederate General Stonewall Jackson will die from a friendly fire wound suffered in the battle.

On July 1, the forces of Union General George Meade confront the Confederate forces under General Robert E. Lee at Gettysburg, Pennsylvania. After two days of battle with more than twenty thousand Confederate casualties and twenty-three thousand Union casualties, Lee's forces retreat south, ending the Confederate campaign into the North. President Lincoln will speak at a ceremony establishing a National Cemetery at Gettysburg on November 19, 1863, offering America the "Gettysburg Address," which will become one of the most impactful speeches of all time.

On July 4, Confederate General John Pemberton surrenders his troops to Union General Ulysses S. Grant, ending the Union siege of Vicksburg, Mississippi. With the victory at Vicksburg, the Union now controls the Mississippi River and has cut the Confederacy into two.

With the loss of the Mississippi River by the Confederates, the importance of Florida beef to the Rebel cause increases significantly. Florida assembles a "Cow Cavalry" to protect the state's cattle on its route north to the Confederate forces.

FIGHT NEAR PALATKA. CAPTAIN DICKISON BEARING THE BODY OF HIS SON FROM THE BATTLE-FIELD.

An 1864 drawing of Captain John Dickison of the Second Florida Cavalry, who successfully attacks and repels the Union forces near Palatka, but at a great price. He is shown here bearing the body of his son, who is killed in the battle.

On October 13, the USS *Tahoma* and the USS *Adda* send shore parties in pursuit of two blockade running ships, the *Scottish Chief* and the *Kate Dale*, which flee up the Hillsborough River in Tampa. The blockade runners are destroyed and five crewmen and two militia men are captured.

In December, Union General Daniel Woodbury occupies and secures Fort Myers, which had been abandoned since the Second Seminole War. Union troops will use the facility to plan and execute attacks on salt works and cattle-trading centers in order to prevent supplies from reaching Confederate forces to the north. The Union efforts are successful. In February 1865, Confederate Major William Footman will lead two companies from Tampa on a failed effort to seize Fort Myers for the Confederacy.

1864

On February 7, Union forces again occupy Jacksonville. Although the Union had controlled Jacksonville in 1862 and 1863, they withdrew from the city each time. This time they will occupy the city for the rest of the war.

On February 20, the most significant Civil War battle in Florida takes place in Olustee, ten miles east of Lake City and about fifty miles west of Jacksonville. More than five thousand Union soldiers led by Brigadier General Truman Seymour set out from Union-controlled Jacksonville in an attempt to cut off the supply of salt, beef, and other supplies from Florida to the remaining Confederacy. After a six-hour battle, the equal-size Confederate forces led by Brigadier General Joseph Finegan force the Union forces to retreat. Ninety-three Confederate and 203 Union soldiers are killed.

During the war, Florida is critical in supplying salt produced at coastal salt works, fish, and cattle to the Confederate armies. At the coastal salt works, salt water is pumped, powered by windmill, to wooden vats. When the water evaporates the salt is gathered. The salt is used extensively by the Confederate troops to preserve meat.

An 1894 lithographic print of the Battle of Olustee

A photograph taken October 23, 1912, of survivors of the Battle of Olustee, who gather to dedicate a monument to the battle

The Union's Florida campaign of 1864 included an effort to recruit black soldiers into the Union army

An April 1864 photograph of the officers of the Seventh U.S. Colored troops in Jacksonville

An 1862 rendering showing the crew of the Union's *Kingfisher* destroying a Confederate salt factory on the Florida coast

Florida provided thirty thousand head of cattle to the Confederacy in 1863 and twenty thousand more in 1864. The Battle of Olustee is the culmination of the Union's Florida Campaign of 1864, an effort to recruit blacks into the Union army, cut off supplies of beef, cotton, timber, turpentine, and other Florida products from the Confederacy and to divert those products to the North, and to bring Florida back into the Union on an expedited basis. One-third of Union troops at Olustee are African American, a reflection of the major role that African American soldiers play in Florida throughout the war on behalf of the North's efforts. The Union's 1864 Florida Campaign ends with the loss at Olustee.

On March 12, General Ulysses S. Grant is named chief of the Union armies, having achieved great success in western battles.

A portrait of Confederate General Joseph Finegan, who leads Confederate forces to victory at the battle of Olustee, the most significant battle in Florida during the Civil War

In April, after shelling by federal gunboats, Fort Brooke, in today's Tampa, falls to Union forces.

On May 6, a federal force arrives and takes control of Tampa. A Confederate contingent of more than thirty men left several days earlier. The Union troops load cannon and other captured supplies into their ship and, before the end of the month, will leave the city.

On July 18, President Lincoln calls for five hundred thousand more volunteers to support the war effort, while General Grant suffers high casualties in his campaign against Richmond.

On August 15, Confederate Colonel Andrew Harris of the 75th Ohio infantry leads a Union force of about 250 infantry and cavalry, including African American soldiers and others from Ohio and Massachusetts, into Gainesville and begins to destroy railroad cars and stores. After initial success, the Union men are confronted by a force of 175 men led by Confederate Captain John Dickison of the Second Flor-

ida Cavalry, who repel the Union force, capture more than one hundred prisoners, and kill and wound many. The target of the Union force was the large supply depot in Gainesville—part of the Union's effort to disrupt Florida supplies from reaching Confederate forces to the north.

An 1864 artist's rendering of the Gainesville battle by the Beville hotel, where the Union troops had gathered to fight, before retreating with Confederate Captain John Dickison in pursuit

On September 27, a Union force from Fort Barrancas at Pensacola, under the command of General Alexander Asboth,

A photograph of an 1864 painting of the CSS *Florida* which, having been captured on October 7, 1864, is sunk in a collision with the U.S. Army transport *Alliance* on November 28, 1864, in Hampton Roads off Norfolk

attacks a small Confederate force in Marianna, Florida, fifty miles northwest of Tallahassee. The Federals are en route to attack and capture Tallahassee. The Union force overwhelms the Confederates and captures the city; however, General Asboth is injured and must return to Pensacola. After much destruction to the city, the Union troops will return to Pensacola the next day with one hundred prisoners. Ten Union and sixty Confederate troops are killed in the battle.

On November 8, Abraham Lincoln is reelected president of the United States, defeating his former general, George McClellan.

On November 15, forces under Union Major General William Tecumseh Sherman leave the captured city of Atlanta, Georgia, and begin "Sherman's March to the Sea" through Georgia toward Savannah. Sherman will accept the surrender of Savannah on December 21 and

will send President Lincoln a telegram offering the city as his Christmas gift.

Also this year, for war purposes, a railroad line is constructed from Dupont, Georgia, to a point on the Florida-Georgia border where the line connects with a railroad line being built north from Live Oak, Florida. It is the first connection of the Florida Railroad line to another state. On November 4, 1879, the line will be sold to Henry Plant, and it will eventually become part of the Atlantic Coast Line.

1865

On February 16, General Sherman takes the South Carolina capital of Columbia. Charleston, South Carolina, where the Civil War began, falls into Union control the next day, February 17, 1865.

On March 4, Abraham Lincoln is sworn into office for his second term as president. In his inaugural address, he anticipates Civil War

Honor Guard at the monument to the Battle of Natural Bridge

victory and urges a conciliatory reunion of the country: ". . . let us strive on to finish the work we are in, to bind up the nation's wounds, to care for him who shall have borne the battle and for his widow and his orphan, to do all which may achieve and cherish a just and lasting peace among ourselves, and with all nations."

On March 6, at the Battle of Natural Bridge, the local militia joined by cadets from the West Florida Seminary, today's Florida State University, successfully defend Tallahassee, leaving the capital city uncaptured until the war's end. The natural bridge, about fifteen miles southeast of Tallahassee, is an area about fifty yards long where the St. Marks River runs underground. The Battle of Natural Bridge is the second largest Civil War battle fought in Florida.

On April 1, Florida Governor John Milton, knowing that the war is lost and preferring death to reunion, kills himself with a shotgun. Abraham K. Allison, as president of Florida's state senate, becomes acting governor.

On April 3, after a long siege, General Grant captures Richmond, Virginia, the capital of the Confederacy. Confederate President Jefferson Davis and his cabinet had abandoned the city in advance of the Union occupation. President Lincoln will visit Richmond on April 4. Montgomery, capital of Alabama, will fall on April 12.

On April 9, General Robert E. Lee surrenders the Confederate Army of Northern Virginia to General Ulysses S. Grant and the Union forces at Appomattox Court House, Virginia.

A drawn portrait of Colonel V.M. Johnson, principal of West Florida Seminary, who commands cadets to defend Tallahassee in the Battle of Natural Bridge

Major General John Newton, Union commander at the Battle of Natural Bridge

A photograph of President Abraham Lincoln and his son Tad in Washington D.C., taken by Matthew Brady on February 9, 1864. The president who had led the nation through the greatest crisis in its history dies six days after Confederate General Robert E. Lee surrenders to Union General Ulysses S. Grant, and less than four weeks before the government of the Confederacy is captured and the war is declared over.

On April 15, President Lincoln dies, having been shot the night before by actor John Wilkes Booth while attending the comedy Our American Cousin *at Ford's Theatre in Washington. Vice President Andrew Johnson assumes the presidency. The assassination conspiracy included plans to kill President Lincoln, Vice President Andrew Johnson, and Secretary of State William Seward. President Lincoln is the only target killed.*

Lewis Powell, a Floridian from Live Oak, eighty miles east of Tallahassee, is part of the conspiracy. Powell stabs Seward in his bedroom several times, then flees. Seward will survive but Powell will be captured and put to death on July 7, 1865.

On May 10, Confederate President Jefferson Davis and a few remaining officials of the Confederate government are captured near Irwinville, Georgia, about 110 miles northeast of Tallahassee. United States President Andrew Johnson declares that the war is over.

Tallahassee is the only state capital east of the Mississippi River that remains unconquered until the end of the war. Also in May, Judah Benjamin, Secretary of State for the Confederacy, escapes federal capture by fleeing to a 3,500-acre sugar cane plantation owned by Major Robert Gamble on the Manatee River in Ellenton. He will remain several weeks before escaping to England.

Also on May 10, Union Brigadier General Edward M. McCook arrives in

Lewis Thornton Powell (alias Lewis Payne), co-assassin of the conspiracy to kill President Lincoln is from Live Oak. He tries to kill Secretary of State William Seward, is caught and hanged.

A 1920s photograph of Confederate veterans at the memorial to Confederate Secretary of State Judah P. Benjamin at Ellenton's Gamble plantation, where Benjamin hid from federal authorities

Union General Edward M. McCook takes formal possession of Tallahassee on May 20, 1865, and raises the United States flag over the capitol. He is occupying commander of Florida.

Tallahassee to receive the surrender of the remaining Florida Confederate forces. He takes up residence in the Hagner home, today known as the Knott House. On May 20, he will take formal possession of Tallahassee, raise the United States flag over the Capitol, and read the Emancipation Proclamation aloud, announcing the end of slavery.

On May 22, Union General McCook places Florida under martial law. Military occupation is established for all principal places in the state. Federal troops are stationed in Tallahassee, Gainesville, Lake City, Madison, Monticello, Palatka, and Tampa. Pensacola, Jacksonville, and Key West are already under Union control. McCook imprisons Abraham Allison, the sitting governor who had replaced Civil War Florida Governor John Milton after Milton's suicide. Allison will be released after a short period.

In July 1865, President Andrew Johnson appoints William Marvin the provisional governor of Florida

On July 23, President Andrew Johnson appoints William Marvin, a former federal judge from Key West and a moderate Unionist, as Florida's provisional governor. Governor Marvin's inaugural address is one of reconciliation with the Union. He stresses the need to accept the new reality: "The war which was commenced among other reasons, for perpetuating the black man's bondage, has… brought him freedom. He can never be enslaved again . . . The spirit of malice and revenge must be banished from among us, and every one of us must embark on a mission of peace and goodwill … Let everyone yield supreme obedience to the laws, and prosperity will follow."

On November 7, Florida, having convened a constitutional convention on October 25, adopts a new state constitution that begrudgingly abolishes slavery in Florida after acknowledging that "slavery has been destroyed in this state by the Government of the United States." The constitution limits the declaration of inherent and indefeasible rights to "all freemen" and limits suffrage to "free white male person[s] of the age of twenty-one years and upward."

On December 18, the Thirteenth Amendment to the United States Constitution, making slavery illegal, is ratified by the twenty-seventh state and is declared law by Secretary of State William Seward.

A portrait of Florida Governor David S. Walker, who is sworn in to office on December 20, 1865

On December 20, David S. Walker, a legislator and former mayor of Tallahassee, is sworn into office as Florida's eighth governor, and the fourth Florida governor to serve in the year 1865. In his lengthy inaugural speech, Governor Walker both defends the positions taken by those who advocated for secession and acknowledges the need to move on: "We have lost much—many of us our all—all but our honor. Let us preserve that, though we lose everything else." With respect to the former slaves, he acknowledges that "they are free. They are no longer our contented and happy slaves, with an abundant supply of food and clothing . . . They are now a discontented and unhappy people . . . doomed to untold sufferings and ultimate extinction, unless we intervene for their protection and preservation." While Governor Walker accepts the former slaves' freedom, he makes it clear that "we could never accede to the demand for negro suffrage."

On December 29, Florida will ratify the Thirteen Amendment "with the understanding that it does not confer on Congress the power to legislate the status of freedmen in the State."

1866

On April 2, President Andrew Johnson declares that the insurrection is at an end in Georgia, South Carolina, Virginia, North Carolina, Tennessee, Alabama, Louisiana, Arkansas, Mississippi, and Florida. He will declare an end to insurrection in Texas, the remaining Confederate state, on August 14.

1867

On March 2, President Johnson vetoes the Reconstruction Act of 1867. Congress responds by overriding the president's veto. The act is Congress' response to the election of ex-Confederates to state and local offices, the enactment of Black Codes designed to oppress former slaves, the defiant attitudes of Southern leaders, and acts of violence against African Americans. It divides the South into five regions, excluding Tennessee, places a military commander in charge of each region and authorizes the military governors, among others, to organize constitutional conventions, remove local officials, impose martial law, require black suffrage, and decide on voter eligibility. New state governments will be recognized by Congress upon adoption of a new constitution guaranteeing black suffrage and state ratification of the Fourteenth Amendment.

On March 4, the oil partnership of John Rockefeller, Samuel Andrews, and Henry M. Flagler is announced in the Cleveland Leader. *On January 11, 1870, the partnership will incorporate as the Standard Oil Company. By 1879, their "Standard Alliance" will control 95 percent of America's oil industry. By 1882, the various stockholders of the alliance companies will combine into the Standard Oil*

Trust, which, at a value of $75 million, will be America's largest business.

On March 30, President Andrew Johnson's Secretary of State William H. Seward signs a treaty with Russia to acquire the Alaska territory for $7.2 million. The Senate will ratify the treaty on April 9 after Seward argues the natural resources and strategic advantage of the land. Many in the media mock the acquisition as "Seward's Folly." The acquisition adds 591,000 square miles to the United States, the nation's second largest single land acquisition to this date after the Louisiana Purchase, which added almost 828,000 square miles.

John Titcomb Sprague, whose proclamation of martial law triggers the second military occupation of the state

On April 8, United States Colonel John T. Sprague, military commander of the District of Florida, proclaims martial law, triggering the second military occupation of Florida. Local governments continue to function subject to intervention by federal forces.

1868

On February 21, Florida's delegates in convention declare the 1861 Ordinance of Secession "null and void."

On February 24, Andrew Johnson becomes the first U.S. president to be impeached by the House of Representatives by a vote of 126-47. He is accused of violating the Tenure of Office Act by dismissing Secretary of War Edwin Stanton. On May 26, 1868, the Senate vote to remove him from office will fail by one vote.

On April 10, Cuban insurgents proclaim independence from Spain, marking the beginning of the "Ten Years' War" for Cuban independence. The 1868 revolution will fall short, but efforts will continue, ultimately resulting in Cuban independence on May 20, 1902.

José Martí on the steps of the Vicente Martínez Ybor Cigar Factory in Tampa, making a speech to supporters of the Cuban revolutionary movement. Martí is in the center of the photograph on the top step with his jacket open and his hands in his pockets.

During the Ten Years' War, thousands of Cuban refugees flee the island to Florida, with the largest exile community settling in Key West. Cuban cigar manufacturers and workers import an industry to Key West that will flourish there and will later grow in an even bigger way in Tampa.

By the 1870s, twenty-nine Key West cigar factories will produce more than 62 million cigars annually. In 1886, Vicente Martínez Ybor will relocate his cigar business from Key West to Tampa, where he will build the world's largest cigar factory. By the turn of the coming century, 150 cigar factories in West Tampa and Ybor City will produce 111 million cigars annually.

On May 6, 7, and 8, Florida's electorate ratifies a new state constitution that modifies many of the objectionable provisions of the 1865 constitution. Among the changes, there is a declaration that "all men are by nature free and equal"; a statement that "no power exists with the people of this State to dissolve its connection" with the United States; and a guarantee that "There shall be no civil or political distinction in this State on account of race, color, or previous condition of servitude." The right to vote is extended to include African American males twenty-one years old and above. Voters must swear allegiance to the United States.

On June 8, Harrison Reed, who came to Florida from Wisconsin as a treasury agent, is sworn into office as Florida's ninth governor and first Republican governor. In his brief address, Governor Reed applauds the end of slavery as "an unmitigated curse" and predicts great things for Florida's future: "All classes of society and all interests of the State demand peace and good government, and if the spirit of our Constitution is appreciated and reciprocated . . . the State may assist from its prostrate condition to a measure unknown in the past, and become one of the brightest luminaries in the galaxy of our glorious Union." Florida's military commander will not recognize the new governor or state constitution until July 4, 1868.

On July 4, the second military occupation of Florida ends with the restoration of civil government.

On July 25, Congress declares that Florida is again a part of the United States.

On November 3, Union general and Civil War hero Ulysses S. Grant is elected president of the United States.

On December 25, President Andrew Johnson grants an unconditional pardon to those accused of treason during the Civil War.

1869

On May 10, the connection between the Union Pacific and Central Pacific Railroads is completed at Promontory Point, Utah, uniting the Atlantic and Pacific oceans by railroad.

On October 6, Abel Miranda settles at Clam Bayou in Point Pinellas, purchasing the Rosa Read property for $500. He will become one of Pinellas' top ranchers, eventually holding more than a thousand head of cattle. During the Civil War, the Florida cattle industry increased due to the needs of the Confederate army. Now, as the cattle industry throughout Florida continues to grow, Florida's ranchers will export cattle to Cuba, receiving over $1.6 million in gold doubloons for cattle shipped to the island during the next decade. The growing cattle industry, along with the merchants and shippers that support it, will help the state recover following the difficult economic times of the Civil War and Reconstruction.

1870

This year, Josiah T. Wells, a former Virginia slave, is elected a U.S. congressman from Gainesville, the first African American to serve from Florida.

A circa 1896 view of the Miami River, twenty-six years after William Brickell establishes a trading post on the river

A post-1969 view of Miami's Brickell Avenue, on the land acquired by William Brickell in 1870

Also this year, William Brickell establishes a trading post on the south side of the Miami River.

1871

William Brickell purchases a large parcel of land from the Miami River south to Coconut Grove.

On April 10, Phineas T. Barnum begins the "Great Travelling Museum, Menagerie, Caravan, and Hippodrome" in Brooklyn, New York. It is the predecessor to the Ringling Bros. Barnum & Bailey Circus.

1873

On January 7, Republican Ossian B. Hart, a farmer, lawyer, and legislator who has lived in different parts of the state, is sworn into office as the tenth and first native-born governor of Florida, having been born in Jacksonville. Governor Hart outlines a very general set of objectives to "punish crime, so that perfect safety alone under the law shall prevail; to stimulate education until it shall, as it ought to do, be universally known as one of the first necessities; to husband all our resources and use them for the public good; to cancel useless paper; to raise money with which to pay all of the state debts with interest promptly." Unfortunately, after becoming

An 1820s photograph of Gilbert's Bar House of Refuge in Stuart, Florida, two miles north of the St. Lucie Inlet and forty miles north of West Palm Beach. It opens in 1876. In 1915 it will be operated by the United States Coast Guard, then beginning in 1941 it will be operated by the U.S. Navy through World War II. The last standing house of refuge, it will become a public museum after 1955.

sick with pneumonia, the governor will die on March 18, 1874.

On September 20, the New York Stock Exchange closes abruptly. The Panic of 1873 precipitates a three-year national economic depression.

1874

On March 18, upon the death of Governor Hart, Lieutenant Governor Marcellus L. Sterns, a former Union soldier, becomes Florida's eleventh governor.

On June 20, a congressional act establishes five houses of refuge along the east coast of Florida from Ft. Pierce Inlet to Biscayne Bay. The houses will be operated by the United States Life-Saving Service to rescue and shelter shipwrecked sailors. The houses of refuge become the foundation for cities along the coast.

1875

On July 31, the town of Orlando is incorporated. It has eighty-five residents, twenty-two of whom were qualified to vote on the incorporation. The town is two miles square, and the Orange County Courthouse is in the middle of the town. William Jackson Brack, a south Florida cattleman, becomes Orlando's first town mayor.

1876

On January 4, John Constantine Williams, known as the General, purchases the Spurlin property in today's downtown St. Petersburg. Williams moved to the city in 1875 from Detroit in an effort to relieve his asthma. His father, General John R. Williams, was commander of the Michigan troops during the Black Hawk War of 1832. John R. Williams (the father) ran a successful mercantile and real estate business, was a founder of the *Detroit Free*

Press, and, in 1824, was elected the first mayor of the city of Detroit.

On March 10, Alexander Graham Bell and his assistant, twenty-two-year-old Thomas H. Watson, successfully transmit the human voice through wire for the first time, the predecessor to the telephone. Bell calls out, "Mr. Watson, come here; I want you." By the fall of 1877 Bell will have 3,000 demonstration telephones; by 1894 almost 300,000; and by 1904, 1,317,000.

Beginning in 1916, Thomas Watson will spend his winters in Pass-a-Grille on St. Pete Beach, painting Florida landscapes until his death at his home in the beach community in 1934.

On November 7, the presidential election between Republican Rutherford B. Hayes and Democrat Samuel Tilden is held. A conflict arises over the election results in Florida, South Carolina, and Louisiana, with the election hanging in the balance.

On November 27, Florida's canvassing board meets to evaluate Florida's presidential election results. The Republicans, who control the board, certify the election for Hayes. Democratic electors meet on the same day and maintain that Tilden carried Florida.

1877

On January 2, George F. Drew, a sawmill and lumberyard operator from Madison County, becomes the first Democratic governor of Florida since the Civil War, and Florida's twelfth governor. Acknowledging the fears of African Americans that a Democrat will not uphold their rights,

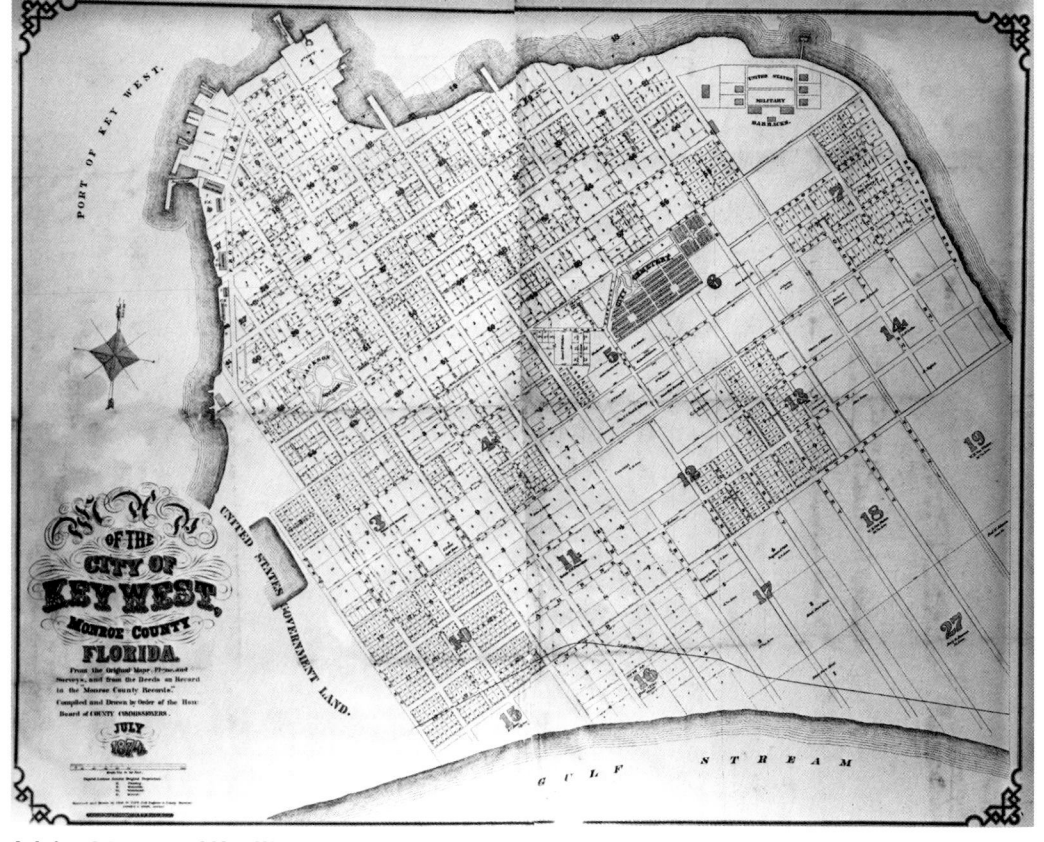

A July 1874 map of Key West

Governor Drew assures all that the "fears are groundless, and our colored fellow-citizens may finally rest assured that their rights, as guaranteed by the Constitution, will be fully sustained."

On January 18, the remaining Reconstruction federal troops begin to leave Florida. They will be gone by January 23.

On March 2, the United States Electoral Commission names Rutherford B. Hayes president. Republicans gain Southern Democratic support for Hayes by agreeing to end Reconstruction and remove federal troops from Louisiana and South Carolina. Hayes will remove the troops in April. This marks the end of Reconstruction.

On May 1, the Silver Springs, Ocala, and Gulf Railroad is chartered to construct a railroad from Palatka to Point Pinellas, today's St. Petersburg. The line will ultimately be built only as far as Homosassa.

Also this year, in Menlo Park, New Jersey, Thomas Edison develops the first phonograph, using a tinfoil cylinder. In 1878, he will play it for President Rutherford B. Hayes and Mrs. Hayes at the White House.

Also this year, Captain Lund brings the steamboat *Pioneer* to the Indian River, starting an era of commercial steamboat transportation in the region that will continue into the early twentieth century. The Indian River, which flows for 121 miles between today's Space Coast beaches and the mainland, is a brackish lagoon forming part of the Intracoastal Waterway from Titusville south to Stuart. It was formerly called the *Rio de Ais,* named after the native tribe that was here when the Spanish arrived.

The steamboat *St. Augustine* on the Indian River. Steamboats along the Indian River are critical to commerce and development in the region around Merritt Island.

> **❝**It is my hope and purpose to secure [the Everglades']
> reclamation and convert what is now unsurveyed
> wasteland into a state asset more valuable than all the
> lands now under cultivation.**❞**

Governor Napoleon Bonaparte Broward, in his 1905 inaugural address, making clear his intent to drain the Glades for use as farmland

Chapter 4
Bringing the Railroad: 1878 through 1919

In the post-Civil War era, transportation is the key to Florida's development, so the state sells and transfers land in order to pay off debt and encourage the development of railroads. Henry Flagler begins his legendary journey down Florida's east coast, building railroads, communities, and hotels, eventually reaching Key West by the end of the era, the southernmost point of the continental United States. In north, central, and southwest Florida, Henry Plant and others also develop railroads. This era will be the greatest period of railroad construction in the United States and Florida. During the 1880s, almost seventy-five thousand miles of railroad are constructed in the nation and about two thousand miles are built in Florida, an increase of almost 500 percent in Florida's total railroad miles during ten years.

On January 22, 1912, crowds greet the first passenger from the mainland to arrive on the inaugural train to Key West, the southernmost point in the continental United States. Railroad builder Henry Flagler, holding a top hat, is in the circle. He is being escorted by Key West Mayor Joseph Fogarty.

During this era, Florida will construct transportation and other infrastructure as development moves south. Utilities are built, social organizations thrive, police and fire departments grow, and banks open to support growth and major industry, including fishing and citrus. Harbors are dredged and trolley systems arrive. In short, Florida's cities are growing into active urban areas.

After the Wright Brothers give birth to flight, airplanes arrive in Florida, and St. Petersburg becomes home to the world's first scheduled passenger airline. President Roosevelt creates a bird sanctuary on Pelican Island, while Florida leaders lay out plans to drain the Everglades and replace wetlands with agriculture.

The state establishes an education system, develops a phosphate industry, organizes and funds a state road department, and plays a major role in the Spanish–American War. Meanwhile, in Ft. Myers, Thomas Edison sets up a winter residence where he continues his break-through scientific work. He is later joined by automobile titan Henry Ford.

Toward the end of the era the United States and Florida enter World War I, then known as the Great War.

Timeline

1878

President Calvin Coolidge on a glass-bottom boat at Silver Springs

Throughout this book events in Florida are set in Roman (non-italics), and events outside Florida are set in *italics*.

A twentieth-century photograph of tourists enjoying the view of Silver Springs in a glass-bottom boat

This year, Hullam Jones constructs a glass viewing box in the floor of a dugout canoe to give tourists a view of the clear water of Silver Springs, seven miles east of Ocala, on the Ocklawaha River.

1879

On October 29, Thomas Edison invents a practical electric light at his laboratory in Menlo Park, New Jersey. Within three years Edison will supply electric service to fifty-nine customers within one mile of his central station system in New York City. Fourteen months later he will be providing electricity to 508 customers with almost 13,000 lights.

Also this year, the Gainesville, Ocala and Charlotte Harbor Railroad is formed. In the early 1880s it will be reorganized under Henry Plant's control and become Florida Southern Railway. Florida Southern will eventually receive 2.58 million acres of railroad land grants from the state government. By the time the Plant System of railroads is sold in 1902, it will have more than 2,200 miles of track and serve much of northern and southwest Florida and southern Georgia. In order to save money, the early lines will be built with narrow gauge rail—three feet between the rails—instead of standard four feet eight and one-half inch gauge.

1880

On January 10, former President Ulysses S. Grant digs the first shovel of dirt for a railroad to connect the St. Johns River at Sanford with Florida's Gulf Coast.

1881

On January 4, Democrat William D. Bloxham, a Florida native from Leon County who has been a lawyer, planter, and legislator, becomes Florida's thirteenth governor. In his inaugural address, Governor Bloxham describes the "three great links in the grand chain of progress upon which we can confidently rely for our future growth and prosperity." The links include that Florida must "invite a healthy immigration; develop our internal improvements by securing proper transportation; and educate the rising generation." He also attempts to reassure Florida's African American population: "As to the colored population, I can but assure them that their rights and liberties are secured by the great fundamental law of the Union as well as those of the state."

Florida Railroad Development

Through Civil War

1836: Tallahassee to Port Leon on the Gulf

1860: Jacksonville to Lake City to Tallahassee

1860: Tocoi (St. Johns River) to St. Augustine (iron rails)

1861: Fernandina to Cedar Key

1861: Pensacola to Pollard, Alabama

1864: Live Oak to DuPont, Georgia

Railroad Era

1880: Orlando to Sanford (on St. Johns River)*

1881: Waycross, Georgia to Jacksonville

1883: Jacksonville to Tallahassee to Pensacola

1884: Tampa to Sanford

1886: Jacksonville to Sanford

1888: St. Petersburg to Longwood (to Sanford 1889)

1889: Jacksonville to Daytona Beach

1894: Jacksonville to West Palm Beach

1896: Jacksonville to Ft. Lauderdale

1896: Jacksonville to Miami

1903: Durant (east of Tampa) to Sarasota

1904: Ft. Myers to Naples

1912: Jacksonville to Key West (Florida's most southern point)

1920: Tampa to Bradenton

1926: Punta Gorda to Ft. Myers

1928: Deep Lake to Everglades City

*Sanford provides access to river transport and, after 1886, to rail to Jacksonville and points north.

Hamilton Disston, who helps save Florida from bankruptcy by purchasing four million acres and then works to drain the Everglades

On February 28, Florida is forced to restructure its debt due to the default on state-guaranteed railroad bond interest. In a deal negotiated by Governor Bloxham, the state agrees to sell four million acres to Hamilton Disston for $1 million, enabling the Florida Internal Improvement Fund to pay off railroad bonds that it had guaranteed. Disston is the thirty-six-year-old heir to a Philadelphia saw manufacturing company. With railroads failing during and after the Civil War, the fund needs cash to make good on the bonds and provide for additional railroad expansion. Most of Disston's purchase roughly resembles a tall pyramid, with Lake Kissimmee on the north, Ft. Myers on the southwest, and Lake Okeechobee on the southeast. The transfers to Disston reduce the pool of Florida land available to homesteaders but

opens up the state's ability to continue the effort to encourage railroad construction.

In addition to the land purchase, under Disston's agreement with Governor Bloxham, Disston will also drain other acres around Lake Okeechobee in exchange for a portion of the lands reclaimed. An engineer for Disston Drainage Company concludes that, by lowering the level of Lake Okeechobee by four feet, a major portion of the land east and west of the lake could be put into agricultural production. Disston's plan is to speed the flow of water draining the lands north of Lake Okeechobee into the lake, via the Kissimmee River, then follow Buckingham Smith's 1848 plan to drain the lake west and east with canals linked to the Caloosahatchee and St. Lucie Rivers. Disston will begin dredging within six months of making the deal with the governor. While Disston will not complete all that he sets out to do, he will make much progress.

North of Lake Okeechobee, Disston:
- dredges canals connecting the Kissimmee River headwaters to Cypress, Hatchincha and Kissimmee lakes;
- dredges a canal connecting Lake Tohopekaliga and East Lake Tohopekaliga, which will then connect to Lake Cypress and ultimately the Kissimmee River and Lake Okeechobee; and
- dredges the Kissimmee River, deepening and straightening it to increase and speed the flow.

South of Lake Okeechobee, Disston works to dredge a canal from the upper Caloosahatchee River to Lake Okeechobee, his objective is to allow steamboat to travel from Kissimmee to Lake Okeechobee to the Gulf of Mexico.

Hamilton Disston's dredge building the St. Cloud Canal. The canal will connect Lake Tohopekaliga to East Lake Tohopekaliga, two of the Kissimmee waterway lakes draining into Lake Okeechobee and the Everglades.

From 1881 through 1887, Disston will dig over eighty miles of canals, receive 1.6 million acres of land, and drain much of the upper Kissimmee River valley, but he fails to successfully drain the water through the canals to the Gulf and Atlantic, thus not draining the Everglades. More canals to the Atlantic will be required. The drainage effort will be advanced again by Florida governors at the beginning of the next century.

On April 25, a railroad line is completed from Waycross, Georgia, to Jacksonville, opening up rail transportation from Florida's east coast to Savannah, Georgia, and points north.

In June, Peter Dementyev (he shortens his name to Demens), a St. Petersburg, Russia, aristocrat and critic of the Czarist regime, arrives in New York after fleeing Russia. He comes to Florida following an acquaintance, probably a distant cousin, who lives in Jacksonville. Demens settles in Longwood, Florida, ten miles southwest of Sanford, and enters the orange grove and lumber businesses. His sawmill produces railroad ties and clapboard siding for railroad stations. He will become the builder of the railroad to Point Pinellas, today's St. Petersburg.

On July 2, President James A. Garfield, having been in office less than two months, is shot by Charles J. Guiteau, a disappointed federal office-seeker, while waiting for a train in Washington, D.C. He will die from the injury on September 19, and Vice President Chester Arthur will assume the presidency.

Also this year, Orlando establishes a telephone exchange with eight phones. By 1911, there will be 498 phones on the exchange with businesses paying $2.50 per month and residents $2.00 per month. The exchange will be acquired by Southern Bell in 1916.

1882

On March 25, Henry Plant's South Florida Railroad line is completed to Kissimmee, Florida, about twenty miles south of Orlando. Along with the steamboat traffic along the Kissimmee River, access to rail expands the town's already thriving cattle industry. By 1934, Kissimmee will be home of the Florida Cattlemen's Association. Florida ranchers breed descendants of the original Florida Andalusian cattle with Brahman (originally from India), Angus, and Hereford stock.

An 1890s photograph of the steamboat *Roseada*, loaded with passengers and supplies, making its way down the Kissimmee River and canals to Lake Okeechobee

A 1910s photograph of cattle being loaded on a train in Kissimmee

On December 2, the Florida Internal Improvement Fund makes an installment transfer of 381,358 acres to Hamilton Disston. More deeds will quickly come as Disston's agents scour the state for good land. Also in December, Disston visits Tarpon Springs and enjoys it so much that he decides to found a town. In 1883, he will hire an attorney to lay out a town and represent his interests in Tarpon Springs.

Also this year, the electric fan is invented by Dr. Schuyler Skaats Wheeler, when he attaches a fan to an electric motor shaft. Sometimes known as the "whirligig," it will be used in Florida homes, hotels, restaurants, courthouses, theaters, barber shops, and other public places.

1883

A 1920s-era photograph of the beautiful Mount Dora hotel that was built in 1883 as the Alexander House. It has been expanded and has remained in continuous operation as a hotel since it was developed.

This year, the Alexander House hotel opens in Mount Dora, about thirty miles northwest of Orlando. The ten-room hotel attracts guests for its Southern charm and lake fishing. It will expand over the years and eventually change its name to the Lakeside Inn. Today, it is still operating as an inn, and it bills itself as Florida's "oldest continuously-operated hotel."

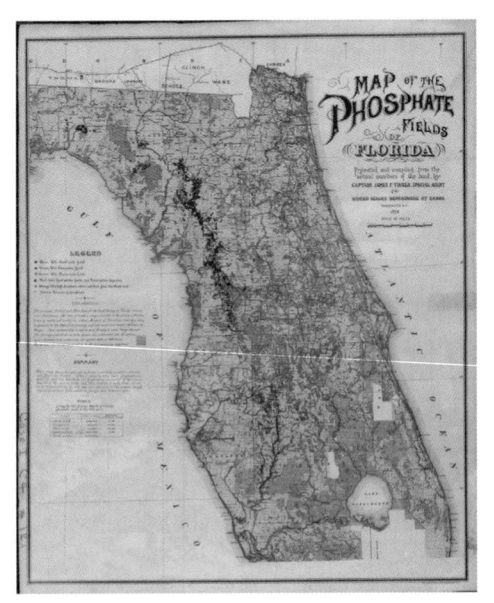

An 1893 map of the phosphate fields in Florida

Also this year, hard rock phosphate deposits are found near Hawthorne, about sixteen miles east of Gainesville. In 1885, railroads will begin transporting phosphate from mines to ships, mostly in Tampa. By 1900, pebble phosphate will be discovered in Polk County. Steam shovels will replace man-based picks and shovels for excavation by 1905. In 1900 it takes a year to mine fifteen acres with picks and shovels, and it will take one month in 2010 to mine the same area with mechanized drag lines. To mine phosphate, the soil above (overburden) is dug out; the phosphate layer is then dug out and sprayed with high-pressure water to create slurry; the slurry is pumped to a plant where the phosphate is separated. The overburden creates hills and the residual clay-water mixture goes into other pits, creating ponds. Most of the phosphate is used to make fertilizer.

In December, Henry Flagler, who has amassed a fortune of up to $20 million while with Standard Oil, honeymoons in Jacksonville and St. Augustine with his second wife. He had originally visited Jacksonville in 1878 with his now-deceased first wife in hopes of improving her health. Flagler and his new wife will stay until March 1884. Flagler feels Florida needs better hotel accommodations. He will return to build both magnificent hotels and an extensive rail system. Before he does, the trip from New York to Florida starts with either a train or steamboat to Savannah, Georgia, then by steamboat (mostly inland) or rail to Jacksonville. The rail trip from Savannah is via Dupont, Georgia (near Valdosta), to Live Oak, Florida, to Jacksonville. From there, the traveler goes south by steamboat, up the St. Johns River waterway to Tocoi, Palatka, Federal Point, and Enterprise. The steamboat burns fat pine, bought along the river.

1884

On January 25, Henry Plant's South Florida Railroad completes construction of a railroad from Kissimmee to Tampa. Plant has also constructed a railroad line from Kissimmee to Sanford on the St. Johns River waterway. In 1886 a line will be completed from Sanford to Jacksonville, thus linking Tampa to Jacksonville. At this time Cedar Key, which prior to the Tampa railroad was the only Gulf coast port with direct rail to northeast Florida, is one of the most important business cities in the state, along with Jacksonville, Fernandina, Pensacola, and Key West.

Cedar Key's development will peak in 1890, then begin a steady decline because of the Plant railroad link to Tampa and the development of Tampa as a port town.

Henry Plant, who brings the railroad to southwest Florida

The parlor of the Tampa Bay Hotel

An 1896 advertisement for the Tampa Bay Hotel and the "Plant System" of hotels and trains

Tampa Bay Hotel and grounds, photographed in 1892

Crew and train of the Tampa Street Railway in April 1886

During the summer, the plat for Hamilton Disston's "Disston City" is filed. The town grows into today's downtown Gulfport. The plat covers twelve thousand acres in today's lower Pinellas County. By 1885, Disston City will have a population of more than one hundred, a wharf, some homes, and three stores.

On July 4, Congress begins providing funds to purchase land for the Seminoles of Florida to homestead. The recent census identifies 236 Seminoles in Florida, including the following bands: Chipco (near today's Blanton in Pasco County), Tustenuggee (northwest of Lake Okeechobee), Old Tiger Tail (in today's Big Cypress reservation), and Young Tiger Tail (near Miami).

On December 24, Christmas Eve, Disston City's Waldorf Hotel opens with twenty-six rooms overlooking the bay.

An 1890 photograph of winter visitors on the porch of the Peacock Inn

An 1885 photograph of Governor E.A. Perry and his cabinet on the steps of the Capitol. Governor Perry is in the front middle with his hands clasped.

Also this year, the Peacock Inn opens in Coconut Grove, the community's first hotel.

1885

On January 7, Democrat Edward A. Perry, a lawyer from Pensacola, becomes the fourteenth governor of Florida. He is a twice-wounded Civil War veteran and brigadier general. In his brief inaugural address, Governor Perry calls for the encouragement of "immigration, investment and labor" and for the increase of educational facilities. He references the "groundless fears entertained by some of our colored citizens that their constitutional rights are endangered" and assures all that such "apprehensions will soon give place to a general rejoicing." During Governor Perry's term, Florida will establish a state board of education.

On March 20, at around noon, Thomas Edison arrives in Ft. Myers (a town of 349 residents) traveling aboard the yacht *Jeannette* up the Caloosahatchee River from Punta Rassa, having learned of the tropical vegetation in the area. He is especially interested in the giant canebrake bamboo, which might be a source for fiber usable as a light bulb filament. He will eventually use imported Japanese bamboo fiber. Earlier in the month, Edison had traveled to Punta Rassa in southwest Florida, intrigued by the underwater telegraph cable that travels from the Caloosahatchee port to Cuba. He took the overnight train from Fernandina to Cedar Key, then the *Jeannette* south along the Gulf coast. At this time Edison has 412 of the 1,093 patents he will eventually possess. While in Ft. Myers, Edison negotiates the purchase of a thirteen-acre riverfront tract on which he will build a home in 1886 and a laboratory in 1887. Beginning in 1901 and until his death in 1931, Edison will spend most winters at his "Florida Eden."

On April 20, T. Arnold, H. Miller, and H. Hall incorporate the Orange Belt Railway, chartered to build a railroad. The line will run from Lake Monroe, near

Sanford on the St. Johns River, thirty-five miles to Lake Apopka, which is northwest of today's Orlando. Shortly after the commencement of the line Peter Demens, the Russian sawmill owner in Longwood, takes over the Orange Belt Railway when its operators fail to pay $9,400 for railroad ties which Demens' lumber company provided. Demens, along with investors Andrew Johnson, his Orlando attorney, Canadian Henry Sweetapple, and his storekeeper A.M. Taylor, form the Orange Belt Investment Company. Together they invest $37,000 and issue $50,000 in bonds for capital to construct the initial phase of the railroad line.

On April 29, noted Baltimore physician Van Bibber announces to the American Medical Society convention meeting in New Orleans that he found Point Pinellas, a "Health City" ideal for maximum good health and longevity. Point Pinellas is today's St. Petersburg. Van Bibber delivers a passage entitled *A Contribution to Sanitary Science. Relating, Especially to the Climate and Healthfulness of Pinellas Peninsula in Florida.* Frank Davis, who will move to the town in 1890, will reprint the article and distribute thousands of copies between 1897 and 1906. Davis will also reprint the article in his medical bulletin distributed to thousands of physicians around the country. Florida is emerging as a place to go if you need to improve your health.

On August 3, the 1885 Florida Constitution is adopted at a state constitutional convention. After submission to the voters for approval in November 1886, it will be effective January 1, 1887. Among other items, the new constitution allows voters at the county level to establish their own prohibition laws. It allows a poll tax as a prerequisite for voting, which effectively

Peter Demens, who brings the railroad to St. Petersburg (St. Petersburg Museum of History)

will disenfranchise poor whites and the vast majority of African Americans. The legislature will exact the poll tax in 1889. Under Article 9, Section 11, the constitution prohibits state tax on "the income of residents or citizens of this State."

The constitution also requires that "white and colored children shall not be taught in the same school, but impartial provision shall be made for both." School segregation will remain the state policy until after the United States Supreme Court's 1954 ruling in *Brown v. The Board of Education of Topeka.*

On November 4, Rollins College opens in Winter Park, about seven miles northeast of Orlando. Daytona, Jacksonville, and Orange City competed for the educational institution founded by the Congregational Church, but Winter Park wins out with a bid of $125,000 in land and cash. The college is named after benefactor Alonzo Rollins.

On November 15, the Orange Belt Railway is completed to the town of Oakland, Florida, on the southern shore of Lake Apopka near today's Winter Garden. Railroad developer Peter Demens had wanted to name the town St. Petersburg after his native town in Russia, but the town's residents insist on retaining the name Oakland, which had been established in the 1850s. The people of the town stage a gala celebration and dinner in honor of the builders of their new railroad. Oakland becomes headquarters for the Orange Belt Railway and the town prospers.

A 1903 photograph showing the collapse of a truss bridge over the St. Johns River at Palatka, along Flagler's Florida East Coast Railway

On December 31, Henry Flagler acquires and sets out to improve the Jacksonville, St. Augustine and Halifax River Railroad, which runs from Jacksonville to St. Augustine. The improved railroad will provide better access to Flagler's Ponce de Leon Hotel in St. Augustine, which started construction on December 1 of this year. In 1888, Flagler will purchase the railroads going from Tocoi (on the St. Johns River) to St. Augustine and from Palatka to Daytona. Flagler will construct railroad lines extending from Daytona to New Smyrna by November 2, 1892; to Titusville by February 6, 1893; to Eau Gallie (today's Melbourne area) by June 26,

1893; and to West Palm Beach by April 2, 1894. After the hard freezes of the winter of 1894–95, Julia Tuttle will convince Flagler to extend his line to Miami, an effort he will complete on April 15, 1896. Flagler's railroad will traverse the east coast of Florida when he completes the line to Key West on January 12, 1912. Flagler's Florida East Coast Railway will obtain between 1,500,000 and 2,000,000 acres in state land grants under an 1893 law giving developers 8,000 acres of land per mile of railroad developed.

1886
In February, during two walks in Manhattan, birdwatcher Frank Chapman identifies feathers from 40 bird species on ladies' hats. Of the 700 hats spotted, 542 had plume feathers. The annual Florida bird-kill for plume hats is estimated at five million, with one Florida agent shipping 130,000 plumes in one year. "Plumer" Jean Chevelier gathers 11,000 skins in south Florida's Ten Thousand Islands in one season. One New York wholesaler

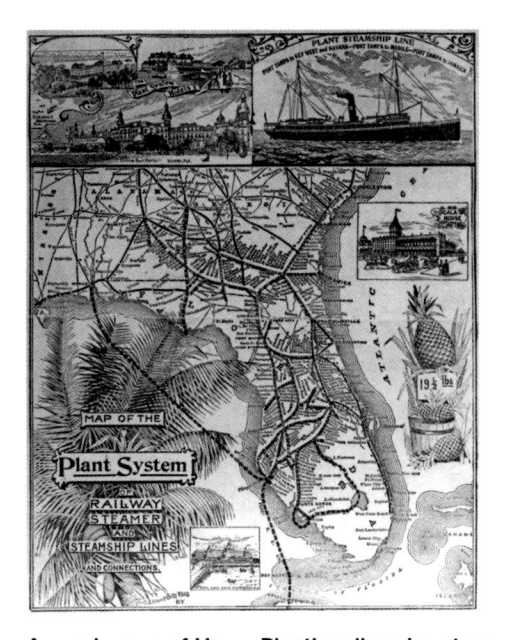

An early map of Henry Plant's railroad system

A plume hunter with a dead heron on Santa Fe Lake, about fifteen miles east of Gainesville

buys $200,000 of plumes for fashion. The $17 million New York millinery industry employs 20,000 people. At risk are forty-two species of Florida birds, including exotic wading and other birds, like the great egrets, great blue herons, ibises, roseate spoonbills, snowy egrets, pelicans, and owls. Plume bird populations shrink dramatically throughout Florida, and and some species vanished from the state.
In 1892 preservationist John Muir will establish the Sierra Club. By 1900 Audubon Societies, named for nature painter and author John James Audubon, will be established around the nation, dedicated to developing laws that protect non-game birds, their eggs, and nests.

In March, the U.S. Post Office approves changing the name of Lake Worth to Palm Beach. The name Palm City had previously been rejected.

On July 24, Henry Plant's Florida Southern Railway opens a line from Bartow (south of Lakeland) to Trabue, later named Punta Gorda, on Charlotte Harbor in southwest Florida. Earlier, in

March, the line opened to Arcadia, with Governor Edward Perry being one of the early passengers. The railroad's real estate division will build the beautiful 150-room Punta Gorda Hotel.

Also this year, the Orlando Street Railway Company establishes the city's first organized transit system for downtown. The transit cars are horse-drawn and are required to stop at all street crossings to allow pedestrians to cross. The line will be disbanded in 1893.

1887

On January 24, after negotiations between John Williams and Henry Sweetapple, Peter Demens' treasurer, Williams agrees to give 250 waterfront acres in today's downtown St. Petersburg to Demens in exchange for bringing the Orange Belt Railway to Point Pinellas. Before the exchange is complete, the town will change its name to St. Petersburg, the name of the city in Demens' homeland, Russia. The railroad line is to extend to a pier reaching a depth of twelve feet in the bay.

On May 30, Henry Flagler completes construction of the Ponce de Leon Hotel in St. Augustine, which will officially open for the tourist season on January 10, 1888. President Grover Cleveland will visit the hotel during the 1888 winter season. The $2.5 million hotel has medieval towers, 450 sleeping apartments, electric lights, steam heat, and a dining hall that seats 700 people. The hotel is the site of today's Flagler College. During the next three decades, as Flagler builds his railroads he will also construct magnificent hotels and develop and expand towns from Jacksonville to Key West in an effort that will transform the east coast of Florida. As he expands, Flagler in some cases will fund city halls, schools, churches, electric lights, water works, sewers, and hospitals. Flagler's early hotels will include St. Augustine's Alcazar and Cordova by 1889. Because of his large holdings in Standard Oil and other investments, Flagler's fortune will continue to grow and will be valued at about $100 million by his death in 1913.

On October 3, the Florida Legislature establishes the State Normal College for Colored Students. "Normal" colleges are established to train teachers. The school opens with fifteen students and two instructors. The school will be renamed Florida Agricultural and Mechanical College in 1909, and Florida Agricultural and Mechanical University (FAMU) in 1953. By 2015, Florida A&M will offer fifty-four bachelor's degrees, twenty-nine master's degrees, and twelve doctoral programs.

1888

On January 1, Elias Disney and Flora Call, residents of Acron, a small town in central Florida, marry in Daytona Beach. Elias Disney had moved to Florida in

An 1891 view of the Ponce de Leon Hotel in St. Augustine, with visitors arriving in horse carriages. Today it is the home of Flagler College.

1884. He has operated the Halifax Hotel in Daytona Beach, worked as a mailman, and purchased an eighty-acre orange grove. After a freeze hits their grove, the Disney family will move to Chicago in 1889, then move to Missouri, where their son Walt will be born. Walt Disney's return to Florida in the 1960s will transform the state forever.

On January 10, the first Pullman passenger train begins direct operation from Jersey City to Jacksonville, with the maiden trip taking twenty-nine hours, fifty minutes. The Pullman railroad cars, named for inventor George M. Pullman, have private compartments or seats that may be converted to sleeping berths.

On April 30, the Orange Belt Railway, after enormous effort on very shaky finances, reaches today's MLK Street and First Avenue South in today's St. Peters-

burg. Engineer Bob Kennedy throttles work train locomotive number six into town. The first regular service train will arrive in the city on June 8 from the eastern end of the line on the St. Johns River waterway. In the early months of 1889, the railroad will extend 3,000 feet into the bay along a pier that reaches a twelve-foot depth. Warehouses will be built along the railroad pier for wholesale fish companies, and a bath house and a toboggan slide will be added for recreation. More than one hundred African Americans have come to the city to help build the railroad. They will come to live in areas called Pepper Town, Cooper's Quarters, and Methodist Town. Later in the year, Demens' lumber company will add the forty-room Detroit Hotel (named in honor of the hometown of city founder John Williams) and a Russian architectural-style passenger depot.

Working on the Orange Belt Railway, linking St. Petersburg to Sanford and ultimately the rest of the nation

An 1895 photograph of St. Petersburg's Detroit Hotel, built by Peter Demens, who brings the Orange Belt Railway to the city

An Orange Belt locomotive, circa 1893. St. Petersburg's Detroit Hotel is in the background. (St. Petersburg Museum of History)

The Orange Belt Railway depot in Clearwater

On June 25, Captain James Cantry begins construction of a 600-foot T-shaped wharf in Ft. Myers. Before construction of the wharf, travelers must transfer from the ship *Fearless* to a smaller tender boat in order to come to shore. Travel by water will continue to be the only way to reach Naples until 1918, when a shell-and-mud road will be completed between Ft. Myers and Naples.

On August 10, the Jacksonville Board of Health announces that the city is experiencing a yellow fever epidemic, which apparently began in late July when R.D. McCormick, a visitor from Tampa, became ill at the Mayflower Hotel. By September the local efforts to contain the spread of the fever will be overwhelmed. As people evacuate, only fourteen thousand of the twenty-five thousand residents remain in the city. Nurses from the north will be brought to the city as part of the relief and treatment effort, which includes systematic bathing, nutrition, and hydration. On October 4, notice will be published of a decision to quarantine Jacksonville. Steamship travel is halted and refugees on trains are refused entry by armed patrols in cities to which they flee. The city suffers food shortages and unemployment as businesses, banks, and schools close. Four days after Thanksgiving, a freeze will trigger the end of the epidemic, but homes will be fumigated

The Fort Myers steamer, *Dixie*, pulls away from the wharf, circa 1920.

A 1920s picture of the city recreation pier in Ft. Myers

A circa 1912 picture of the Royal Palm Hotel in Ft. Myers

before people are allowed to enter. Before the fever is gone, 4,704 people will be infected, and 427 will die. Yellow fever will spread in other parts of Florida this year with reports in Tampa, Fernandina, and Gainesville.

At this time, Dade County extends from the St. Lucie River to Key West and has a population of 257.

1889

On January 8, Francis P. Fleming, a lawyer born in Duval County and Civil War commander of volunteers at Tallahassee's Battle of Natural Bridge, takes office as the fifteenth governor of Florida. His inaugural address's primary focus is on the need to take quick action in response to the yellow fever epidemic that has stricken Florida. Governor Fleming will call for a special session of the legislature to address the

As yellow fever rages in Jacksonville and other Florida cities in 1888, a drawing in *Frank Leslie's Illustrated Newspaper* shows Florida being dragged down by "Yellow Jack" while Columbia comes to rescue.

subject, resulting in the establishment of a state board of health.

On April 12, the Orange Belt Railway completes a 3.4-mile extension from Longwood to Sanford, connecting St. Petersburg to Sanford, which has rail and steamship connections to Jacksonville and the northeast United States. On June 4, the Orange Belt Railway will begin operating discount railroad excursions for visitors to visit "St. Petersburg-by-the-Sea." The city is promoted as a seaside summer resort that is cooler than the inland areas.

1890

On January 10, the Naples Town Improvement Company goes up for sale. The company was started in 1887. It acquired much of today's Naples. For the first few years the company operated largely for fishing and hunting excursions. Now the company needs money. Walter Haldeman pays $50,000 to purchase the company, which includes 8,600 acres, the pier, a hotel, and the *Fearless* ship, transporting passengers back and forth between Naples and Ft. Myers.

On January 20, a railroad bridge over the St. Johns River in Jacksonville is completed, enabling railroad traffic from the northern states through Jacksonville to connect to Sanford and central Florida. Financed by Henry Flagler, the Strauss Trunnion Bascule Bridge is the Jacksonville's first bridge over the St. Johns. Before the bridge was built, tourists had to disembark from the train and cross the St. Johns by ferry to connect again to the trains heading south. The railroad bridge will be replaced with a double track version in 1925. As an alternative to rail, steamship companies offer routes from Sanford up the St. Johns River to Jacksonville and then up the Atlantic Coast

Caption for this circa 1888 picture identifies it as the first building in Naples. It is described as the temporary office for the "Naples Company" (probably the Naples Town Improvement Company) that is used while the hotel and pier are being constructed.

The Naples Hotel framed by Australian pines. A south wing is added to the hotel in 1916 and a north wing is built in 1920.

The 1890 Strauss Trunnion Bascule Bridge over the St. Johns River in Jacksonville will be replaced in 1925 with a double rail bridge, shown here under construction.

to cities such as Charleston, Boston, and New York. As one steamship company map boasts, steamship travel is a way of avoiding "the inconvenience of changes and the annoyance of dust incidental to railway travel."

Late in the year, the Tampa Bay Ice Co. begins operation of an ice plant for fish packing on Second Street and First Avenue South near the railroad pier in St. Petersburg. Before construction of the new plant, local fish packers had to rely on ice brought in by rail from Oakland, on Lake Apopka in central Florida. With an ice-making plant and the ability to sell catches on the wharves by the railroad, commercial fishing is the city's main indus-

A February 1960 photograph of fishermen on the Naples Pier. Later that year, on September 10, this pier will be destroyed by Hurricane Donna.

A 1960 photograph of bridges in Jacksonville. Notice the train on the railroad bridge.

try, especially mackerel and snapper. The citrus industry also expands. By the end of the decade, fish houses will work with about 250 fishermen and ship over three million pounds of fish a year.

On December 29, at Wounded Knee Creek in South Dakota, the U.S. Cavalry attacks an encampment of Sioux. At least sixty U.S. cavalrymen and two hundred Sioux (including women and children) are killed. Wounded Knee is considered the last significant armed engagement between the United States troops and natives of North America.

1891

Ladies of the town of St. Petersburg raise money, by selling ice cream and lemonade and giving "entertainments" and picnics, to provide funds to build a wooden sidewalk on Central Avenue from Ninth Street to the bay. It is the first recorded public improvement in the town's history. On September 13 of next year, the town council will pass an ordinance requiring all able men between twenty-one and forty-five years old to work on the public streets for up to six days a year. Ministers and town officers are exempt.

Also this year, Orlando's city council approves an expenditure of $150 to pave Pine Street, the city's first paved street. Until now, the streets are made of sand. Clay is brought in from Bartow Junction for the job.

1892

On February 29, St. Petersburg citizens assemble at Cooper's Hall and vote fifteen to eleven to incorporate as a town. In 1903 the town will be reincorporated as a city and, on March 1, 1904, Robert H. Thomas, an Illinois native whose business interests include insurance, banking, and real estate, will win the first mayoral election of the new city.

1893

On January 3, Henry L. Mitchell, a lawyer and legislator from Tampa, takes office as the sixteenth governor of Florida. In his inaugural address, Governor Mitchell focuses on fiscal responsibility and the expansion of the common school education: "I mean to see that every unnecessary expense of the state government is stopped as far as possible, and that the state take by taxation from her citizens no money that is not necessary for the purposes of obtaining those benefits."

A circa 1900 photograph of U.S. Mail Number 4 stagecoach in which Louis McClenithan delivers the mail in Arcadia, about 40 miles southeast of Sarasota.

A 1906 photograph of Frank Stranahan's home on the New River in Ft. Lauderdale. The home is built in 1901 on the site of the city's original trading post. Stanahan builds a large porch so that Seminoles who come to trade can camp there.

On January 26, Frank Stranahan arrives at the New River in southeast Florida to operate a ferry and overnight camp for the new Lantana–Lemon City stage line. He establishes a trading post that he names "Fort Lauderdale."

On March 27, Thomas Edison installs the first electric lights in Ft. Myers at the Seminole Lodge. Later in the year Ft. Myers will be struck by a yellow fever epidemic, forcing quarantine.

Also on March 27, Wallace Fisher Stovall publishes the first *Tampa Morning Tribune*. He had moved his operations from Bartow. Stovall will begin the *Tampa Tribune* daily newspaper in 1895.

In April, Henry Flagler acquires hundreds of acres on the west side of Lake Worth across from Palm Beach and, in August, lays out the town site for

West Palm Beach. With his railroad to arrive here by April of next year, Flagler intends for West Palm Beach to become the commercial center, while Palm Beach hosts winter visitors. West Palm Beach will incorporate as a town on November 10, 1894, and will be part of Dade County until 1909.

By this year, with post–Civil War improvements to transportation and access to northern markets, Florida's commercial citrus production exceeds five million boxes.

1894

A March 18, 1893, photograph of a group posing by a hammerhead shark that was caught off Palm Beach

On February 11, Henry Flagler opens the Royal Poinciana Hotel in Palm Beach. The hotel, on one hundred acres, has 540 bedrooms and a dining hall for 1,600 people. Thought to be the largest resort hotel in the world, it boasts two 18-hole golf courses, tennis courts, and boats.

The Royal Poinciana Hotel will close in 1934 after suffering two hurricanes and the Great Depression. In January of 1896, Flagler will add a second Palm Beach hotel called the Palm Beach Inn, later renamed the Breakers. After a 1903 fire, the Breakers will be replaced in 1906 and is still open today.

In the fall, Reverend Richard J. Morgan purchases the *West Hillsborough Times*, moves the newspaper's operations from Clearwater to St. Petersburg, and later will rename it the *St. Petersburg Times*.

The *Times* will be joined in Florida by the *Miami Evening Record* on September 15, 1903, which will change its name to the *Miami Herald* in 1910. The two newspapers will become the state's largest by the twenty-first century.

On November 5, West Palm Beach votes to incorporate, with about five hundred inhabitants. Residents had considered naming the town Flagler, in honor of Henry Flagler's bringing the railroad and building town amenities such as fire station, churches, and other public

An 1893 photo of the plumbers and mechanics who are building Flagler's Royal Poinciana Hotel in Palm Beach

Among the Royal Poinciana Hotel guests in this March 14, 1896, photograph are railroad and shipping businessman Cornelius Vanderbilt (far right) and Mrs. Cornelius Vanderbilt (third from left). Notice the train between the guests and the hotel.

A June 9, 1903, photograph of a fire at the original Breakers Hotel in Palm Beach. The hotel will be rebuilt in 1906.

An aerial view of the great hotels of Palm Beach. The Royal Poinciana is on the left in the foreground, the Whitehall on the right in the foreground, and the Breakers in the background.

An early view of sunbathers on the beach at Flagler's Breakers Hotel, which is built in Palm Beach in 1896

buildings. They decide instead to stick with the name West Palm Beach, which had originally been used as just one word: "Westpalmbeach." At this time the town's "calaboose" houses the jail and town hall on Poinsettia, later known as Dixie Highway.

The "Great Freeze" of 1894 and 1895 decimated orange groves throughout the state, as shown in this 1894 photograph of Streaty Parker's orange grove in Bartow. The second freeze, which begins with a blizzard on February 7, 1895, freezes many of the trees as well. Temperatures in some places drop to the low 20s for three successive nights.

On December 26–27, a blizzard passes through the state. In Titusville, the temperature is recorded at eighteen degrees for over twenty-four hours. As in other parts of Florida, the citrus on the local trees is lost, along with the jobs of workers who would have picked, shipped, and transported the fruit. Another hard freeze will follow in early February 1895. Young citrus seedlings and older trees are frozen to the core. In Orlando, many smaller citrus farms are forced to sell out to larger landowners, and seven of the eight local banks close. Florida citrus production will fall from 5,000,000 boxes in 1894 to 46,580 in 1896. The state will not reach the million-box level for citrus again until 1901. Many growers move farther south in the state. One result of the freeze is that groves that survive achieve some level of fame. When trees survive the freeze in Keystone City, about seventy-five miles east of Tampa, the town is renamed "Frostproof." Prior significant freezes impacting the state in this century came in 1835 and 1886.

After the freeze, Julia Tuttle, the "Mother of Miami," reportedly sends Henry Flagler orange blossoms as proof that the freeze had not impacted the citrus in her city. Tuttle proposes a deal to Flagler that, if he extends his railroad to Biscayne Bay and builds a significant hotel, then she will give him half of her holdings north of the Miami River. Flagler agrees.

Also this year, the St. James Colored Missionary Baptist Church is organized. They will build their first church in Mims, five miles north of Titusville.

1895

On April 5, the St. Petersburg Town Council passes an ordinance precluding cows with bells from wandering within the town limits.

1896

On April 15, Henry Flagler's Florida East Coast Railway reaches Miami. Before the railroad arrives, "barefoot mailmen" carried the post along the beach from Palm Beach to Miami.

On May 1, obituaries in three New York newspapers and the Washington *Post* report that Florida land barron Hamilton Disston is dead from an apparent heart attack in his bed in Philadelphia, after a night of dinner and theater with his wife and the Philadelphia mayor. One paper, the *Philadelphia Press,* will report, apparently incorrectly, that Disston committed suicide.

On May 15, the first edition of the *Miami Metropolis* is published. It will later become the *Miami Daily News.*

On July 28, Miami, the former Fort Dallas, is incorporated as a city with 502 voters. The town has grown from four houses and one store in 1874 as noted by

a traveler, to two thousand inhabitants today.

An 1898 view of visitors enjoying the pool at Flagler's new Royal Palm hotel in Miami

On December 31, 1896, a gala New Year's Eve ball will be held at Flagler's newest magnificent hotel in Miami, the Royal Palm. The hotel will officially open on January 16, 1897, located on fifteen acres where the Miami River meets Biscayne Bay. The hotel will be damaged in the 1926 hurricane and closed shortly thereafter. The magnificent Royal Palm will be torn down in 1930, with the contents and fixtures sold to Miami residents

A 1914 view of the *Osceola* at the port in Jacksonville

Also this year, Frank A. Davis, a Philadelphia publisher, issues a 132-page book entitled *Facts and Suggestions for Persons Forced to Seek Permanent or Temporary Homes on the Pinellas Peninsula for Relief from Consumption. Chronic Bronchitis. Rheumatism. Gout. Neurasthenia and Kindred Diseases.* Davis will pay for and distribute (including to thousands of physicians) extensive advertising to promote St. Petersburg as a health resort, including the reprinting of Dr. Van Bibber's 1885 report on the "Health City."

1897

Governor William Bloxham and President William F. McKinley at the Tallahassee capitol

On January 5, William D. Bloxham, Democrat, becomes the seventeenth governor of Florida, Florida's first two-term governor, and the state's only governor to serve split terms, having first served in 1881. Governor Bloxham restates his first term call for immigration and transportation facilities and argues that Florida "should fully sustain the paramount claim of public education." His stated philosophy is that the "best government is that which interferes the least with the legitimate business vocations of its citizens and imposes the lightest burdens on property and labor."

Henry Plant's Belleview Hotel in Clearwater. Notice the Plant System train in front.

On January 15, the Belleview resort opens in Clearwater with a six-hole golf course. It was built on a bluff overlooking the Gulf by railroad builder Henry Plant.

On February 2, Frank Davis obtains from voters a twenty-year electric utilities franchise. He moves his fifty-watt, wood-burning boiler power plant from Tarpon Springs to St. Petersburg. On July 18, 1899, a charter for the company will be signed by Florida Governor William D. Bloxham with the name St. Petersburg Electric Light & Power Company. It is today's Duke Energy Florida.

Also this year, John Cheney organizes the Orlando Water and Light Company. It will receive a contract to construct twenty-eight electric-arc streetlights in 1901 and a twenty-year franchise to supply the city's water in 1902. In 1923, the City of Orlando will purchase the company for $975,000.

1898

In January, in anticipation of conflict with Spain in Cuba, Mullet Key and Egmont Key are fortified with coastal artillery units.

On the night of February 15, the USS Maine *explodes in Havana, killing 252. On April 20, President McKinley declares war on Spain. The war will be over by the end of the year.*

U.S. Army transports loading soldiers at Port Tampa in 1898 during the Spanish-American War

Cannons being loaded on a transport at the Tampa port in 1898, bound for Cuba during the Spanish-American War

Reportedly, the first United States mainland receipt of the news that the *Maine* has been sunk in Havana harbor reaches Ft. Myers at the Punta Rassa terminus of the underwater cable line to Cuba. During the war, United States military camps will be established in Tampa, Lakeland, Jacksonville, Fernandina, and Miami. The military training center in Jacksonville will house more than twelve thousand troops in what will be known as "Camp Cuba Libre."

On April 7, Henry Plant's steamer *Olivette* begins shuttling American refugees from Havana to Port Tampa under a $15,000 contract between the United States government and the Plant Steamship Company. The U.S. will designate Port Tampa as the principal port of embarkation for the Cuban theater of the Spanish-American War. During the war, with the permission of the town council, water is piped from St. Petersburg's Reservoir Lake, today's Mirror Lake, to boats on the railroad pier, then taken to Hillsborough County for use by troops stationed in Tampa.

During the war, the Key West sponge industry that started around 1830 moves to Tarpon Springs because of the threat of Spanish warships. As the sponges available in the Keys diminish, the industry will take root in Tarpon Springs. Greeks will come to the city in the early 1900s, and Tarpon Springs will eventually have almost five hundred divers, fifty sponge boats, and, in 1907, an exchange for divers to sell their sponges. After many sponge beds are destroyed by blight in the 1950s and artificially made sponges become cheaper, the industry will fall off but will remain as a tourist attraction.

On July 1, Theodore Roosevelt and the Rough Riders take the San Juan Heights overlooking Santiago, Cuba.

Buyers checking out the merchandise at a Key West sponge market on June 11, 1898

On August 12, fighting stops after Spain agrees to surrender. Among the terms agreed in the protocol, the United States occupies Cuba.

After the war, all soldiers returning from Cuba will spend ten days at a thousand-tent hospital and quarantine station at Egmont Key's Fort Dade by St. Petersburg, where soldiers endure the miseries of sunstroke, dehydration, and mosquitoes.

1899

On May 1, Albertus Vogt discovers phosphate near Dunnellon, twenty-five miles southwest of Ocala. Phosphate was found in the Peace River Valley in southwest Florida in 1881 and had been shipped from there in 1888. Phosphate, used to manufacture fertilizer, comes from the bones of prehistoric animals. Mulberry, about ten miles south of Lakeland, will become known as the "Phosphate Capital of the World," complete with a Mulberry Phosphate Museum.

Future president Colonel Theodore Roosevelt and other officers of the First U.S. Volunteer Cavalry Regiment in Tampa

Workers mining phosphate in Dunnellon with shovels and wheelbarrows

A circa 1910s photograph of the phosphate washer plant and power house of the Florida Mining Company in Mulberry

Phosphate being unloaded from railroad boxcars into barges below for the Dunnellon Phosphate Company

During the summer, a yellow fever epidemic strikes Miami, killing fourteen people. The city will be quarantined from October of this year until January 15, 1900.

Late in the year, St. Petersburg's first public telephone system is established on the second floor of a building on Central Avenue and Third Street. Eighteen subscribers sign up for service. In 1898, the city got its first telephone when Arthur Noorwood connected his two stores, four blocks apart, with two receivers and two thousand feet of wire. In June 1900, Bell-affiliate St. Petersburg Telephone Company will be granted a franchise by the town council. Long distance will be added on June 24, 1902, enabling calls to Tampa at a cost of 25 cents. The development of telephone service from single user to local system to long distance mimics the progression in other Florida cities.

1900

On February 12, the song "Lift Every Voice and Sing," sometimes called the Black National Anthem, is sung for the first time by five hundred schoolchildren at the segregated Stanton School in Jacksonville as part of a celebration of Abraham Lincoln's birthday. The song was written by Jacksonville native James Weldon Johnson, principal of the school, and was put to music by his brother, John Rosamond Johnson.

On March 2, a group gathers in Maitland, Florida, about ten miles north of Orlando, to form the Florida Audubon Society. The group's formation is, in part, a response to the large-scale slaughter of beautiful native Florida birds for their plumes to adorn ladies' hats. *(See 1886.)*

In May, the federal government enacts the Lacy Act, which prohibits interstate commerce in birds that are protected under state laws. The leaders of the newly formed Florida Audubon ramp up efforts to protect the state birds from slaughter for plume hats worn by fashionable ladies in the North and, in May 1901, the Florida legislature will pass a model bird protection law. Despite the law, bird killings will continue due to the lack of wardens to enforce the prohibition. Florida Audubon will begin a campaign in 1908 to discourage women from wearing hats with plumes. While poachers will remain active in Florida for almost two more decades, the collective efforts will result in a diminished demand for feathers and an increase in bird sanctuaries by 1920.

On September 6, President William McKinley is shot by anarchist Leon Czolgosz at the Pan American Exposition in Buffalo, New York. He will die from the wound on September 14. Vice President Theodore Roosevelt assumes the presidency.

1901

On January 8, William Sherman Jennings, an Illinois-born lawyer who has lived in Brooksville and Miami, is sworn into office as Florida's eighteenth governor. A major portion of his inaugural address

focuses on the problems of delays in the legal system caused by increased caseloads and insufficient judicial resources at both the state supreme court and circuit court levels: "The Florida Supreme Court is five years behind with its work." Governor Jennings calls for tax reform, noting that some counties assess property at 90 percent of its value while others assess at 20 percent; praises the state board of health for its success at controlling smallpox; and calls for "the most liberal support and development of the public school system."

On May 3, a lunchtime kitchen fire ignites piles of drying Spanish moss (used to stuff mattresses) at the Cleveland Fibre Factory, a mattress factory, on Davis and Beaver streets in Jacksonville. The fire quickly spreads throughout the downtown, including to nearby factories containing pine, feathers, and other flammable materials. By the time the fire is under control, at 8:30 P.M., 2,368 buildings are destroyed,

Jacksonville City Hall after the 1901 fire

The Methodist Church in Jacksonville burning during the 1901 fire

The charred remains of Jacksonville's port after the 1901 fire

Corner of Bay and Main Streets in Jacksonville after the 1901 fire

An overhead view of destruction in downtown Jacksonville after the 1901 fire

10,000 residents are homeless, and seven people are dead, out of Jacksonville's population of 28,000. It is one of the greatest fires in Southern history. The fire impacts 146 city blocks. Twenty-three churches, ten hotels, and thousands of homes are destroyed. Governor William Jennings will declare martial law and send in the state militia, which will maintain authority until May 17. In the next twelve years, more than twelve thousand buildings will be built as the city recovers and moves forward.

1902

On July 17, the world's first scientific air-conditioning system is designed by Willis H. Carrier. The system, which controls both humidity and temperature, is installed at the Sackett-Wilhelms Lithographing and Publishing Company of Brooklyn, New York. It will complete its first successful summer operation in 1903.

Air conditioning will transform Florida and be one catalyst for the boom in population during the second half of this century.

1903

On March 14, President Theodore Roosevelt declares the nation's first federal bird sanctuary at a five-acre mangrove key named Pelican Island in the Indian River Lagoon, between today's Sebastian and Wabasso, south of Melbourne. As poachers continue to slaughter Florida's native birds for plumes on women's hats, the sanctuary is intended to protect a prime bird roosting and nesting area. By 1920, there will be ten federal bird refuges in Florida's coastal nesting areas. *(See 1886 and 1900.)*

Over 500 additional national wildlife refuges will also be established, and President Roosevelt will protect 230 million acres of public land, including Mount Olympus and the Grand Canyon.

On March 23, a Seaboard passenger train arrives in Sarasota for the first time on a fifty-one mile line constructed from Durant (south of today's Plant City) through Parrish, Manatee, and Oneco (today's Bradenton area). An Atlantic Coast Line subsidiary will connect Sarasota more directly with Tampa through Bradenton and Palmetto. Railroad yard tracks will be constructed to accommodate circus trains after Ringling Brothers and Barnum and Bailey Circus establishes Sarasota as its winter home this decade.

On July 23, Henry Ford sells his first gasoline-powered Model A to a Detroit physician at a price of $850.

On December 17, Orville Wright becomes the first man to fly an airplane, remaining in the air for twelve seconds in Kitty Hawk, North Carolina. Later that day his brother Wilbur will complete a fifty-nine-second flight.

1904

On May 10, Atlantic Coast Line brings the first passenger train to Ft. Myers from Punta Gorda. The railroad brings passengers and commerce to the Gulf coast town and will spark a renaissance of development. Seaboard's railroad will reach Ft. Myers in 1926.

Also this year, Mary McLeod Bethune opens the Daytona Educational and

Mary McLeod Bethune, founder of today's Bethune-Cookman University

Industrial Training School for Negro Girls. It will become a coeducational school in 1923 after merging with the Cookman Institute in Jacksonville. Bethune-Cookman will become a junior college in 1931, and a four-year college in 1941. In 2007, the former Bethune-Cookman College will become Bethune-Cookman University.

1905

On January 3, Napoleon Bonaparte Broward of Jacksonville is sworn into office as Florida's nineteenth governor. The Southern progressive's career includes logging, phosphate, Cuban gunrunning, steamboat operations, as well as city commissioner, legislator, and sheriff. He will advocate for public schools, trust regulation, and prohibition. In his inaugural address, Governor Broward urges the need to continue the growth of Florida's railroad system, expand the "fish, oyster and sponge business," and replace wetlands with agricultural industries: "We have millions of acres of fertile lands in Florida that will produce crops of great value long after our forests have become things of the past . . . to be drained and reclaimed for our people. I refer to the overflowed lands of the Everglades and Lake Okeechobee . . . land especially adapted for the cultivation of sugarcane."

A 1905 photograph of automobiles on Daytona Beach

The wreck of Frank Croker in the surf. Croker and co-racer Alexander Raoul are the first recorded racer fatalities at Daytona Beach.

During Governor Broward's term, the state's universities will be reorganized and roads will be improved, but his most aggressive effort will be to drain the Everglades. His plan is to build canals draining Lake Okeechobee to the Atlantic and to also expand the Caloosahatchee River canal draining the lake west to the Gulf of Mexico. The land is believed to have great agricultural potential.

On January 21, during a timed auto-racing run on Daytona Beach, amateur racer Frank Croker's Simplex racer glances off the side of another racer and crashes into the surf. Croker's chauffeur and mechanic, Alexander Raoul, is riding with Croker and is thrown from the car. Both Croker and Raoul die from injuries sustained in the race. It is the first recorded death of racers on Daytona Beach.

A cartoon of Uncle Sam offering "Miss Florida" the Florida Everglades. All she needs to do is drain and develop vast wetland for farming and settlement.

In May, the Florida legislature passes a law creating a Board of Drainage Commissioners, and empowers the group to develop a plan to drain and reclaim swampland, build a system of levees, locks, and canals, and assess annual drainage taxes of up to ten cents per acre within drainage districts. The board is appointed and establishes

the Everglades Drainage District, 60 miles wide and 150 miles long, including 4.3 million acres. They will focus on draining swampland around Lake Okeechobee in order to create farmland and expand the state's agricultural sector.

On July 8, Guy Bradley, game warden for the Florida Keys and Everglades, is ambushed and shot to death by poachers of birds for plumes. The murder galvanizes many to support the Audubon efforts to protect Florida's native birds. *Bird-Lore* editorializes, "A brave man shot at his post, defending the helpless against the brutality, and for what? A feather to adorn the head of some woman!" *(See 1886, 1900, and 1902.)* The fight with poachers will continue, as will be evidenced by the 1916 destruction of southwest Florida's Alligator Bay Rookery, when poachers will shoot an estimated eight hundred birds and burn the entire rookery.

Everglades game warden Guy Bradley, who is shot and killed when he attempts to arrest a Florida native bird plume poacher

On July 31, the *Miami Metropolis* publishes a special edition announcing Henry Flagler's intention to extend his railroad from Miami to Key West. A workforce reaching four thousand men (some losing their lives) will work seven years encountering heat, hurricanes, and mosquitoes.

This monument erected by the Florida Audubon Society in the Everglades honors Guy Bradley. It reads, in part, "He gave his life for the cause to which he was pledged."

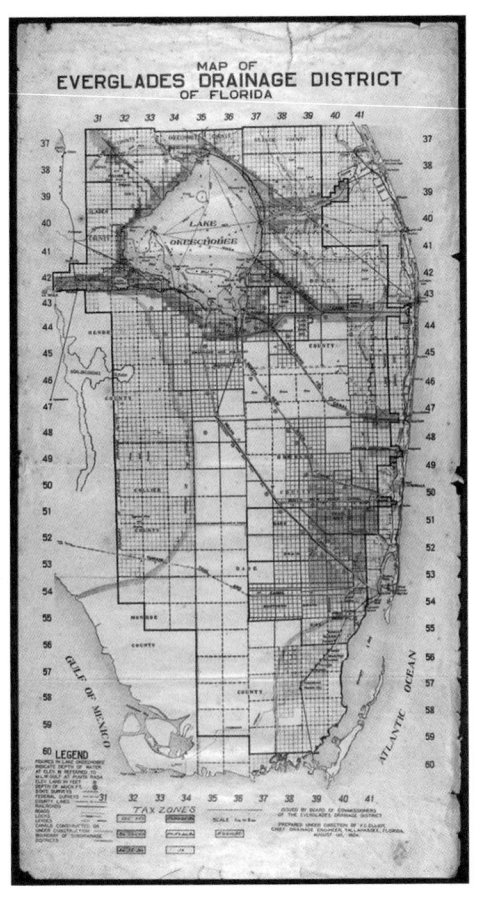

A 1924 map issued by the Board of Commissioners of the Everglades Drainage District. The map identifies the drainage canals and tax zones for the district. (Courtesy of University of Florida Digital Collections)

They will build on thirty islands and cover over 155 miles before the goal of completion will be reached in 1912. *(See 1912.)*

On December 12, the Florida Board of Drainage Commissioners decides that the first canal to drain Lake Okeechobee into the Atlantic will be Ft. Lauderdale's North New River Canal. On July 8, 1906, the dredge "Everglades" will begin dredging the canal (to be fifty feet wide and ten to fourteen feet deep), which will go northwest to Lake Okeechobee from the north fork of the New River. In April 1907, the dredge "Okeechobee" will begin work on the canal from the south fork of the New River, which will proceed west to connect with the Miami canal. Governor Broward's vision of draining the Everglades is in sight as construction commences on the dredging of the following canals (with locks):

- North New River Canal, connecting Lake Okeechobee southeast to the North New River and entering the

A 1906 photograph showing former Florida Governor William Jennings (top left) and current Florida Governor Napoleon Bonaparte Broward (top right) on a tour of the Everglades drainage project. Governor Broward selects his predecessor, Governor Jennings, to serve as general counsel for the Trustees of the Internal Improvement Fund.

Kissimmee - Lake Okeechobee - Everglades Drainage Area

Governor Broward, Hamilton Disston, and other early Floridians dreamed of converting the rich land around the Kissimmee River and Lake Okeechobee into an agricultural engine for Florida. By the twenty-first century the success of that plan is apparent, although it comes at a cost to the Everglades ecosystem.

County	Boxes of Citrus[1]	Heads of Cattle and Calves[3]	Value of Agriculture Products Sold[4][5]	Harvested Acres of Sugarcane[6]
	2010	2010	2012	2009
Broward		3,000	$47,000,000	
Collier	7,416,000	11,000	$203,000,000	
DeSoto	17,956,000	73,000	$198,000,000	
Glades	2,132,000	56,000	$107,000,000	36,000
Hardee	13,027,000	86,000	$218,000,000	
Hendry	16,330,000	58,000	$499,000,000	34,000
Highlands	21,592,000	110,000	$273,000,000	
Miami Dade		3,000	$604,000,000	
Monroe			$11,000,000	
Okeechobee	1,678,000	145,000	$257,000,000	
Orange	1,368,000	11,000	$262,000,000	
Osceola	3,115,000	105,000	$109,000,000	
Palm Beach[2]		4,000	$999,000,000	300,000
Polk	27,875,000	100,000	$350,000,000	
St. Lucie	10,219,000	21,000	$168,000,000	
Total	122,708,000	783,000	$4,305,000,000	370,000

1. 2011 Florida Agriculture by the Numbers, Florida Department of Agriculture, p. 19.
2. Palm Beach and four other counties totaled 207,000 citrus boxes.
3. 2011 Florida Agriculture by the Numbers, Florida Department of Agriculture, 49.
4. Florida Agriculture Overview and Statistics (2014), Florida Agricultural Statistics Service, p. 5.
5. The leading Florida fruit and vegetable production in 2009, in order, is tomatoes, strawberries, sweet corn, bell peppers, watermelons, potatoes, snap beans, cucumbers and blueberries. 2011 Florida by numbers p. 11.
6. 2011 Florida Agriculture by the Numbers, Florida Department of Agriculture, p.39.

Atlantic Ocean at Ft. Lauderdale. It begins in 1906 and will be completed in 1912.

- The Miami Canal to the southeast—completed in 1913;
- The Hillsboro Canal to the southeast, entering the Atlantic Ocean south of Boca Raton, near Hillsboro Beach—completed in 1915;
- The West Palm Beach Canal to the east—completed in 1920;
- The St. Lucie Canal to the St. Lucie River twenty-five miles to the east, entering the Atlantic near Stuart and Port St. Lucie—completed in 1926;
- The Caloosahatchee Canal, which was initially dredged by Hamilton Disston in 1883, connecting to the Caloosahatchee River, entering into the Gulf of Mexico at Cape Coral, near Ft. Myers.

A 1918 photograph of the dredge *Roseada* digging the West Palm Beach Canal, running from Lake Okeechobee east

A 1921 photograph of the dredge *Culebra* digging the St. Lucie Canal, connecting Lake Okeechobee to the St. Lucie River to the east

1906

On October 18, a hurricane with winds reaching 125 miles per hour strikes Miami after sweeping through the Florida Keys. One hundred sixty-four workers on Flagler's railroad to Key West perish when their floating work camp breaks loose from its anchors. Last month, on September 26–27, a Category 2 hurricane struck Pensacola, killing 134 people.

A view of the damage to Pensacola Harbor after a Category 2 hurricane strikes on September 26-27, 1906

A 1913 photograph of an Everglades surveying team

St. Petersburg's famous green benches will be a hub of activity downtown until the 1960s. (St. Petersburg Museum of History)

1907

On March 18, real estate salesman Noel Mitchell, called St. Petersburg's "sand man" because of his ability to sell real estate, becomes president of the Board of Trade. Next year, he will place the first benches, which are bright orange, in front of his office. The benches become very popular with tourists buying real estate in the city, and soon benches of various colors pop up downtown. In 1916, Mayor Al Lang will push through an ordinance requiring all benches to be a standard size and green. Eventually there will be an estimated three thousand green benches on downtown streets, and St. Petersburg will become known as the "City of Green Benches." Because St. Petersburg is a segregated city, African Americans will not be permitted to use the downtown green benches.

On August 1, the Charlotte Harbor and Northern railroad opens between Boca Grande and Arcadia. Later the line will be extended north from Arcadia to the phosphate mines near Mulberry. A 3,000-foot phosphate dock will be built at South Boca Grande on Gasparilla Island, connecting central Florida's phosphate mines

to a deep-water port. The railroad and port will support the major and growing industry in phosphate, a key ingredient in fertilizer that will be shipped around the world. In 1970, a new phosphate port loading facility on Tampa Bay will begin construction, taking over the phosphate business. On September 30, 1979, the last phosphate shipment will be loaded at Port Boca Grande. By the twenty-first century, phosphate mines in Polk, Hillsborough, Hardee, Manatee, and Hamilton counties will account for over half of the national annual production, and $1.3 billion in fertilizer will be exported from Florida. The Mosaic Company, CF Industries, and PCS Phosphate Company all will operate mines.

A pre-February 1920 photograph of the steamship *Jacob Luckenbach* from New York at the Port Tampa dock phosphate elevator

1908

In October, the Florida Sanitarium and Hospital is opened in today's Orlando. In 1908 the Sanitarium, constructed on seventy-two acres along Lake Estelle, will be sold to the Seventh-Day Adventist Church Conference of Florida. By the mid-1920s the hospital will have sixteen buildings and about 175 employees serving 125 patients. It is today's Florida Hospital.

Also this year, the Ocala National Forest is established on more than 440,000 acres east of Ocala. Today, it is the oldest national forest east of the Mississippi River and the largest forest of sand pines in the world. It lies between the St. Johns River and the Ocklawaha River. Today, other significant national forests in the state are the Apalachicola National Forest, a 564,000-acre forest southwest of Tallahassee that contains the largest population of red-cockaded woodpeckers in the world; and the Osceola National Forest, to be established in 1931, a 200,000-acre forest located about fifty miles west of Jacksonville.

1909

On January 5, Albert W. Gilchrist, a bachelor who grew up in Quincy and later lived in Punta Gorda, where he has been a civil engineer and orange grower, is sworn into office as Florida's twentieth governor. Governor Gilchrist's lengthy inaugural speech covers a wide variety of topics, including the need for good roads; the treatment of convicts; his desire to add Abraham Lincoln's birthday as a state holiday in addition to those holidays that exist honoring Robert E. Lee and George Washington; his pleasure in the growth of Florida's phosphate industry; the value in using Everglades land to produce sugar; and the desirability of good public educa-

tion. The new governor summarizes the inherent conflict true in any era: "Many of our people advocate changes, all of which cost money, yet they all want a reduction of taxation."

A 1916 view of Clematis Street in West Palm Beach

On July 1, Palm Beach County separates from Dade County. Residents of Palm Beach have felt that, despite paying 60 percent of the total taxes in Dade County, the majority of tax dollars were being spent in Miami. After earlier attempts failed, this year the legislature votes to split off the new county.

Also this year, the Florida legislature passes the Public Records Law, providing that any documents coming into the possession of a public agency doing official business are subject to request and inspection by the public, unless exempted by law. Computer information, cell phone records, photographs, and tapes will all come to constitute "public records."

1910

Bertha Honoré Palmer, widow of Chicago merchant Potter Palmer, takes a winter home in Sarasota and becomes a major force in Florida cattle ranching and farming

In February, Bertha Honoré Palmer arrives in Sarasota to establish a winter home. Her husband, Potter Palmer, wealthy Chicago merchant and real estate promoter, had died in 1902. Bertha Palmer will accumulate large land holdings in west Florida, engage in cattle ranching and farming, and build a magnificent estate at Osprey Point called The Oaks. Palmer's twenty-five mile tract of land will extend from Oneco, through Sarasota, to Venice.

On March 16, Barney Oldfield breaks the Daytona Measured Mile world speed record at 131.72 mph. During the week of February 12, 1919, Ralph DePalma will break the Measured Mile record again, with a speed of 149.875. His V-12 engine is based on the Liberty aircraft engine used in World War I. Daytona and speed are becoming synonymous.

On May 1, the National Association for the Advancement of Colored People is founded.

On June 24, much of downtown Clearwater is destroyed by a fire that engulfs many of the buildings on the north side of Cleveland Street.

Barney Oldfield in the "Lightening Benz" on Daytona Beach, where he sets a "Measured Mile" record in 1910

Ralph DePalma sets a "Measured Mile" record on Daytona Beach in 1919 in his Packard V-12.

The north side of Cleveland Street in Clearwater after the 1910 fire

Newspaper readers receiving free copies of the *Evening Independent* from a paper carrier on March 19, 1947, one of the Sunshine City's few days with no sunshine

On September 1, Lew Brown, owner of the *St. Petersburg Evening Independent*, proclaims his hometown to be the "Sunshine City" and declares that "To prove our faith in the recurrence daily of gladsome sunshine throughout fall and winter, when all is cloud and gloom in the Northland, the *Evening Independent* challenges the world by inaugurating today a standing offer to give away—ABSOLUTELY FREE—WITHOUT COST OR CONDITION—to subscribers and strangers alike—at the office, or on the carrier routes or on the streets—FREE—*The Evening Independent*— Free Every Day The Sun Doesn't Shine on St. Petersburg." The free papers will be given out less than five days per year. The city will enter the Guinness Book of World Records for having 768 consecutive days of sunshine from February 9, 1967 to March 17, 1969.

1911

Former Governor William S. Jennings (1901-1905) tours the Everglades drainage project in 1907. Governor Jennings is second from the left. Speculator Richard Bolles is seventh from the left with the bowler hat and right hand on his knee.

The Hotel Bolles built in 1910-11 by speculator and land developer Richard Bolles in Ritta, five miles east of Clewiston on the south shore of Lake Okeechobee. The hotel hosts prospective Everglades land buyers. From the cupola, purchasers are told that their land is "somewhere over there." The land is usually underwater.

On March 27, Ft. Lauderdale is overwhelmed by thousands participating in a land lottery for land in the Everglades that has not yet been drained. Speculator Richard Bolles sells plots in anticipation of the land being drained and becoming useable. One tactic of land sellers is to get people to buy into lotteries for a chance to win the not-yet drained land in amounts as diverse as 10 or 640 acres. The influx of new residents will lead to the incorporation of the city.

Carl Fisher, developer of Miami Beach and creator of the Indianapolis 500, in a 1915 photograph sitting on the Packard he used as the pace car in that year's Indianapolis 500

On May 30, Memorial Day, Ray Harroun drives his Marmon Wasp to victory at the inaugural Indianapolis 500 Mile Race. The Indy race track is the idea of Indiana auto dealer Carl Fisher, who proposes it as a car manufacturers testing facility. Harroun's average speed is almost 75 miles per hour and he takes home a prize of more than $14,000. In preparation for the race, Harroun invents and installs on the Wasp the first automobile rear-view mirror so he can see approaching cars without the aid of a mechanic sitting next to him. By 2005, when IndyCar racing makes its debut at today's Firestone Grand Prix of St. Petersburg, the Indianapolis 500 will be known as the "Greatest Spectacle in Racing" and, with attendance in the hundreds of thousands, as the largest single-day sporting event in the world. Indy 500 founder Carl Fisher will later become a significant promoter and developer of Miami Beach in the 1910s and 1920s.

A photograph taken between 1905 and 1912 of workers on Florida East Coast Railway's locomotive engine #12 during construction of the Overseas Railway

President William Howard Taft (on the left) in Key West

1912

On January 12, Henry Flagler completes the Overseas Railway, an extension of his Florida East Coast Railway to Key West. The line, which cost $28 million

Henry Flagler arrives on the first train to reach Key West.

twenty thousand parcels of swampland will be sold with the promise that the land will be drained for agricultural use. When the water remains, an Iowa purchaser will declare that he has bought land by the foot and acre but "by God, I have never before bought land by the gallon." Indictments will follow and the phrase "buying swampland in Florida" will be born to describe one who has been foolishly swindled.

Nevertheless, by 1920, thirty-four thousand acres of the Everglades will become farmland. Northwest of Miami, along the new Miami canal, Pennsylvania Sugar Company will begin Florida's sugar industry with cane fields and a mill in Pennsuco. Towns around Lake Okeechobee develop as Henry Flagler's railroad reaches today's Okeechobee on the north end of the lake and Henry Plant's railroad reaches Moore Haven on

to complete, includes ninety-one miles of roadbed and thirty-four railway bridges. Flagler rides on the first train to Key West.

On February 16, W.L. Bonney, "dare devil aviator," brings a brand new Wright biplane to St. Petersburg and makes the first flight in Pinellas County. He takes off from a strip of land near Bayboro Harbor and lands on the waterfront near the Electric Pier. Bonney raises $186.75 by charging adults twenty-five cents and children fifteen cents to watch.

On April 14, at 11:40 P.M., the White Star Line Steamship R.M.S. Titanic strikes an iceberg and sinks in the North Atlantic; 1,517 passengers and crew die at sea, while 700 are saved.

Also in April, a dry period, Florida's Internal Improvement Board hosts media from the North to promote the Everglades, with its reclaimed farms and canals. Soon,

An early map of the Florida East Coast Railroad and hotels

the lake's southwest shore in 1918 and Clewiston in 1922. The two railroads will connect at Lake Harbor on the south tip of the lake. Belle Glade, South Bay, and Clewiston will also develop in an agricultural area south of the lake. Pond Apple Swamp, a natural habitat in that area, disappears.

A 1923 photograph of the Pennsylvania Sugar Company factory in northwest Dade County, an area named "Pennsuco" after the sugar company. Sugar production will arrive in a very big way to that portion of the Everglades east and south of Lake Okeechobee.

1913

On January 7, Park M. Trammell, a lawyer and former mayor of Lakeland, becomes Florida's twenty-first governor. His inaugural address discusses his many priorities, including campaign finance reform; raising the standards for common schools; the need to drain and reclaim the Florida Everglades for agricultural purposes; the development of a program to eradicate cow ticks; the use of convicts to build roads; and changing the state tax system by discontinuing the state levy of ad valorem state tax and supporting the state government solely with license and franchise taxes.

On February 25, the Sixteenth Amendment to the United States Constitution goes into effect, permitting the imposition of an *income tax. Although an income tax had been in effect briefly during the Civil War, the U.S. Supreme Court held income taxes to be unconstitutional in 1895.*

The paddle steamer *City of Jacksonville*, along with other steamboats and ships, moored at the dock in Jacksonville in 1912, the year before the Phillies come to train in the city

Also in February, Major League Baseball's Chicago Cubs hold spring training in Tampa. Next year other Major League teams will come to spring train in Florida, including the St. Louis Browns, managed by Branch Rickey, in St. Petersburg, the St. Louis Cardinals in St. Augustine, and the Philadelphia Phillies in Jacksonville.

The opening of the Collins Bridge linking Miami and Miami Beach

Sign identifying various tolls for the Collins Bridge. A one-way one-horse dray (horse-drawn cart or other vehicle) costs 15 cents, while a horse with a rider is only 10 cents.

On June 12, Collins Bridge opens, connecting Miami to Miami Beach by automobile for the first time. At 2 ½ miles, it is called the "longest wooden bridge in the world." South Florida land developer John S. Collins builds the toll bridge with financial assistance from Carl Fisher, Miami Beach's developer. The bridge will be replaced in 1925 and renamed the Venetian Causeway.

On October 9, the U.S. Secretary of the Navy starts the process to select a location for a naval air training station. The process will result in the establishment of the Pensacola Naval Air Station in 1914.

1914

On New Year's Day, at 10:00 A.M., Tony Jannus flies a type-14 Benoist Flying Boat on a twenty-three-minute flight from St. Petersburg to Tampa as the first scheduled commercial passenger flight in the world. The world's first scheduled passenger airline, established in St. Petersburg, will be called the St. Petersburg-Tampa Airboat Line and will operate two daily round trips through March 31, the end of the 1914 tourist season. The plane is powered by

a sixty-five-horsepower Roberts engine connected to the propeller by a roller chain. It is designed to carry two people and, fully loaded, can reach sixty-four miles per hour. After prevailing at an auction, former St. Petersburg mayor A.C. Pheil pays $400 for the honor of becoming the first passenger. Later, passengers will pay five dollars per flight or ten dollars per round trip. Two round trips are scheduled daily leaving St. Petersburg at 10:00 A.M. and 2:00 P.M. Two years later, on October 12, 1916, Jannus will die in a plane crash while training pilots in Russia during World War I.

The world's first scheduled airline is based in St. Petersburg. Shown here (l-r) are Percy Fansler, general manager of the St. Petersburg-Tampa Air Boat Line; former St. Petersburg Mayor A.C. Pheil, the first passenger; and Tony Jannus, pilot of the first flight.

Take-off of the world's first scheduled airline with Tony Jannus as pilot as the crowd in St. Petersburg watches history take place (Courtesy of St. Petersburg Museum of History)

A photo-collage of the world's first scheduled passenger flight, which takes off from St. Petersburg on January 1, 1914

On January 2, Miss Mae Peabody of Dubuque, Iowa, takes a flight from St. Petersburg on the Benoist Flying Boat, becoming the first woman passenger on a scheduled airline.

In March, Morton F. Plant, son of railroad builder Henry Plant, donates $100,000 as an endowment for a hospital in Clearwater which, when it opens in 1915, will be named after its benefactor.

A 1917 photograph of a Navy blimp and hangar at the Naval Air Station in Pensacola

In April, nine Navy officers and twenty-three sailors from the USS *Mississippi* and the USS *Orion,* along with seven

A 1921 photo of pilots at Pensacola Naval Air Station.

aircraft, arrive at the former Pensacola Navy Yard to establish a navy flying school. Navy Air Station Pensacola will add multiple airfields and grow to be one of the world's most significant naval air training facilities.

On June 28, a Serb student assassinates Austrian Archduke Ferdinand and his wife in Sarajevo, Bosnia. A month later Germany invades France and Russia invades Germany. The Central Powers of Germany and Austria line up against the Allies of England, France and Russia as World War I begins.

On the night of November 10, Edward F. Sherman, a St. Petersburg winter resident who is a photographer and developer, is murdered by a shotgun blast to the head while asleep in his bed at home. His wife is beaten and assaulted. Mrs. Sherman, recuperating at Augusta Memorial Hospital, tells authorities that two Negroes are responsible. A manhunt is undertaken by a posse with hundreds of armed volunteers combing the area swamps with bloodhounds. Two days after the attack, arrested suspect John Evans, a black laborer whom Sherman had fired, is removed from his jail cell, tortured, and lynched by a mob estimated at 1,500.

Also this year, automobile builder Henry Ford travels with Thomas Edison to Ft. Myers. In 1916, Ford will purchase a winter residence in the town, naming his home "the Mangoes." Rubber and tire businessman Harvey Firestone will become a frequent visitor to his friends Edison and Ford in Ft. Myers.

1915

On May 7, a German submarine torpedoes and sinks the British Cunard liner Lusitania, *killing 7,200, including more than one hundred Americans. The United States draws closer to war.*

On April 30, Broward County is created out of southern Palm Beach County and northern Dade County. It is named after former Governor Napoleon Bonaparte Broward, who worked to drain the Everglades. Governor Broward died in 1910. The new county is mostly uninhabitable Everglades and has a population of about 4,700.

On October 8, the first board meeting is held in Tallahassee for the Florida State Road Department. The department was formed by the 1915 legislature for the purpose of developing a system of state roads that cross county lines. Prior to this time, most Florida roads were developed by and within the counties. The legislature provides funding for the new effort by dedicating 15 percent of the auto license money raised in the counties to the road department. The department's annual revenues for the first fiscal year will be about $16,000, but will exceed $6.7 million by 1924. During the twenty-nine years from 1915 through 1944, the State Road Department will receive total revenues, from federal and state sources, of over $295 million to spend on Florida's roads.

Henry C. Mustin in his Curtis airplane being catapulted from the USS *North Carolina* off Pensacola on November 5, 1915. It is history's first catapult of an airplane from a moving vessel.

A Martin aircraft on the catapult of the USS *Huntington* at the Pensacola Naval Air Station

On November 5, at Pensacola, Henry C. Mustin launches his Curtis airplane from a catapult on the USS *North Carolina*. It is the first catapult of an airplane from a moving vessel.

Also this year, the Florida East Coast Railway completes an extension from New Smyrna through Maytown to the town of Okeechobee on the Nosohatchee River, two miles northeast of Lake Okeechobee. The "Okeechobee division" of the railroad will be extended around the eastern shores of the lake and south to Lake Harbor. The extension of the railroad, combined with drainage and flood control in this part of the Florida Everglades, will stimulate the growth of a substantial agricultural industry here, with beans, cabbage, peas, tomatoes, sugar, and molasses

1916

In November, four thousand acres of land, including Paradise Key, are dedicated as Florida's first state park. Named Royal Palm State Park and located near the southeast point of the state, it is the beginning of what will become the Everglades National Park. The park results from legislation written by former Governor William Jennings and promoted by his wife, May Mann Jennings. The late Henry Flagler's company donates land around Paradise Key for the new park.

Also this year, the Atlantic Coast Line decides to extend the railroad to Immokalee, southeast of Ft. Myers. By the 1940s and 1950s, packinghouses will spread along the Immokalee branch, which experiences significant shipments of fruits, vegetables, and timber. Cypress logs are loaded on the train in Copeland, south of Immokalee in Collier County, and are bound for milling in Perry, Florida. By 1957, the cypress will be significantly depleted.

Preparing for war. A 1916 of the USS *Florida* in dry dock. The ship was commissioned in 1911 and is armed with more than thirty guns.

1917

On January 2, Sidney J. Catts, a former Baptist minister from DeFuniak Springs, is sworn into office as the twenty-second governor of Florida. In a speech containing many references to faith, Governor Catts stresses that the "most important thing facing Florida today is the draining of the Everglades . . . an event of as much moment will have transpired in the history of Florida as the opening of the Panama Canal was to the world." He also emphasizes the need to eliminate waste from the administration; the need to give more power to the "board of equalization of taxes"; the upcoming prohibition question; and his desire to expand industrial schools and training: "If we desire to retain the respect of ourselves and the nations of the earth we must educate the hand as well as the brain."

On April 6, at 1:11 P.M., President Woodrow Wilson signs a resolution of Congress declaring war on Germany. The United States enters World War I. The declaration follows German submarine torpedoing of U.S. ships and the publication of the Zimmermann telegram, an attempt by Germany to form a war alliance with Mexico. The "Great War" will continue until late 1918, when Germany is defeated and an armistice is signed.

The day after President Wilson's declaration of war, Florida residents will receive news of persistent but unconfirmed reports of German submarines in the Gulf of Mexico. The Florida economy, by this

Ocala volunteers going to war

World War I student pilot sitting on a wing of his crashed "Jenny" near Carlstrom Field training center in DeSoto County, near Arcadia

World War I Pilots and their airplane at the Dorr Field training center near Arcadia

Shipbuilding for the war effort in Jacksonville

time largely based on winter residents and tourists, will be devastated by World War I, but the bust that comes in 1918 will be short-lived.

On April 8, the Florida Naval Militia is ordered to duty. During the war, 42,030 Floridians will serve in the military. In 1918, two United States Army Air Service pilot training centers will be established in the Arcadia area, about sixty miles south of Lakeland, at Dorr Field and Carlstrom Field.

On June 12, the Pinellas County School Board decides that only single women will be employed as teachers. Married women who are already teaching

A 1917 Tampa parade in honor of Americans at war. Notice that the men march in the street and the women on the sidewalk.

World War I soldiers at Camp Joseph E. Johnston in Jacksonville. Today it is the Jacksonville Naval Air Station.

World War I soldiers manning guns at Fort Taylor in Key West

will be retained as long as desired. The board will later determine that married women whose husbands are in the navy or army may be hired as teachers.

1918

On May 13, the Atlantic Coast Line's first passenger train arrives in Moore Haven, on the southwest coast of Lake Okeechobee. The new line connects the western lake area to the north through Harrisburg, Sebring, and Haines City. By 1921, the line will be extended fourteen miles south to Clewiston by the Moore Haven and Clewiston Railway. By the 1930s, Clewiston will become a major sugar center, with U.S. Sugar owning one hundred miles of track and its own railroad system.

Coast Guardsmen Paul Webb, on left, and Harold Myers, seated, both from St. Petersburg, are among the 116 Coast Guardsmen who lose their lives when the Coast Guard Cutter *Tampa* sinks. (Courtesy of Frances Rose, sister of Harold Myers)

When the U.S. Coast Guard Cutter *Tampa* sinks on September 26, 1918, it is the second largest naval loss of American life in World War I.

On September 26, the U.S. Coast Guard Cutter *Tampa* is torpedoed by a German U-boat off the south coast of Wales while en route to its English base in Milord Haven, Wales. One hundred and sixteen U.S. Coast Guardsmen are lost, making it the greatest Coast Guard disaster of World War I and the second largest individual loss sustained by any U.S. naval force in the war.

A 1922 photograph of the Aeromarine Airways *Curtis* passenger airplane on the Miami-Bimini-Nassau route

On October 27, Aeromarine Company begins passenger airline service between Havana and Key West.

On November 5, Florida voters pass a referendum prohibiting the sale and manufacture of alcoholic beverages.

On November 11, the armistice with Germany is signed. More than 50,000 Americans have died in battle during the Great War.

News of the armistice reaches St. Petersburg at 3:50 A.M. when a local Western Union telegraph operator, who had been persuaded by *St. Petersburg Times* editor E.E. Naugle to stay up all night, receives the news that as of 6 A.M. the war will be officially over. Mayor Al Lang is awakened with the news and the city's "big siren" sounds, waking the entire city. By 4:30 A.M. Central Avenue is filled with people wild with joy. In the *Times* Armistice Extra, on the street within twenty minutes after the news arrives, Mayor Lang implores the city to suspend business, close school, stop all labor and "cut everything loose."

Armistice Day parade in Cocoa

1919

A circa 1920 view of the Everglades Club, designed by architect Addison Mizner, on Lake Worth in Palm Beach

On January 25, the Everglades Club opens on Worth Avenue in Palm Beach. The Spanish mission-style club is designed by architect Addison Mizner. Mizner, who will become known for his Mediterranean Revival style and his vision for Boca Raton, will design more than fifty villas and mansions for wealthy Americans. Examples will include many boom-era homes in Palm Beach such as the El Solano (future home of John Lennon), William Gray Warden House, and La Guerida, which will become the winter White House for President John Kennedy. As magnificent mansions are built on the island, Palm Beach becomes known for residences of the wealthy and famous. By the early twenty-first century, the *Palm Beach Daily News* will list twenty-nine billionaires with local ties.

On January 29, the Eighteenth Amendment to the United States Constitution, prohibiting the manufacture or sale of "intoxicating liquors," is declared ratified. Prohibition will go into effect on January 16, 1920, and will continue as the law of the land until the ratification of the Twenty-First Amendment in 1933.

During Prohibition, that portion of the Atlantic eastern seaboard just outside of the territorial limits of the United States is known as "Rum Row." Vessels containing liquor for illegal smuggling into the country sit more than three miles offshore to sell to smugglers willing to risk transporting the liquor onto shore. Most illegal liquor arriving in Florida comes from the Bahamas, a British colony, especially from West End, sixty miles east of West Palm Beach, and from Bimini, fifty-seven miles east of Miami. After President Calvin Coolidge persuades Congress to improve the Coast Guard fleet, torpedo boat destroyers, cabin cruisers, and motorboats of the Coast Guard vigorously pursue Rum Row and the rum-running business from 1927 to 1930, inflicting severe damage to the illegal effort.

A chain gang building Florida roads in 1925

On May 24, the Florida Legislature abolishes the system of leasing state prisoners to private businesses. Before the law, prisoners were leased to phosphate operators, turpentine businesses, sawmills, and others, but the conditions of the convict camps were often unsanitary and inhumane. Under the 1919 act, prisoners will go to work in the State Convict Road Force building Florida's highways. As the state road system expands, the number of "Road Prisons" will reach thirty-five, with each being located on about twenty acres of land and holding fifty-five prisoners. The wearing of leg chains by road prisoners will be eliminated in the mid-1940s.

During the fall, Florida is invaded with tourists traveling by automobile and train. The visitors are flush with money from the post-war economic boom.

On September 10, a strong hurricane strikes just south of Key West as a Category 4 storm. It will continue northwest across the Gulf of Mexico making landfall again south of Corpus Christi, Texas. The storm will inflict $22 million in damages within the United States, and will cause 600–900 deaths, including 488 souls lost aboard when the steamer *Valbanera* sinks. It will later be found between Key West and the Dry Tortugas.

Chapter 5

Boom and Bust:
1920 through 1940

The nation pivots quickly from World War I and roars through the 1920s while Florida welcomes the world to its sunny shores. A future Florida governor will describe the

frugal nature of Florida's "tin can tourists," while a governor from this era sets out to form a marketing bureau to provide "truthful advertising" to attract other states' residents here. While visiting the state, tourists fuel a "lot boom," buying an estimated 20 million lots for residential and investment purposes. Other states warn their residents against the purchase of Florida's real estate.

A January 1926 photograph of the Vinoy Park Hotel in St. Petersburg. The magnificent hotel opens on New Year's Day, seventeen days before this picture was taken, just in time to greet the Florida real estate collapse and the Great Depression.

Florida officials continue to build roads, improve public education, drain the Everglades, and expand agriculture. Throughout the state, developers plan new cities, build magnificent hotels, sell lots in real estate developments, and create amenities like dog tracks and horse tracks. Car racing sets records on Daytona Beach. The railroad reaches southwest Florida, while new bridges come to Jacksonville and St. Petersburg. Miami begins a boom that will continue throughout the century and beyond.

Meanwhile, the development of an air-conditioned movie theater in Texas provides a glimpse into Florida's future and Florida executes its first prisoner by electrocution.

As the boom peaks, the Florida real estate market collapses, followed by the stock market crash, signaling an end to the good times.

As the United States enters the Great Depression, Florida mirrors the national crisis. Statewide, over 150 of Florida's cities and towns default on their municipal bonds. A state commission will later conclude that the ad valorem tax base had been inflated by lot sales and that more bonds had been issued than the taxpaying ability could stand. Depression-era governors argue

A portable field conveyor loading juice oranges near the Indian River in Cocoa

An early photograph of the interior of a packinghouse in Winter Haven

against increasing taxes on residents and for more efficiency in government spending. Meanwhile, almost 150 banks in the state close their doors.

Hurricanes kill thousands in central and south Florida and a plan is developed to build a dike around Lake Okeechobee to control water flow. After another hurricane severely damages Flagler's railroad through the Florida Keys, the track is abandoned and replaced with an overseas highway. As the era comes to close, a world war has begun overseas and the nation and state brace and prepare.

Timeline

1920

This year, Dr. Phillip Phillips moves from Memphis to the Orlando area, where he will build a citrus empire. In 1927, he will develop a process of "flash Pasteurization" for orange juice that allows the juice to retain its content of vitamin C. He develops a canning plant, a fertilizer plant, and the world's largest packinghouse. By the late 1920s, Phillips will be the world's largest owner of citrus acreage. In 1954, he will sell his citrus holdings to Granada Groves, a subsidiary of Minute Maid.

Also by this year, Carl Fisher, who invented the automobile headlight and started the Indianapolis 500, converts the barrier islands off Miami into Miami Beach. It is a tourist destination with millions of cubic yards of sand dredged from the bottom of Biscayne Bay. During its first decade, property assessments on Miami Beach will grow from $250,000 to $44 million.

On April 6, St. Petersburg real estate developer Noel A. Mitchell, who calls himself "the sand man" and who established the city's first green benches, is elected mayor. During the campaign, Mitchell, who had spent time in a mental institution, waves his competency papers to the crowd and declares himself "the only candidate proved not crazy." He will be recalled from office after one and a half years on November 15, 1921, after police raid a Prohibition-era booze party at city hall.

On August 26, the Nineteenth Amendment to the United States Constitution is ratified, giving women the right to vote in national elections.

On September 17, Mary Gill Patterson of Orlando will register to vote. This year she will be the first Orlando woman to vote in the 1920 presidential election.

A circa 1920s view of Opa-locka's opulent City Hall

A November 1924 photograph of the construction of the Coral Gables Inn, part of the aggressive development of George Merrick's master planned community

Part of Glenn Curtiss' vision of growth for Hialeah is a horse track, under construction in this November 26, 1924, photograph

Boom-era Coral Gables developer George Merrick rides the Coral Gables streetcar on April 30, 1925, its first day of operations.

During five years of the boom, the value of Miami's building permits increases 1,300 percent and the number of transactions increases 1,700 percent. Having one skyscraper in 1920, by 1925 Miami will have thirty under construction. Land in Miami that costs $15,000 an acre in January of 1922 will go for $150,000 five months later. Around Miami, communities will grow, including Coral Gables, master-planned by George Merrick to include the University of Miami, Spanish architecture, and Venetian canals; and Hialeah, developed by Glenn Curtiss with casinos, greyhound and horse tracks, and a jai alai fronton. Curtiss will also help develop nearby Miami Springs and Opa-locka.

1921

On January 4, Cary A. Hardee, a Live Oak banker and lawyer, becomes Florida's twenty-third governor. Governor Hardee sets out his agenda of building public roads with convicts and discontinuing the convict lease program, which will end in 1923; developing a plan to conserve resources like timber, fish, and game; continuing the Everglades drainage and reclamation program; developing a state road system paid for from state funds; improving rural public education; amending the constitution to allow for an intangible tax rate; and developing a marketing bureau "to give people of other states some conception of the greatness, the attractiveness and beauty of Florida through truthful advertising." At the onset of the Roaring Twenties, Governor Hardee warns against the extravagant nature of the times: "Individual thrift and frugality have been largely discarded, and erstwhile luxuries are now being classed as necessities. Thoughtful men have known that such an orgy of inflation could not continue, and with prophetic voice have all along wooed the people back to safer ground."

Tin Can Tourists on the Atlantic beach in Indialantic, three miles east of Melbourne

In May, responding to concerns that the "tin can tourists" are not the type of visitors that St. Petersburg wishes to attract, the city commission abolishes the publicly financed tent cities. Tin can tourists have invaded all parts of Florida. They arrive by automobile and truck and bring their own food and tents. Tampa has its own "tin-canners club." Fuller Warren, a future Florida governor, will say of the tin can tourists, "They came to Florida with one suit of underwear and one twenty dollar bill, and changed neither." As Florida develops, the mobile home industry will replace tents for those seeking a low-cost entry into the state.

Tin Can Tourists invade Florida. In 1921, some gather here by their tent in Gainesville.

An early view of the Acosta Bridge over the St. Johns River in Jacksonville, alongside the railroad bridge

A 1960 view of the Florida East Coast (railroad) Bridge and Acosta Bridge, each to the left, along with the Alsop Bridge to the right, crossing the St. Johns River in Jacksonville

A 1953 photograph of the ribbon cutting for Jacksonville's Mathews Bridge. Left to right are Florida Governor Fuller Warren, Mrs. John Mathews, Justice John Mathews, who had advocated for the bridge, and Jacksonville Mayor Haydon Burns.

On July 1, the St. Johns River Bridge opens in Jacksonville, the first automobile bridge over the river. The "vertical lift" bridge will be renamed the St. Elmo W. Acosta Bridge in 1949 after the city councilman who advocated for funding and construction of the bridge. Before the bridge opens, automobile traffic crossed the river by ferry. As the city grows, the Acosta Bridge will be replaced in 1993 and other bridges will cross the river, including

The schooner *Thomas B. Garland*, aground in Tampa along with other rubble after the 1921 hurricane

the John T. Alsop, Jr. (Main Street) Bridge to open in 1941 (replaced in 2002); the John E. Mathews Bridge, to open in 1953; the Fuller Warren Bridge, to open in 1954; and the Isiah David Hart Bridge.

On October 25, at 3:00 A.M., a major hurricane strikes west-central Florida. The storm had developed in the western Caribbean Sea, blew west of Cuba, traveled north until it reached the latitude of Tampa Bay, and then moved inland. Gusts exceed 100 mph.

Damage to the Safety Harbor public school after the 1921 hurricane

On November 9, the United States Congress passes the Federal Highway Act, providing $75 million for highway construction, developing a system for providing federal aid

to states for construction and making available surplus war materials for states to use in road work. From the first federal highway aid authorized under the Bankhead Act of 1916 through 1923, Florida will receive over $4.6 million in federal highway funds.

1922

St. Petersburg Mayor Frank Pulver, the millionaire bachelor mayor, resting up from his demanding duties as the city's bathing suit inspector (Courtesy of St. Petersburg Museum of History)

On March 14, *The Tourist News* prints a tongue-in-cheek column labeling the "Purity League" a sham and calling for the resignation of St. Petersburg Mayor Frank Pulver as bathing suit inspector. The Purity League is a contrived organization created a couple of months ago by publicist John Lodwick. Lodwick wrote a letter, copying national media, demanding that "something be done to make female bathers at beaches wear decent and respectable bathing suits," saying, "They make Eve's

The "Golden Arrow," in which Major Henry Seagrave breaks the world speed record on Daytona Beach on March 11, 1929

fig leaf look like a complete disguise." The resulting front-page national media alternatively labels St. Petersburg as a "disgrace" or "the nicest place this side of heaven." The columnist, Harry King, even suggests a replacement bathing suit inspector: Harry King!

On April 7, Sig Haugdahl drives his Wisconsin Special very fast and becomes the first man to reach 180 miles per hour on Daytona Beach. On March 29, 1927, Major Henry Seagrave will set the world's land speed record at Daytona Beach with a speed of 203.79 mph. He will return to break his own record on March 11, 1929,

Sig Haugdahl shaking hands with Mayor Bailey after breaking the 180 m.p.h. mark at Daytona Beach in his Wisconsin Special on April 7, 1922

Fellow racer Sig Haugdahl shakes hands with Major Henry Seagrave, who breaks the world speed record on Daytona Beach on March 11, 1929. Seagrave's achievement results in his being knighted "Sir Henry Seagrave."

when he reaches 231.362 mph. Daytona Beach's is clearly "roaring" through the 1920s. Seagrave, who served in the Royal Air Force during World War I, will be knighted for his achievements.

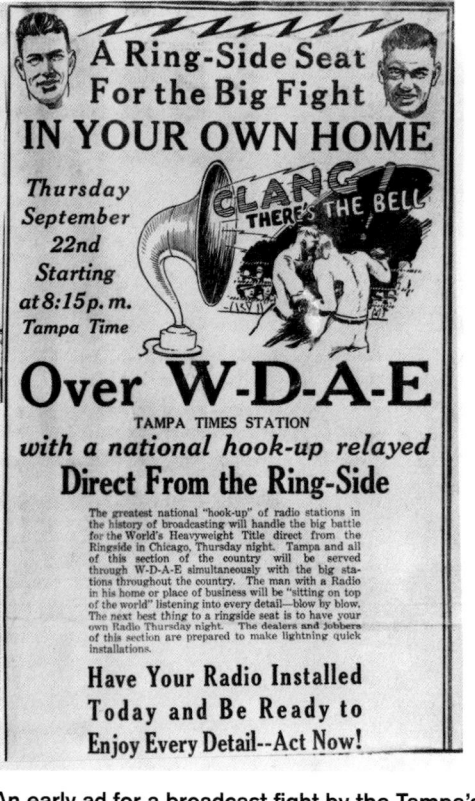

A Ring-Side Seat For the Big Fight
IN YOUR OWN HOME

Thursday
September
22nd
Starting
at 8:15 p.m.
Tampa Time

CLANG THERE'S THE BELL

Over W-D-A-E
TAMPA TIMES STATION
with a national hook-up relayed
Direct From the Ring-Side

The greatest national "hook-up" of radio stations in the history of broadcasting will handle the big battle for the World's Heavyweight Title direct from the Ringside in Chicago, Thursday night. Tampa and all of this section of the country will be served through W-D-A-E simultaneously with the big stations throughout the country. The man with a Radio in his home or place of business will be "sitting on top of the world" listening into every detail—blow by blow. The next best thing to a ringside seat is to have your own Radio Thursday night. The dealers and jobbers of this section are prepared to make lightning quick installations.

Have Your Radio Installed Today and Be Ready to Enjoy Every Detail--Act Now!

An early ad for a broadcast fight by the Tampa's WDAE, Florida's first licensed radio station to go on the air

On May 15, WDAE in Tampa becomes the first licensed radio station to operate in the state, broadcasting baseball scores and playing records. WCAN in Jacksonville receives a license on May 8 of this year but reportedly does not go on the air until August. Miami's WQAM (We Quit At Midnight) site indicates that it went on the air in February 1921, but was not licensed as WQAM until January 1923. Radio stations will quickly spread around the state, including WDBO in Orlando

(1924), WSAG in St. Petersburg (1924), WFLA in Clearwater (1927), and others. Also this year, the *Miami Herald* is the heaviest newspaper in the nation due to the large number of real estate advertisements selling the city's property. "Binder boys" around the state find willing buyers for lot sales and take a down payment or "binder" before turning the buyer over to the realtor.

1923

A home burns during the vicious racial attack on the African American community in Rosewood

On January 4, white mobs in Rosewood, Florida, about fifty miles southwest of Gainesville, burn African American churches and homes, killing six and forcing all others to permanently leave. The attack follows an assault upon a white woman. In 1995, nine elderly Rosewood survivors and descendants of deceased Rosewood victims will collectively receive $2 million in compensation awarded by the Florida Legislature to make amends for the tragedy.

Observing the damage at the smoldering remains of an African American home in Rosewood

The "Tamiami Trail Blazers" set out on a drive through the Everglades to gain support for the completion of the road linking south Florida's east and west coasts.

A 1924 photograph of Barron Collier and Florida Governor Cary Hardee aboard Collier's yacht. Collier, a pioneer and passionate supporter of development in southwest Florida, helps finance the Tamiami Trail.

In April, the "Tamiami Trail Blazers" launch an automobile caravan in the Florida Everglades across the unfinished portion of the Tamiami Trail, from Ft. Myers to Miami. The group includes a truck and seven Model T Fords. It will take ten days, but it will help convince the state to restart construction and finish the road.

On May 8, the Florida legislature creates Collier County, splitting it off from Lee County. The new county is named after Barron Gift Collier, a businessman who is passionate about the development of southwest Florida. In 1911, Collier began purchasing land in the Ft. Myers/ Naples area until he owned over a million acres in the state. When the state needs money to finish the Tamiami Trail, Collier pledges to complete it himself. Having earned his fortune selling advertising for subway, trolley, and train lines, Collier has set down roots on the Gulf coast and envisions bold development for southwest Florida. He brings the community its first telephone service, railroad, newspapers, and buses.

On August 2, President Warren G. Harding dies of apoplexy in San Francisco. Vice President Calvin Coolidge assumes the presidency.

The stately home of Barron Collier on Useppa Island, off Ft. Myers

A 1949 photograph of the Gulfstream Polo Club in Delray Beach

On November 1, the Florida Road Condition Map describes the completed Dixie Highway, then State Road 4 and today U.S. Highway 1, running from the Georgia state line down the Atlantic coast to Miami and Homestead. The road surface alternates with shell, hardtop, sand, clay, paving, limerock, and brick. The trip is described as teeth-rattling.

Also this year, in the midst of the Florida boom, the Gulfstream Polo Club opens along the ocean in the Delray Beach area. It is the first, and will become the longest, operating polo club in Florida. Following Gulfstream's lead, multiple other polo clubs will open on Florida's east coast.

1924

In the summer, Willis Carrier's air conditioning system is installed in a motion picture theater for the first time at the Palace Theater in Dallas, Texas. "Air-cooled" movie theaters mark the beginning of use of air conditioners for comfort instead of industrial purposes. Until now, movie houses have closed during the hot summer months. Between 1924 and 1930, Carrier will install three hundred air conditioners in theaters.

On July 4, the fifty-one-mile Conners Highway, a toll road, is completed from Palm Beach to Okeechobee. Its builder,

Florida's east coast will see polo come to Delray Beach, Lake Worth, Boca Raton, and other cities. Here is a February 21, 1920, portrait of a polo team in Miami Beach.

William J. "Fingey" Conners, wants to connect his farm on the east end of Lake Okeechobee to Palm Beach. It cost $1.8 million to build, and the starting toll is 1.5 cents/mile. It is intended to be the first link in the state's first hard-surfaced cross-state highway to join the St. Petersburg/Tampa area and the Florida west coast with Palm Beach and the east coast.

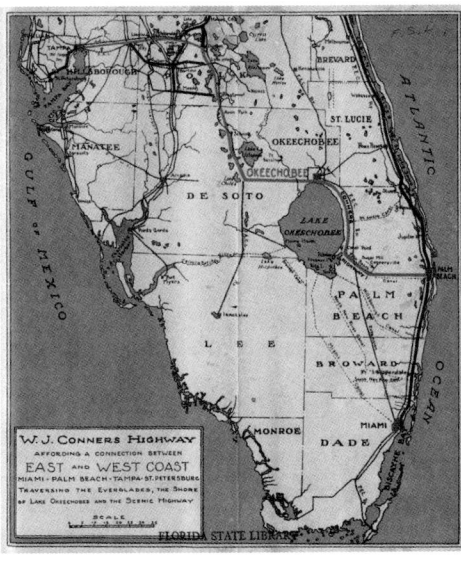

A circa 1924 map of the Conners Highway and connecting roads in Florida

A 1936 photograph of the electric chair at Raiford Prison, about thirty-five miles north of Gainesville

On October 7, Frank Johnson becomes the first convict to die in Florida's electric chair, which is nicknamed "Old Sparky." The Duval County man had been convicted of murdering a railroad engineer

for his watch and $100. The death penalty will be struck down by the U.S. Supreme Court in 1972 because of arbitrary application. After a new law is drafted, Florida executions will commence again in 1979. The first American use of the electric chair was in New York on August 8, 1890. Use of the electric chair in Florida will again be suspended by the U.S. Supreme Court in 1999. In 2000, the Florida legislature will change the method of execution to provide for lethal injection.

On October 14, the Smithsonian Institution publishes a report entitled *Preliminary Archeological Explorations at Weedon Island, Florida.* The study discusses and displays the stone, aboriginal pottery, and skeletal remains unearthed from the "Weedon cemetery" in St. Petersburg, whose occupants "probably never saw a white man or heard of a European." During the excavations, local publicists waste no time marketing the excavation as a tourist attraction, promising that visitors will "Stand where Narváez and DeSoto ... stood when they first set foot on our soil."

The Gandy Bridge, connecting St. Petersburg and Tampa, opens in 1924 at the height of the boom.

On November 20, Governor Cary Hardee unties a knot holding a rope of flowers to officially open the 2.5-mile Gandy Bridge connecting St. Petersburg and Tampa, including an additional 2.5 miles of causeways. Governors from fifteen other states, Hawaii, and Alaska, along with city officials, join in the celebration of the historic bridge. Public celebrations follow at Williams Park. The St. Petersburg Chamber of Commerce presents honors to Gandy at a Huntington Hotel banquet. Construction of the bridge took more than two years, having commenced on September 24, 1922. The new bridge reduces the St. Petersburg to Tampa trip from forty-three miles to nineteen miles.

1925

The heading to the picture reads "Greyhound Racing at the St. Petersburg Kennel Club, World's Oldest Greyhound Track."

Dizzy Dean (holding #2) and Babe Ruth (holding #1) at the St. Petersburg Kennel Club, circa 1930. Today it is called Derby Lane. (Courtesy of St. Petersburg Museum of History)

On January 3, the St. Petersburg Kennel Club runs its first greyhound races at its new track on Gandy Boulevard. The races continue today, and the club, now known as Derby Lane, is the world's oldest greyhound track. After the Florida legislature legalizes pari-mutuel wagering at horse and dog tracks in 1931, the Broward County Kennel Club will be established in southeast Florida, opening on December 12, 1934, with an admission cost of ten cents. Other dog and horse tracks around the state will follow suit.

On January 6, John W. Martin, a lawyer and former mayor of Jacksonville, becomes Florida's twenty-fourth governor. Governor Martin pledges to secure "a reduction and equalization of taxes, economy and efficiency in office, the building and maintenance of good roads, the improvement of the public school and its facilities, prompt and impartial administration of the law, the safe-guarding of public health, encouragement to the agricultural, citrus, horticultural and mining industries, the conservation of the oyster and fish resources of the state, drainage of the Everglades, justice to labor and capital and all other interests that tend to the welfare and happiness of the people." Governor Martin's term will see free textbooks for public school students, direct state appropriations for public schools, and state highway expansion.

Construction on the Miami Biltmore Hotel in Coral Gables commences on March 14, 1925. This is the completed landmark hotel in 1926.

A circa 1917 drawing of Fort Lauderdale's Hotel Broward, which will be completed in 1919 on the corner of Andrews Avenue and Las Olas Boulevard

On February 6, 1926, the Cloister Inn opens in Boca Raton as the most expensive 100-room hotel of the day. After many renovations, as shown in this post-1988 photograph, the hotel will be called the Boca Raton Resort & Club.

The Hollywood Beach Hotel, built in 1925

Exterior and interior views of the Hotel Floridan in Tampa, built during the boom and opening on January 31, 1927

A circa 1920s view of the Palm Beach Biltmore, earlier known as the Ambassador

Members of the Ku Klux Klan in the funeral procession for slain Miami police officer Laurie Lafayette Wever

On March 14, the magnificent Biltmore Hotel begins construction in George Merrick's Coral Gables. During the boom, signature hotels will be constructed throughout the state as the real estate and tourism industries explode. Examples are the Floridan in Tampa, the Vinoy Park in St. Petersburg, the Hotel Carling in Jacksonville, the Hollywood Beach Hotel, the Boca Raton Cloister Inn, the Don CeSar in St. Petersburg Beach, and others.

On March 15, Miami police motorcycle officer Laurie Lafayette Wever is shot and killed by two armed robbers. The Ku Klux Klan will send a delegation to participate in his funeral procession. The Klan is active in many parts of Florida, and will be for decades.

In August, the Florida East Coast Railway significantly reduces its service in Florida in order to repair damaged track. Only food, livestock, and perishables are permitted to enter the state. By October every other rail line in Florida will follow Florida East Coast's lead, and Florida's construction and tourist industries, unable to obtain supplies and visitors, are seriously impacted.

Also in October, the Minnesota Department of Conservation issues an "Immigration Bulletin" warning its state citizens against investing in Florida and

A Ku Klux Klan gathering in front of a burning cross in Tallahassee, September 1, 1956

predicting that a "terrible crash is sure to come." The bulletin is one of many alarms issued throughout Northern states. A *Barron's* magazine article estimates that 20 million real estate lots have been laid out for speculation sale in Florida, enough to house half of the United States. Ohio passes a law prohibiting the sale of Florida real estate in Ohio. The Massachusetts Savings Bank Association cautions depositors after one hundred thousand accounts in the state are drawn upon for Florida investments, totaling $20 million.

Boom-era real estate salesmen in Coral Gables, February 12, 1925

On November 22, the Sunday edition of the *St. Petersburg Times* consumes 90 of its 134 pages for real estate advertising, 55 pages of which offer vacant lots for sale. This year there are almost six thousand real estate salesmen in the city, over one third of the population. They are known as "knickerbockers boys" due to their fashion of the day, and use "binder boys" to drum up contacts. The massive purchase and sale of vacant lots is driven not by potential homeowners but by investors hoping to profit greatly from the escalating values of Florida real estate.

The week of December 7 is cold and rainy while Florida is hosting a thousand members of the Investment Bankers Association of America. An effort is launched at the convention to promote restrictions on the sale of speculative Florida real estate being sold by "pirates of promotion." The inclement weather and harsh criticism of wild land speculation forecast the imminent downfall of the Florida's real estate industry. During 1926, the Florida real estate industry will collapse. Walter P. Fuller, historian and one of the major developers of the era, will later attribute the bust to the fact that "The 1925 Florida lot boom just ran out of fuel in the late fall of 1925 and quit . . . We just ran out of suckers. That's all. We got all their money, then started trading with overdues. We became the suckers." A newspaper editorial will lament that "many Florida cities, forgot [they were] in the tourist business as a means of livelihood, and that the real estate business was a side line that had developed . . . as a result many of the tourists became disgusted."

By this year, Henry Ford will build one Model T every ten seconds.

Massive destruction from the 1926 hurricane in Everglades City

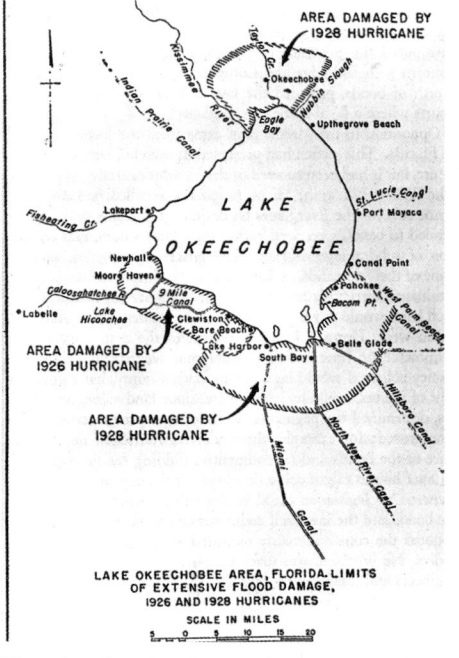

LAKE OKEECHOBEE AREA, FLORIDA. LIMITS
OF EXTENSIVE FLOOD DAMAGE,
1926 AND 1928 HURRICANES
SCALE IN MILES

Map showing the destruction around Lake
Okeechobee caused by the 1926 and 1928
hurricanes

The schooner *Rose Mahoney* is washed up
onto Biscayne Boulevard in Miami by the force
of the 1926 hurricane. The storm kills 400.

1926

On New Year's Day, after a gala New
Year's Eve party, the Vinoy Park Hotel
opens, having cost a reported $3.5 million.
The hotel is developed by Aymer Vinoy
Laughner, who came to St. Petersburg
with his father, Perry, in 1918. Architect

for the Vinoy, Henry Taylor, also designs
two other magnificent St. Petersburg
hotels: the Rolyat (Taylor spelled backward), which opens on the same day as the
Vinoy, and the Jungle Hotel, which will
open next month.

On January 10, a four-masted schooner
Prinz Valdemar capsizes in Miami's harbor
entrance, impeding shipping to the city.

*On March 16, physicist Robert H.
Goddard launches the world's first flight of a
liquid-fueled rocket. The lift-off takes place at
the Auburn, Massachusetts, farm of Goddard's
Aunt Effie.*

During the night of September 17 and
morning of September 18, Miami, Ft. Lauderdale, and south Florida are struck by the
"Great Miami Hurricane," one of the most
powerful hurricanes in their history. The
path of the Category 4 storm goes directly
through downtown Miami, damaging or
destroying most buildings. Wind gusts of
up to 140 mph and storm surges up to
fifteen feet violently slam the city. When
the eye of the storm passes around 6 A.M.,
some residents go out to survey the damage, not realizing that the storm will return
when the eye passes. Flood waters flow out
of Lake Okeechobee, destroying property
and killing hundreds in Moore Haven, on
the lake's south side. In total, almost four
hundred people die from the storm and
more than forty thousand are rendered
homeless. The storm causes almost $80
million in damage. The disaster accelerates
the path that Florida is on toward a real
estate collapse.

After the 1926 hurricane, Governor
Martin supports $20 million of drainage
bonds, which pass in the legislature. The
St. Lucie Canal will be completed, but
plans to strengthen the dike around Lake
Okeechobee and build more canals are not

developed further after a lawsuit blocks the taxes intended to support the bonds.

Seaboard Airline Railway's *Orange Blossom Special* arrives in Naples on January 7, 1927, with the governor and the railroad's president on board.

On December 27, the first Atlantic Coast Line (ACL) passenger train arrives in Naples, traveling south from Ft. Myers with stops in Estero and Bonita Springs. A Seaboard freight train arrived on a new line in the city six weeks earlier, on November 10. Just eleven days after the ACL brings passenger service to the city, the Seaboard Airline Railway' *Orange Blossom Special* will bring a second line to Naples on January 7, 1927. Governor John Martin and Seaboard president Davies Warfield arrive on board the *Orange Blossom Special* and attend the grand celebration that includes bands, waving flags, beach visits, and a luncheon.

ACL will reach Collier City, today's Marco Island, in June 1927.

Alfred I. duPont, who invests his fortune in Jacksonville and the Florida Panhandle

Also this year, Alfred I. duPont moves from Delaware to Jacksonville. He is one of the heirs to the duPont family fortune. The historic duPont businesses include gunpowder, chemicals, plastics, paint, and others. By the time of his Florida move, duPont owns 100,000 acres in Florida. He will invest $34 million in banks, land, bonds, and buildings in Jacksonville and the Florida Panhandle. In 1933, he purchases 240,000 Florida acres in the panhandle counties (southwest of Tallahassee) of Gulf, Bay, Liberty, and Franklin. In St. Joe (today's Port St. Joe), on the Gulf coast about a hundred miles southwest of Tallahassee, he will acquire a sawmill, dock, and terminal company, a telephone company, and the Apalachicola Northern Railroad Company. DuPont's objective is to revive St. Joe and its historic timber industry. He will invest in town improvements and build a paper mill, receiving timber from his land holdings.

Cattle-raising has been a major industry in Florida since the Spanish arrived, as will ultimately be exemplified by two large ranches: the Mormon Church's Deseret Ranch across central Florida and the Lykes family ranch in Glades County west of Lake Okeechobee. This cattle roundup took place in Kissimmee in 1974.

Also this year, the Lykes family acquires 274,000 acres in Glades County, on the west side of Lake Okeechobee. The family will ultimately develop a 300,000-acre cattle ranch along with meat-processing plants, orange groves, and citrus pack-inghouses, becoming one of the largest ranches east of the Mississippi River. The Mormon Church, starting in 1950, will assemble land across central Florida in Brevard, Osceola, and Orange Counties, ultimately evolving into the Deseret Ranch, the largest ranch in Florida, with citrus, timber, and 50,000 head of cattle. The ranch is self-described as "a beautiful and productive cattle ranch in the heart of Central Florida."

1927

The sweeping veranda of Marjorie Merriweather Post's magnificent Mar-a-Lago mansion in Palm Beach, completed in 1927. It will acquired by developer and future president Donald Trump in 1985.

In January, Marjorie Merriweather Post completes *Mar-a-Lago* (Spanish for "sea to lake") on Palm Beach. The 115-room mansion sits on 17 acres stretching the width of the island from the Atlantic to Lake Worth. Post is the daughter of Charles Post who developed Postum Cereal Company, today's General Foods. Developer and future president Donald Trump will acquire the property in 1985.

On April 7, the first public demonstration of television takes place. The New York event is organized by American Telephone and Tele-graph and features a Washington, D.C., speech by Secretary of Commerce Herbert Hoover.

On May 21, Charles Lindbergh arrives in Paris after crossing the Atlantic by air, traveling 3,600 miles in thirty-three and one-half hours.

In the fall, St. Petersburg Junior College holds its first classes in the east wing of the former St. Petersburg High School building at Second Avenue North and Fifth Street, with 111 students and 15 faculty members. The college, supported with a $10,000 annual payment from the city, is Florida's first junior college. In 2001, the college will begin offering baccalaureate degrees, becoming a four-year institution renamed St. Petersburg College. The move will be replicated by other community colleges throughout Florida.

The first flight of Pan American Airway's *American Clipper* in Miami

On October 28, Pan American World Airways flies its first flight from Key West to Havana. The flight provides passenger and mail service. On September 15, 1928, Pan Am will move its home base from Key West to Miami. By 1935, the airline will connect Miami to thirty-two other Central and South American countries. In 1930, Eastern Air Transport will begin flights between Miami and New York.

Also this year, John Ringling brings the Ringling Bros. & Barnum and Bailey Circus to Sarasota and makes Sarasota the circus's winter home.

Crowds and an elephant line up for the Sarasota premiere of the movie *The Greatest Show on Earth*. The 1952 Cecil B. DeMille movie is filmed in Sarasota, the winter home of the Ringling Brothers & Barnum and Bailey Circus.

1928

On January 1, the twenty-one-story Milam office building opens in San Antonio, Texas. It is the world's first office tower originally constructed with air conditioning.

On January 8, Key West is incorporated. It is seven miles long and one mile wide.

An early view of the Don CeSar Hotel, which opens in 1928 on St. Petersburg Beach

On January 16, the Don CeSar Hotel opens on Pass-a-Grille Beach, today's St. Pete Beach. Builder Thomas J. Rowe, who started construction of the 300-room, $1.5 million facility in 1925, also builds an adjoining subdivision of Spanish-style houses. A week of parties celebrates the hotel, which is named after the hero of Rowe's favorite American opera, *Maritana*. On opening night, 1,500 guests in formal attire dine on the fifth floor and dance in the grand ballroom.

A cargo ship docked at the Port Everglades refrigeration company

On February 22, 85 percent of Broward County's residents gather for the official dedication ceremony of Port Everglades. President Calvin Coolidge was scheduled to push a button from the White House detonating explosives to clear the rock barrier separating the harbor from the ocean. Although the blast did not occur, the rocks will later be cleared. Located near Ft. Lauderdale in Broward County, the port will become one of Florida's leading container and petroleum products ports. By 2015, the port will lead the state in containers and exports.

An excavator constructing the Tamiami Trail in 1927. The road is being built with rock dredged up from digging the canal that runs alongside the road.

On April 25, the cross-Everglades route of the Tamiami Trail opens, linking Tampa to Miami. The road is 108 miles between Naples and Miami through swamp, wetlands, sawgrass, hammock islands, mosquitoes, and alligators. Three million pounds of dynamite were exploded building the $7 million inhospitable Everglades stretch that cost many workmen their lives. The Tamiami Trail will effectively block the natural flow of water, which has run from Lake Okeechobee through the Everglades to Florida Bay, jeopardizing the ecosystem. Additionally, the road, along with lower water tables in the Everglades, makes canoe travel in the Everglades more difficult for the Seminoles. Many Seminole camps move to areas near the road, with some becoming tourist attractions.

In June, the Atlantic Coast Line's first passenger train arrives in Everglades City, completing the railroad's reach to the southwest corner of Florida. At the port, grapefruit from Barron Collier's Deep Lake Hammock arrive for shipment by cargo boat. Pine and cypress are brought to the sawmill in Everglades City.

Mass funeral service for the victims of the 1928 hurricane that wipes out Pelican Bay and kills 2,000

SCENE OF DESOLATION AND RUIN SOUTH OF COURT HOUSE, WEST PALM BEACH

The caption of this photo of West Palm Beach following the 1928 hurricane says "scene of desolation and ruin."

A grim scene of workers in Belle Glade loading bodies of those who perished in the Everglades during the 1928 hurricane

On September 16, a major hurricane strikes Palm Beach and West Palm Beach with winds up to 145 miles per hour. At the time of the storm, many people live near Lake Okeechobee because of the

valuable soil. The lake's water level rises and falls as much as a foot in just a few hours due to regular regional rainfalls. Farmers have constructed a series of canals and dirt levees to hold back the waters and reclaim the flood plain for planting, but these improvements are no match for the storm. The storm causes Lake Okeechobee to overflow and kills two thousand. All 450 residents of Pelican Bay perish. The monetary damage is $25 million. The loss of human life is so great that mass graves and cremation become the only means of providing dignity and sanitation in the cleanup process.

The disaster will lead newly elected President Herbert Hoover to tour the hurricane-damaged area around Lake Okeechobee in February 1929 and commit to "help you fix this thing." He tasks the Army Corps of Engineers with finding a solution to prevent future flooding disasters. During the following ten years, the Army Corps of Engineers will spend $20 million to construct a four-story-high dike around the lake, to be named the Herbert Hoover Dike. The 1930 Rivers and Harbor Act will call for the deepening and widening of the St. Lucie and Caloosahatchee canals to allow more rapid drainage of Lake Okeechobee during storms.

On November 6, Republican Herbert Hoover is elected president of the United States over Democrat Al Smith.

State Democrats are shocked as Florida breaks from the "Solid South" and votes for Republican residential nominee Herbert Hoover for the first time since Reconstruction. By a vote of 6,607 to 5,621, St. Petersburg sends Republican Albert R. Welsh to the Florida Senate, Florida's first Republican legislator since Reconstruction.

Also in this election, Edna Giles Fuller of Orlando becomes the first woman elected to the Florida House of Representatives. Orlando's Beth Johnson will become the first woman elected to the Florida Senate in 1962.

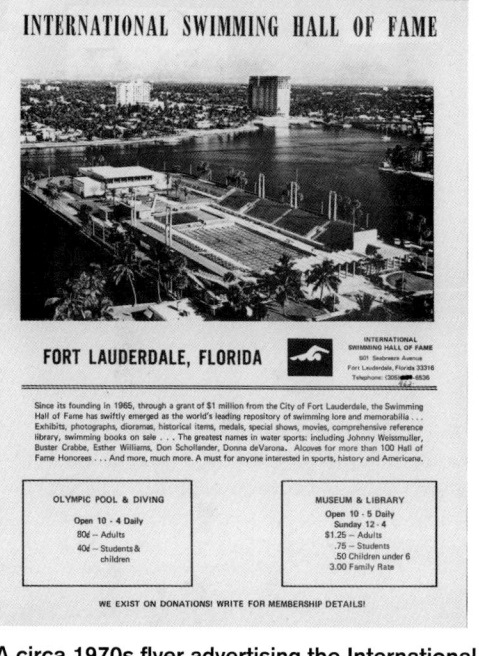

INTERNATIONAL SWIMMING HALL OF FAME

FORT LAUDERDALE, FLORIDA

INTERNATIONAL
SWIMMING HALL OF FAME
501 Seabreeze Avenue
Fort Lauderdale, Florida 33316
Telephone: (305) ▒▒ 6536

Since its founding in 1965, through a grant of $1 million from the City of Fort Lauderdale, the Swimming Hall of Fame has swiftly emerged as the world's leading repository of swimming lore and memorabilia . . . Exhibits, photographs, dioramas, historical items, medals, special shows, movies, comprehensive reference library, swimming books on sale . . . The greatest names in water sports: including Johnny Weissmuller, Buster Crabbe, Esther Williams, Don Schollander, Donna deVarona. Alcoves for more than 100 Hall of Fame Honorees . . . And more, much more. A must for anyone interested in sports, history and Americana.

OLYMPIC POOL & DIVING	MUSEUM & LIBRARY
Open 10 - 4 Daily	Open 10 - 5 Daily
	Sunday 12 - 4
80¢ — Adults	$1.25 — Adults
40¢ — Students &	.75 — Students
children	.50 Children under 6
	3.00 Family Rate

WE EXIST ON DONATIONS! WRITE FOR MEMBERSHIP DETAILS!

A circa 1970s flyer advertising the International Swimming Hall of Fame in Ft. Lauderdale. The complex includes an Olympic pool, a museum, and a library.

Also this year, the Las Olas Casino Pool opens in Ft. Lauderdale. The $118,000 Spanish-style structure provides showers and locker rooms. In the future, the pool will host national and international swimming competitions, with competitors breaking world records. The 1928 pool opens east of today's International Swimming Hall of Fame, which will be established in 1965 with a grant of one million dollars from the city. In 1938, the pool will host the first College Coaches Swim Forum, exposing the college world to Ft. Lauderdale. The event sets the stage for the college student spring break phenomenon that will come to Florida.

Also this year, Ernest Hemingway arrives in Key West. He is attracted to the island and makes a home here. He becomes a fixture of Key West history. Among his many great works will be *The Old Man and the Sea.*

1929

On January 8, Doyle E. Carlton, a lawyer and legislator from Tampa, takes office as the twenty-fifth governor of Florida. Much of Governor Carlton's inaugural address discusses the need to get the state's fiscal affairs in order: "Weak spots have developed in our financial structure. Public expenditures—and I speak of county and municipal as well as state—have become excessive. Our disbursements have exceeded our receipts to an alarming degree, with taxes far too high . . . This gap cannot continue to widen without disaster." The governor calls for a policy of "rigid retrenchment." As governor, Carlton will support a sales tax to raise money and oppose a state income tax. Although Governor Carlton opposes gambling, in 1931 the legislature will create a State Racing Commission and legalize pari-mutuel betting, providing added tax revenues.

President-elect Hoover riding in a parade in Miami on January 22, 1929

President-elect Herbert Hoover with Henry
Ford, Thomas Edison, and Harvey Firestone in
Ft. Myers

A portrait of Congresswoman Ruth Bryan
Owen, Florida's first woman in Congress. She
serves in Congress from 1929 to 1932 and
will later serve as the American Minister to
Denmark from 1933 to 1936.

In February, President-elect Herbert
Hoover visits Thomas Edison in Ft. Myers
to recognize the fiftieth anniversary of the
electric lamp. President Theodore Roosevelt had visited Edison's Ft. Myers home
in 1917.

On March 4, Ruth Bryan Owen of
Miami takes her seat in the United States
House of Representatives, the first Florida
woman to serve in Congress. She is the
daughter of William Jennings Bryan,
three-time Democratic Party nominee for
president.

A 1940s era photograph of author Ernest
Hemingway posing with sailfish in Key West.
He makes a home in the city.

Lou Gehrig and Babe Ruth at the New York
Yankees training camp in St. Petersburg

After his baseball career was over, legendary player Ted Williams made a home in Islamorada, where he is shown here being inducted into the Florida Sports Hall of Fame.

New York Yankees manager Ralph Houk with Mickey Mantle, Governor Bryant, Roger Maris, and Wendell Jarrard, the chair of the Florida Development Commission. After retiring from baseball, Maris will settle in Gainesville to run a beer distributorship.

By this spring, ten of the sixteen Major League baseball teams hold spring training in Florida. By 2010, fifteen major league teams will play in Florida's "Grapefruit League" spring season:

- the Detroit Tigers will have played in Lakeland since 1934 (except for the war years);
- the Philadelphia Phillies will have played in Clearwater since 1947;
- the Pittsburgh Pirates will have played in Bradenton since 1969;
- the Toronto Blue Jays will have played in Dunedin since 1977;
- the Houston Astros will have played in Kissimmee since 1985;
- the New York Mets will have played in Port St. Lucie since 1988;
- the Minnesota Twins and Boston Red Sox will have played in Ft. Myers since 1991 and 1992, respectively;
- the St. Louis Cardinals and the Florida (today's Miami) Marlins will have played in Jupiter since 1998 and 2002, respectively;
- the New York Yankees will have played in Tampa since 1996;
- the Atlanta Braves will have played in Lake Buena Vista (Orlando) since 1997;
- the Montreal Expos and Washington Nationals will have played in Viera (on the Space Coast) since 2002;
- the Tampa Bay Rays will have played in Port Charlotte since 2009; and
- the Baltimore Orioles will play in Sarasota.

Legends like Ted Williams, Babe Ruth, Roger Maris, Mickey Mantle, and many others will become regulars in the Sunshine State.

On October 29, dubbed "Black Tuesday," the stocks listed on the New York Stock Market lose $9 billion in value. The market crash, which began on October 24, "Black Thurs-

day," totals $16 billion in losses for October. America enters the Great Depression.

The Great Depression will deal a blow to Florida's tourism and financial industries.

In November, Dale Mabry Field is opened in Tallahassee. The field is the city's first municipal airport and is named after World War I Army pilot and Tallahassee native Captain Dale Mabry.

The Mediterranean fruit fly, menace to Florida citrus

Also this year, the state experiences an infestation of the Mediterranean fruit fly, requiring citrus to be destroyed in twenty Florida counties. The fruit fly will return to Florida in 1956 and 1962.

1930

A 1925 photograph of the Goodyear blimp *Vigilant* **over the streets of New Port Richey**

In January, the Goodyear blimp arrives in St. Petersburg. A blimp hangar was completed at Albert Whitted Airport in December 1929 and, through the efforts of publicist John Lodwick, Goodyear agreed to come. Goodyear blimps will call the city home for fifteen years.

On April 14, Carrier tests the first air-conditioning system on a railroad diner car along a run between Baltimore and Cumberland. As Pullman passenger cars and diners are cooled, traveling businessmen will discover and spread the word about the air-conditioning comfort.

A run on an Orlando bank.

Worried looks and hard days ahead. A run on a bank in Lakeland.

A run on St. Petersburg's Central National Bank & Trust Company. From 1926 to 1930, 146 Florida banks close their doors, with combined deposits of over $100 million. (Courtesy of the Tampa Bay Times)

On April 25, two St. Petersburg banks fail and close their doors: American Bank & Trust Company with $2,450,000 in deposits, and the Fidelity Bank & Trust Company, with $181,413 in deposits. On June 9, First National Bank of St. Petersburg, the city's largest and oldest bank, will close along with affiliate First Security Bank. Three days later, the Ninth Street Bank & Trust Company closes. Within a year, every existing bank in the city will close. From 1926 through 1930, 146 Florida banks close their doors, with combined deposits of over $100 million.

In the years following the stock market crash, 25 percent of Ft. Lauderdale homes will be foreclosed upon for liens and taxes, along with about 80 percent of vacant lots and 85 percent of non-farm acreage in the city. Ft. Lauderdale's founder,

Frank Stranahan, becomes so depressed by the failure of his bank and mounting foreclosures brought on by two hurricanes and the Depression that he dramatically commits suicide by tying a sewer grate to himself and jumping into the New River.

Between 1926 and 1935, more than 150 of Florida's 237 cities and towns will default on their municipal bonds. Debt liability of cities, counties, and districts had increased from $110 million in 1922 to over $600 million in 1929. A 1939 report of the Florida State Planning Board will conclude that:

> The first and primary cause of the local government financial crisis was the optimistic speculation in town lots. Hundreds of thousands of town lots were laid out, far in excess of any possible immediate need, and many were

improved by municipal bond issues. Of more importance, this speculation drove values skywards, and tax assessment rolls climbed on the bandwagon. With swollen assessment rolls, containing large quantities of vacant lands, a highly untruthful picture of taxable resources was presented. Thus, more bonds were issued than the real taxpaying ability could stand.

A circa 1930s photograph of a United States Sugar Corporation mill with water cooling tank in the foreground

Even in the midst of the Depression, Clearwater Beach knows how to have a good time. Here in a contest on the beach described as a "Pseudo-Miss America event," these women are chosen as (l-r): America's Healthiest Girl, Miss St. Petersburg, Miss America (Tampa's Margaret Ekdahl), and Miss Clearwater.

A 1946 photograph of a U.S. Sugar Corporation hoist at the Miami Locks Plantation moving sugar cane from the field cars to rail cars for transport to mills in Clewiston

1931

The crowd at the official opening on January 19 of Southern Sugar Corporation's (pre-U.S. Sugar) new mill in Clewiston, southwest of Lake Okeechobee

On April 29, Charles Stewart Mott purchases Southern Sugar Corporation, a failed sugarcane farming and processing company located on the southwest shore of Lake Okeechobee. Mott, who had been an investor and officer of General Motors, reincorporates the company as United States Sugar Corporation. In order to expand sugar-processing capabilities beyond the Clewiston Sugar House opened in 1929, Mott will open the Bryant Sugar House in 1964. By the next century, after Fidel Castro takes over Cuba and the United States embargoes Cuban sugar, United States Sugar will own a sugarcane refinery, orange groves, citrus- and juice-processing facilities, and 215,000 acres of farmland, along with its own irrigation system of ditches, levees, and pumps. Together with Florida Crystals, which will come to the state in 1960, the two companies will be known as "Big Sugar" and will collectively control 400,000 acres south of Lake Okeechobee.

On May 1, the eighty-six-story Empire State Building opens in New York City. It is the world's tallest building.

On October 7, after the failure of eight hundred U.S. banks, President Hoover announces plans to provide a privately financed pool of funds to assist financially troubled banks and federal loans to industry.

On October 18, inventor Thomas Edison dies.

In 1947, Thomas Edison's widow will donate Edison's Ft. Myers estate to the city for a museum.

In 1997, Life magazine will name *Thomas Edison the "Man of the Millennium."*

Also this year, John Ringling opens the 21-gallery John and Mable Ringling Museum of Art in Sarasota to house his remarkable collections of paintings and art objects. Ringling's stated purpose for the museum is to "promote education and art appreciation, especially among young people." Upon his death five years after the opening, the museum will be bequeathed to the State of Florida. Today it is the state art museum of Florida, governed since 2000 by Florida State University, and is promoted as the home of one of the preeminent art and cultural collections in the United States.

1932

On June 27, reflecting Depression-era finances, the Pinellas County School Board lays off its entire maintenance

staff, and telephones are disconnected at most schools. On September 15, teachers will receive only 30 percent of their first month's salary. In 1933, lights at all schools are ordered to be kept off except in emergencies. At one point during the Depression, tuition is charged for local public schools and childless couples are asked to pay tuition for poor children.

On November 8, Franklin Delano Roosevelt, governor of New York and fifth cousin to former President Theodore Roosevelt, is elected president of the United States pledging a "new deal" for the Depression-era country. Roosevelt will be elected to four terms, the only president in U.S. history elected to more than two terms. In 1951, the nation will ratify the Twenty-Second Amendment to the U.S. Constitution, prohibiting future presidents from serving more than two terms.

Florida Governor David Sholtz (middle seat) and Jacksonville Mayor John Alsop (seated on the picture's right side) enjoy a ride with President Franklin D. Roosevelt in Jacksonville.

1933

On January 4, David Sholtz, a Daytona Beach lawyer and legislator, is sworn into office as the twenty-sixth governor of Florida. Governor Sholtz dedicates much of his inaugural address to a discussion of the financial condition of his Depression-era state. He warns against communist influences, promises a more efficient government, and commits to not burden Floridians with additional taxes in an effort to balance his budget: "Florida needs to encourage instead of discourage her payrolls; Florida needs to encourage instead of discourage her citizens who now constitute

Fatally wounded Chicago Mayor Anton Cermak being led to a car after he is shot on February 15, 1933, in Miami during the attempt on President-elect Franklin D. Roosevelt's life

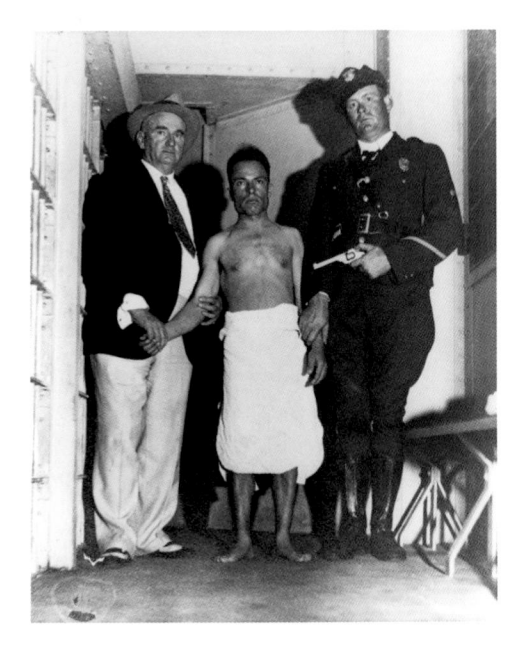

Giuseppe Zangara, an unemployed bricklayer who kills Chicago Mayor Cermak while trying to assassinate President-elect Roosevelt. Zangara will die in Raiford's electric chair.

her economic and industrial life. For these reasons, I have heretofore said and I now again say that the welfare of Florida will be best subserved discouraging all efforts for new and additional sources of revenue."

On February 15, an assassin fires pistol shots at President-elect Franklin Roosevelt while he is speaking in Miami's Bayfront Park, missing Roosevelt but killing Chicago Mayor Anton Cermak. Giuseppe Zangara, an unemployed bricklayer, will be arrested for the shooting. By March 20, Zangara will be put to death in Florida's Raiford Prison electric chair. When asked by Sheriff Hardie if he has a final comment, Zangara replies, "Push the button."

On February 20, the U.S. Congress adopts a resolution to repeal the Eighteenth Amendment, which had adopted Prohibition. On November 14, Florida will vote to ratify the repeal amendment. *On December 5, Utah will become the thirty-sixth state to ratify the amendment and "intoxicating liquors" will no longer be constitutionally prohibited.*

On March 5, President Franklin Roosevelt, in office for less than two days, closes the nation's banks for a four-day holiday, orders an embargo on exports of gold and silver, and calls Congress into special session to address the banking crisis.

Florida Governor David Sholtz calls on Floridians to have courage during the banking crisis, asserting that "no one has ever frozen to death or starved to death in Florida. We still have our wonderful climate and our wonderful soil."

Also this year, John and Mary Haslam establish Haslam's Book Store in St. Petersburg. Their son Charles will work to grow the store in many ways, including with a fifteen-year television show called "The Wonderful World of Books" and a radio show reviewing books. Ray and Suzanne (Haslam) Hinst will take over the business in 1973, and by 2010, the store on Central Avenue will contain over three hundred thousand books and be billed as "Florida's Largest New and Used Book Store."

John and Mary Haslam in front of their growing book store on Central Avenue in St. Petersburg (Courtesy of Ray Hinst)

1934

On June 18, President Roosevelt signs the Indian Reorganization Act of 1934 providing for, among others, the expansion of Native American reservations. In 1935, a U.S. special commissioner will be instructed to begin negotiations to purchase land requested by the Seminoles for reservation property. The Seminole reservations today include the Big Cypress Reservation and Immokalee Farms (southwest Florida), Brighton Reservation (northwest of lake Okeechobee), Miccosukee Reservation

Ed Ball, who builds St. Joe Paper Company, his sister Mrs. Alfred I. duPont, and Roger Main

(east of Big Cypress National Reserve), Tampa Orient Road Reservation, and the State Reservation and Dania-Hollywood Reservation (Southeast Florida).

On June 28, the 9.5-mile Davis Causeway toll road opens from Clearwater to Tampa. It will become the Courtney Campbell Causeway after World War II. In 1940 U.S. Senator Claude Pepper will persuade the federal government to eliminate the toll.

Also this year, William J. Porter University, a two-year college located along the St. Johns River, is founded. The school's name will change to Jacksonville Junior College in 1935, will relocate and, in 1956, will change its name again to Jacksonville University.

Also this year, as Florida's cattle industry grows, the Florida Cattlemen's Association is formed in Kissimmee, and in 1938 the Kissimmee Livestock Auction Market will be established to sell cattle weekly. An arena will be built alongside the Auction Market and, in 1944, the first Silver Spurs Rodeo will be held, attended by an estimated one thousand people. Today the air-conditioned indoor arena seats 8,300, with twelve skyboxes, and hosts the largest rodeo east of the Mississippi River. By 2010, there will be 105,000 head of

A circa 1960s view of three ships loading paper from St. Joe Paper Company's large Port St. Joe operation

cattle in Kissimmee's Osceola County, and an estimated 1.72 million head of cattle in Florida, with the largest producing counties, in order, being Okeechobee, Osceola, Polk, Highlands, Hardee, and Hendry.

1935

On April 28, Alfred duPont dies. He has been a significant investor in Jacksonville, Port St. Joe, and the Florida Panhandle. He leaves much of his fortune and holdings to a charitable trust to be managed by his wife Jessie and her brother, Ed Ball. The trust benefits crippled children. Ed Ball will focus on building St. Joe Paper Company, which will eventually own over one million acres in Florida and Georgia. In 1961, he will acquire the Florida East Coast Railway Corporation, originally established by Henry Flagler. Ball will expand the paper products business, build the telephone business established by DuPont, and engage in other enterprises.

On September 2, a Category 5 hurricane strikes the middle Florida Keys, with a devastating blow to Islamorada. Of the 485 deaths in the Keys attributed to the storm, 228 are civilians and 257 are World War I veterans working on road construction in the Keys and living in work camps on Lower Matecumbe. Islamorada's Russell family loses thirty-eight of their fifty-three family members in the storm. They had become one of Islamorada's founding families in 1882 when Mary Ann Russell received a land grant for the upper one-third of the island. Because of the massive number of deaths, funeral pyres will be built to burn the bodies. Multiple burial sites are established around Islamorada to take the resulting ashes.

The eleven-car rescue train that was swept off the track near Islamorada by the 1935 hurricane. The train was sent to rescue World War I veterans, many of whom were in a New Deal Civilian Conservation Corps work camp in Windley Key, just south of Islamorada. The veterans were building roads under the Veterans Rehabilitation Program. About 250 veterans die as a result of the hurricane.

Makeshift caskets containing over 250 victims of the 1935 hurricane are cremated on the banks of Snake Creek, about fourteen miles southwest of Key Largo, near Islamorada. Key West resident Ernest Hemingway will write a critical magazine article called "Who Killed the Vets" about the needless deaths of the veterans and failure of the rescue effort.

A photograph taken about two years before the 1935 hurricane that decimates Islamorada. Floyd Russell (second from left) survives the storm with his father, Clifton, but his mother, Charlotte, and four siblings perish, including his younger brother Glenwood, seated next to him (third from left). Floyd's cousin Irene (fourth from left) is lost in the storm along with her mother and two sisters. Of the 53 members of the Russell family, 38 die in the storm, which inflicts a dramatic tragedy on the island and its people. (Courtesy of Floyd Russell)

The September 2 hurricane largely destroys Flagler's overseas railroad. The damage is so severe that the Florida East Coast Railway abandons the Florida Keys line. The right of way, bridge, and trestles will be purchased by the Florida Road and Bridge District for the purpose of building an overseas highway to Key West, which will be completed in 1938. Much of the roadwork will be financed by the Federal Emergency Relief Administration.

On September 19, at 1 P.M., President Franklin Roosevelt sends a telegraph message that triggers the explosion of fifty pounds of dynamite and the commencement of construction of the Atlantic Gulf Ship Canal in Florida. The canal is a New Deal transportation project designed to connect shipping from the Mississippi River and Gulf of Mexico to the Atlantic Ocean and the northeast United States coast without having to travel south around the Florida Straits. The canal will allow ships to enter the St. Johns River by

Jacksonville, travel south to Palatka, then along the Ocklawaha River toward Silver Springs, then travel west along a newly built channel south of Ocala to Dunnellon, then west along the Withlacoochee River to the Gulf, near Yankeetown.

While the Army Corps of Engineers initially recommended a lock canal in order to avoid harming the state groundwater table, the final design is for a sea-level canal. At a projected cost of almost $143 million, the 195-mile route will be twice the length of the Suez Canal and four times longer than the Panama Canal. It will cut a new 90-mile channel through the Central Florida Ridge and double the depth of more than 105 miles of existing waterways.

1936

President Franklin Roosevelt leaving for a fishing trip at Port Everglades, near Fort Lauderdale. The photo is taken on March 24, 1936, a few weeks before the president halts the funding for the Florida Atlantic Gulf Ship Canal.

On April 15, President Roosevelt announces that he will not forward further relief funds to the Florida Atlantic Gulf Ship Canal project until Congress authorizes the expenditure. A U.S. Geological Survey report had concluded that a sea-level canal would cut through the Florida aquifers and risk south Florida's fresh water supply. In the seven months since the canal's construction began, strong opposition has been building, with concerns that it would adversely impact communities south of the canal that depend on the aquifer for drinking water and agriculture. Railroads fear competition from the canal. Concerned with harms to tourism and trade, St. Petersburg, Miami, and Tampa have been fighting the project. Others argue that the canal is a waste of federal money and that the marginal savings in time and travel costs created by the canal do not justify the cost. On June 18, the United States House of Representatives will vote 108 to 62 to kill funding for the canal. Work on the canal stops with only 3 percent of the project complete. The push for a Florida canal will resurface in the 1960s.

FACTS ABOUT
The Singing Tower and Sanctuary
LAKE WALES, FLORIDA

Also Items of Interest About
Lake Wales, Florida
"THE CITY OF THE CARILLON"

A 1936 pamphlet entitled "Facts about the Singing Tower and Sanctuary, Lake Wales, Florida." It is commonly known as the Bok Tower.

The dolphin show at the Aquatarium on St. Petersburg Beach

A circa 1920s photograph of Arthur McKee, founder of McKee Jungle in Vero Beach

A circa 1934 post card of Parrot Jungle on Red Road in Miami

A 1939 view of Miami's Monkey Jungle, "Where the humans are caged and the monkeys run wild."

The world famous water ski team at Cypress Gardens in Winter Haven

Young women posing at the entrance to Sunken Gardens in St. Petersburg in 1964

On November 29, the opening of George Turner's Sunken Gardens is announced in the *St. Petersburg Times*. The attraction, located at 305 Eighteenth Avenue North, displays royal palms, banana trees, azaleas, gardenias, a rock garden and pool, and a large variety of rare tropical plants. Early Florida tourist attractions draw visitors around the state, such as Jacksonville's Ostrich Farm (opened in 1892, now closed), Dixieland Park in Jacksonville, Parrot Jungle in Miami, the Aquatarium on St. Petersburg Beach, St. Augustine's Alligator Farm (1893, still open), McKee Jungle in Vero Beach, the Black Hills Passion Play in Lake Wales, Miami's Monkey Jungle, and Winter Haven's Cypress Gardens (1936, now open in conjunction with Legoland).

A 1953 photograph of an actor portraying Jesus Christ bearing the cross at the Black Hills Passion Play in Lake Wales

An early view, probably circa 1910, of Dixieland Park in Jacksonville

1937

This January 1937 photograph provides a reminder that, as a new Florida governor takes office, many in the state are still hurting. This family, originally from Tallahassee, lives in this shelter near a packing plant in Winter Haven.

These Live Oak residents are participants in the New Deal-era National Youth Administration work-relief program for youth, providing them with school and job skills.

On January 5, Fred P. Cone, a Lake City lawyer, banker and legislator, becomes the twenty-seventh governor of Florida. In his inaugural address, Governor Cone spends the large portion of his time discussing the need to keep taxes low, run the government more efficiently, and move spending authority solely to the legislature, away from boards and commissions. His comments directed to law enforcement display little concern for the rights of the accused: "I will tell all sheriffs and police officers, 'When you deal with criminal, don't be too particular how you handle them, because the governor of your state is behind you, and our people must be protected in this state.' " Regarding the president, Governor Cone has confidence that "peace all over the world shall prevail . . . I have no fear of war as long as Franklin D. Roosevelt is president of the United States."

On February 6, the Liberty Square Housing Complex opens 243 single-family units as a New Deal public housing project in the Liberty City neighborhood of Miami. Many families will move in from the Overtown neighborhood (formerly "Colored Town"), an area with poor living conditions.

On June 1, in the morning, Amelia Earhart takes off from Miami Municipal Airport on the first leg of her journey to fly around the world. She will land in Puerto Rico in the afternoon.

Amelia Earhart will make stops in South America, Africa, and Southeast Asia. On July 2, she will take off from New Guinea, intending to fly to Howland Island. She will never reach her destination and will be lost in the Pacific. Miami Municipal Airport will be rededicated as Amelia Earhart Field in 1947.

On September 1, Congress passes the National Housing Act, establishing the U.S. Housing Authority, which will finance low-income housing throughout the nation.

1938

On January 17, renowned architect Frank Lloyd Wright appears on the cover of *Time* magazine. Later this year, the cornerstone will be laid on the Annie Pfeiffer Chapel, designed by Wright at Florida Southern College in Lakeland. The chapel is the first of many buildings at the campus that will be designed by Wright. As more buildings are completed, FSC's campus will become the largest collection of Frank Lloyd Wright's architecture in the world.

On March 29, the Overseas Highway is completed through the Florida Keys to Key West after fifteen months of construction. The road, which makes Key West the southern terminus for US 1, requires a toll of one dollar per car and driver and

The Annie Pfeiffer Chapel at Florida Southern College is the first of a collection of buildings on the campus designed by architect Frank Lloyd Wright.

twenty-five cents per passenger. US 1 begins in Kent, Maine. During its first year of operation, 800 cars per day will use the new highway.

A circa 1940s photograph of Marjorie Kinnan Rawlings with her dog in Cross Creek. In 1939, Rawlings wins the Pulitzer Prize for *The Yearling*, her novel about life in rural central Florida

Also this year, Marjorie Kinnan Rawlings releases her novel *The Yearling*, the story of the Baxter family and their life in remote central Florida. In 1939, she will win the Pulitzer Prize for the book, which will be read by school children for generations. In 1942, Rawlings will release the book *Cross Creek*, the story of Rawling's experiences when she lived in the rural Florida community with the same name, located fifteen miles southeast of Gainesville.

1939

On March 15, Adolf Hitler's Nazi army enters Prague and assumes control of Czechoslovakia.

As war approaches in Europe, the U.S. Coast Guard is assigned the task of training sailors for the U.S. Merchant Marines.

The ships *American Seaman* and *Joseph Conrad* arrive in Florida from New York with 250 apprentice seamen, for training. In 1942 the job of training the seamen will shift to the U.S. Maritime Service.

On June 4, Packard Motor Car Company publicly exhibits the first air-conditioned car at an automobile show in Chicago.

On September 4, France and Great Britain declare war on Germany, three days after Adolf Hitler's army attacks Poland. The United States remains neutral as Europe enters World War II.

On October 22, the *St. Petersburg Times* begins publication of a weekly insert called *News of Negroes of St. Petersburg and Pinellas County.* The first edition has articles about African American schools including Gibbs High and Davis Elementary.

Also in October, President Roosevelt issues a proclamation prohibiting submarines of belligerent nations from cruising offshore the United States. The U.S. Coast Guard begins to conduct anti-submarine air patrols over the Gulf of Mexico.

Also in October, John V. Atanasoff, a professor of physics at Iowa State University, working with graduate student Clifford E. Berry, operates a successful prototype of the world's first all-electronic binary computer. It will lead to the development of the Atanasoff-Berry Computer (ABC) in 1942, but further work will not continue due to World War II. ABC will be followed by the Electronic Numerical Integrator and Computer (ENIAC) developed as a "general-purpose" computer for the U.S. Army in the winter of 1944–1945, and the Universal Automatic Computer (UNIVAC), developed as a commercial-use computer, which will go into operation for the U.S. Census Bureau in March 1951. With the invention of the transistor in

1947 at Bell Laboratories, computers developed after the late 1950s will replace vacuum tubes with transistor circuits.

1940

On May 26, the British Expeditionary Force in Europe evacuates from Dunkirk as France falls to Germany.

On September 16, Congress passes the Selective Service Training and Service Act. The nation's first peacetime military draft lottery will take place in Washington, D.C. On October 29, sixteen million men register.

On November 8, George Jenkins opens his first Publix Super Market in Winter Haven, with marble, glass, stucco, fluorescent lighting, and air conditioning. He had previously opened two Publix Food Stores in Winter Haven in the 1930s, but had closed both. In 1945 he will purchase a warehouse and nineteen All American Stores from the Lakeland Grocery Company. With a commitment to "putting people first," he will add Publix supermarkets throughout the southeast United States. By the twenty-first century, the grocery store, headquartered in Lakeland, will have over one thousand supermarkets, with annual sales approaching $30 billion.

Also in November, Florida Governor Cone, preparing for the possibility of an Axis Powers attack on the United States east coast, creates the State Defense Council to organize civilian preparedness and defense throughout the state. Among the council's responsibilities are promoting the sale of war bonds and stamps, providing rationing information, promoting victory gardens, encouraging increased agriculture, regulating blackouts and dim-outs, conducting air raid drills, and many others.

A circa 1946 photograph of the first Publix Supermarket opened by George W. Jenkins in 1940 in Winter Haven, fifteen miles east of Lakeland. The store is air-conditioned, and customers enter through "electric-eye" doors.

A 1961 photograph of George Jenkins, founder of Publix Supermarkets, a legend in the Florida grocery business

> ❝*Florida has become the veritable spearhead of that most vital part of the defense program . . . Numerous military and naval bases are already clustered in Florida, extending in a great arc from Pensacola to Key West . . . Tens of thousands of our American boys will train here . . . Floridians are . . . eager to fulfill the grave and unusual responsibilities.*❞
>
> **Florida Governor Spessard Holland, in his January 8, 1941, inaugural speech**

Chapter 6

World War II and Post-War Years: 1941 through 1959

As the United States' involvement in World War II appears imminent, the nation and state prepare. Florida's wartime governor Spessard Holland outlines a strategy to develop military bases and training facilities throughout the state and strengthen local protection through a state defense council.

After Pearl Harbor, America turns to Florida to train its military in a warm climate. Florida cities convert boom-era hotels into military barracks. Military tent cities occupy golf courses. Around the state, Coast Guard, Army, Navy, and Merchant Marine bases expand and develop, along with connected air bases. Thousands of trainees come to the Sunshine State for the first time.

Sailors getting ready for World War II action at the Naval Air Technical Training Center in Jacksonville

The nation and state send their sons to battle, ration supplies, and collect raw materials. Blackouts, coastal anti-aircraft batteries, and the presence of enemy submarines in the Atlantic and Gulf of Mexico reflect the homefront seriousness of the fighting.

As the war ends, Florida joins the nation in celebrating victory. The Great Depression and World War II melt into history.

America emerges from the war years as the strongest and most prosperous nation on Earth, but the rest of the world is not content to let that status go unchallenged. The Soviet Union works to develop a space program and nuclear bomb capabilities, while China becomes a communist nation and forms an alliance with the Soviets.

As Florida enters the post-war years, its leaders' focus turns to the economy—tourism, industry, and agriculture—and the need to upgrade transportation and other infrastructure. A rocket-launching base is established at Cape Canaveral. Population rises dramatically, and Florida begins to emerge as one of the nation's major states. An auto racing tradition is established in Sebring, and Daytona, a legendary city for racing, opens a new speedway.

The air conditioning industry grows and Florida's population booms, a trend that will continue for the rest of this century and into the next.

Marjory Stoneman Douglas issues a wake-up call on the need to protect the Everglades ecosystem, and President Truman dedicates a portion of the "River of Grass" as a national park. Toward the end of the era, a former Tallahassee lawyer who becomes Florida's governor engages the discussion of race and integration—topics that will intensify in the next era.

Throughout this book events in Florida are set in Roman (non-italics), and events outside Florida are set in *italics*.

Timeline

1941

In front of the governor's mansion, Governor Spessard Holland (far right) is sworn into office on January 7, 1941. The other three in the picture are (l-r) Mildred Cone, Mary Holland, and Governor Frederick Preston Cone, who is leaving office. Holland is destined to be Florida's wartime governor.

On January 7, Spessard L. Holland, a lawyer, judge, and legislator from Bartow, becomes the twenty-eighth governor of Florida. Governor Holland's inaugural address contains a broad discussion of his five guiding principles for state leadership, the many issues challenging the state, and the need to find revenues to replace the state ad valorem tax, which voters have repealed—as well as the upcoming effort that he believes will repeal the gross receipts tax. As Germany invades its European neighbors and America strengthens its defense, Governor Holland outlines the strategic role Florida will play, including military bases, statewide training facilities, and strengthening of local protection through the newly created State Defense Council. While he prays for peace, the new governor argues that "peace is possible only to that nation which is so strong that none dare attack it . . . sacrifices will be required, in many fields and in an unpredictable number of instances." After completing his term as governor, Holland will be elected to represent Florida for four terms in the United States Senate.

On March 12, President Roosevelt signs into law the Lend-Lease Act, authorizing the president to loan or lease war materials to the countries fighting the Axis powers, even though the source of repayment is uncertain.

In Florida, women form "Bundles for Britain" sewing groups to provide garments in support of Britain's war effort.

On July 26, the United States freezes all Japanese assets within the United States in response to Japan's occupation of French Indochina.

On the morning of December 7, the Japanese launch a surprise attack against Pearl Harbor, Hawaii, killing more than 2,300. The next day the United States Congress declares war on Japan, and on December 11, Germany and Italy declare war on the United States. World War II has begun and will continue through 1945. Over 248,000 Floridians will serve in the military during the war.

Also, during the war, rationing boards are established in every county in Florida, with authority to regulate the sale of 90 percent of all civilian commodities, while home defense units teach volunteers first aid, fire control, the manual of arms, and military maneuvers. The U.S. Office of Price Administration rations nonessential motorists up to six gallons of gas weekly. Sugar rationing cards are issued, with each stamp being good for one pound of sugar, a two-week supply. The supply of tires is rationed. One local board calls the number of available tires "meager." Rationing will cause a reduction of beach tourism and transit on toll roads. Scrap metal will be gathered for the war effort. The metal comes in the form of World War I hel-

mets, radiators, lawn mowers, bed frames, broken tools, and other scrap.

1942

Having been struck by a German submarine, the tanker *Gulfland* is burning in the water off Hobe Sound, about thirty-five miles north of Palm Beach.

Scrap metal collection in Pensacola in 1943 for the war effort.

In January, German submarines begin Operation Drumbeat, attacking Gulf Stream shipping. With the greatest intensity being between February and July 1942, twenty-four freighters and tankers will be sunk on Florida's Atlantic and Gulf coasts. By the end of the German submarine offensive, four hundred American ships will be sunk and thousands of lives will be lost. The Germans use the lights of coastal cities to silhouette their targets. Within a few weeks after Pearl Harbor, the 252nd Coast Artillery Battery occupies Pass-a-

Grille Beach in Pinellas County, taking over most of the community's dwellings and establishing defenses. Anti-aircraft guns, observation towers, and tent camps are constructed.

Also in January, Hollywood legend Clark Gable graduates from gunnery training school at Tyndall Army Air Base in Panama City. Gable had previously attended Officer Candidate School in Miami Beach.

On February 19, President Roosevelt issues Executive Order 9006, authorizing the creation of exclusion zones (about one-third of the country) in which persons of identified national origin are not permitted to reside. In the nation, about 120,000 Japanese-Americans, 11,000 German-Americans, and 3,000 Italian-Americans will be detained. The cases of Florida detainees are reviewed by an "enemy alien board" in Miami and detainees are housed temporarily beneath the Orange Bowl stadium.

Also in February, B-17 bomber pilots train by dropping fake bombs containing sand on Pinellas County's Mullet Key. As war production improves, armed bombs will be used. P-51s use Egmont Key as a machine gun strafing range. Unexploded bombs will be discovered by Fort DeSoto park employees on Mullet Key in 1968, 1980, and 1988.

In March, training takes place at Eglin Field near Ft. Walton Beach for Lt. Col Jimmy Doolittle's strike force Tokyo raid on April 18, 1942. Doolittle's sixteen American B-25 bombers will strike Tokyo and other Japanese cities, raising American morale. Among the other war-era Florida Army Air Corps bases are Eglin Field in Valparaiso (near Ft. Walton Beach), Drew and MacDill Airfield in Tampa, Dale Mabry Field in Tallahassee, Buckingham and Page Airfields in Ft. Myers, Tyndall Army Airfield in Panama City, along with army airfields in Avon Park, Boca Raton, Homestead, St. Petersburg, Sarasota, and Venice. The Jacksonville Naval Air Station will become one of the three largest naval air stations in the world.

America's young men come to Florida to train and prepare to go to war. Here, sailors relax for a while watching a boxing match at the Naval Air Technical Training Center in Jacksonville.

On April 10, at 10:20 P.M., U–123, a German submarine torpedoes the tanker *Gulfamerica* in the shipping lane off Jacksonville Beach, scoring a direct hit. The *Gulfamerica* is a Gulf Oil Corporation ship on its maiden voyage to New York with 90,000 barrels of fuel oil, a crew of forty-one, and seven Navy armed guards. Fire from the resulting explosions can be seen by residents viewing from the beach as the ship burns and is severed in two. A destroyer will inflict damage on the U-boat, but it will make it back to its home port in France. On April 11, local authorities will enact rules designed to prevent ships being lighted up from shore,

A convoy transporting the Ninety-seventh Bombardment Group along U.S. 41 from MacDill Army Air Field in Tampa to Sarasota Army Air Field

"Colored" troops in Tallahassee, in the segregated military of World War II.

Portrait of military couples at Dale Mabry Field near Tallahassee, a moment's break from the war

A photograph of the reunion of the surviving airmen who trained at Eglin Air Force Base and participated in Doolittle's Tokyo air raid on April 18, 1942. The group selects Sarasota for their fifty-fourth reunion in 1996, shown here, and for their fifty-sixth reunion in 1998.

A 1942 postcard featuring MacDill Air Field in Tampa

including prohibitions against bright or neon lights on shore, requiring black-out curtains in beach homes and prohibiting cars on the beach at night.

Cities throughout the state become home to servicemen training for war. In Miami, by August 1943 the United States government will take over for military housing purposes Miami hotels, 108 apartment houses, and 18 private homes. Hotels in Daytona Beach also become housing for trainees.

On June 5, former U.S. Ambassador to England Joseph Kennedy pins naval aviator wings on his son, and future president of the United States, John F. Kennedy at Naval Air Station Jacksonville.

On June 13, four Nazi spies come ashore at Ponte Vedra near Jacksonville

A 1944 gathering at the Tampa Shipyard

A 1940s view of the St. Johns River Shipbuilding Company in Jacksonville

with plans to destroy power plants and factories. After joining four other spies in Chicago and Washington, D.C., they will be caught by the FBI and six of the eight will be put to death on August 8, 1942.

On June 30, Congress passes a $42.8 billion military budget, the largest in U.S. history to this time.

Shipyards throughout Florida will support the war effort, including Panama City's Wainwright Shipyard (108 ships), Tampa Shipbuilding and Engineering Company, Tampa's Hooker Point Yard, Jacksonville's St. Johns River Shipbuilding Company (82 Liberty ships and 12 tankers), and Miami Shipbuilding Company (patrol torpedo [PT] boats).

Also in July, the United States Congress authorizes construction of the Cross Florida Barge Canal. The move is in response to German U-Boat attacks on merchant ships on Florida's Atlantic and Gulf coasts and the desire to bring oil and gas from Texas to the Atlantic without the hazard of traveling the length of Florida. Responding to concerns that killed the canal attempt in 1936, this time the canal will have locks and dams and will be only twelve feet deep—presumably not harming the aquifer. But no funds will be appropriated to build the canal until the 1960s.

A 1941 aerial view of Camp Blanding, near Starke, Florida

On September 24, Germans captured from sunken U-boats and sailors from a sunken German battleship are taken as prisoners to Camp Blanding, near Starke, about forty-five miles southwest of Jacksonville. During the war, prisoner-of-war camps will be established throughout Florida, with the base camps being Camp Blanding and Camp Gordon Johnston in Carrabelle on the Gulf of Mexico about twenty miles east of Apalachicola.

By the end of 1942, there are more than seventy thousand Army Air Corps trainees in Miami and Miami Beach hotels, while tens of thousands of other servicemen are housed in hotels throughout Florida.

1943

In January, the U.S. Maritime Service enlarges the Merchant Marine training base at St. Petersburg's Bayboro Harbor. By this year, the Florida Defense Force (later Florida State Guard) will have 2,100 men in thirty-six units. The force was created to replace the Florida National Guard, which had been mobilized in 1940 and 1941 to join the war effort.

Spring baseball training is discontinued until after the war.

On June 4, Governor Spessard Holland signs into law the Women's Emancipation Bill, which had been introduced in the Florida Legislature by Mary Lou Baker, the legislature's only female member. The law gives women greater rights regarding the management of their separate estates and involvement in contracts separate from their husbands.

On July 16, Whiting Field in Milton is commissioned as an auxiliary to Naval Air Station Pensacola, which will have eight main and auxiliary stations during the war. Other Florida war-era naval bases and naval air stations include Daytona Beach, DeLand, Ft. Lauderdale, Green Cove Springs, Jacksonville, Key West, Melbourne, Miami, St. Petersburg, Richmond, Sanford, and Vero Beach. NAS Pensacola and NAS Jacksonville, along with NAS Corpus Christi, train the nation's naval pilots, with Pensacola alone training 28,000 during the war.

On September 13, a storm strikes the Panhandle at Port Leon, near St. Marks on the Gulf Coast, south of Tallahassee. The storm reaches hurricane strength and destroys most of the town, killing one boy. After the storm, Port Leon residents vote to abandon their town and move north to higher ground, forming Newport.

"Jiu-jitsu" training at the Naval Air Technical Training Center in Jacksonville during World War I

Chinese cadets training at Dale Mabry Field in Tallahassee during World War II

Crowds gather around Jefferson County's only oil well on January 19, 1926. The well proves to be dry. Other oil wells are attempted throughout Florida, including in Oldsmar (Pinellas County), Cedar Key, Palmetto (Manatee County), Jay (north of Pensacola), and others, until a successful well hits in Collier County in 1943.

Officials inspecting Sunniland Oil Well #1 in Collier County on December 20, 1943. This had become Florida's first working oil well the previous September.

On September 26, Humble Oil Co. strikes oil in Collier County at the Sunniland Oil Field, twelve miles south of Immokalee and about thirty miles northeast of Naples. It is Florida's first successful oil well. The discovery follows unsuccessful Florida oil exploration efforts stretching back to those in the Florida Panhandle in 1901 and other failed wells that followed throughout the

state. The success also follows a relentless pursuit by Barron Collier, who assured doubters that "I can smell it." Sadly, Collier died in 1939, four years before the discovery.

The Sunniland well initially produces 140 barrels of oil per day. By 1954, the wells at the Sunniland Oil Field will produce 500,000 barrels per year. In 1964, Sun Oil Company will discover oil in Hendry County, which is northeast of Collier County and extends to the south shore of Lake Okeechobee. From 1943 to the second decade of the next century, over 120 million barrels of oil will be extracted from eight commercial wells along the "Sunniland Trend," an oil reserve running from Miami to Ft. Myers. By the next century, the oil reserve will continue to produce almost 2,800 barrels per day.

Men on horses at Rosemere Farm, the birthplace of Ocala's Thoroughbred horse training tradition

Also this year, Carl Rose, a road builder from Indiana, buys farm property on Highway 200 in Ocala, and names it Rosemere Farm. He breeds racehorses on the farm and next year, his filly Gornil will win at Tropical Park in Miami, the first horse bred in Florida to do so. By the twenty-first century, Marion County (Ocala) will have 4,500 registered Thoroughbred foals and 450 Thoroughbred farms. Horses bred in the Ocala area will win many races in the future including the Kentucky Derby, Preakness Stakes, and others. In 1978, Affirmed, born at Ocala's Harbor View Farm, will win the Triple Crown of horse racing.

1944

On April 3, the United States Supreme Court, in Smith v. Allwright *holds that it is unconstitutional for the Democratic Party in Texas to exclude African Americans from membership when the state of Texas places Democratic nominees on the ballot. The practice, known as the "white primary," has been used in Southern cities, including in Florida, to disenfranchise African Americans.*

On June 6, the Allied forces, in Operation Overlord, land 150,000 troops on France's Normandy beaches to commence the invasion of France. It is D-Day!

1945

On January 2, Millard Fillmore Caldwell, a Democratic lawyer and legislator from Milton, is sworn into office as the twenty-ninth governor of Florida. Anticipating

Florida Governor Millard Caldwell and naval officers at the Pensacola Naval Air Station

an upcoming victory in World War II, Governor Caldwell focuses his inaugural remarks on Florida's transition to a peace-time economy: "The permanent solution lies in measures to increase the flow of trade, to expand our industries, to enhance the prosperity of agricultural industries and to stimulate our tourist business . . . We must expand travel facilities by building good roads and encouraging air, rail and motor facilities and transportation."

From February 19 to March 16, Americans fight the Battle of Iwo Jima, and from April 1 to June 22, Americans fight the Battle of Okinawa.

Practice landings on the Gulf of Mexico at Camp Gordon Johnston's Amphibian Training Center in 1943. The camp is on the Panhandle near Carrabelle, about fifty miles southwest of Tallahassee. The first amphibian infantry assault teams to land in France during the Normandy Invasion were from the Fourth Infantry Division, which trained for the assault at Camp Gordon Johnston. They landed on Utah Beach.

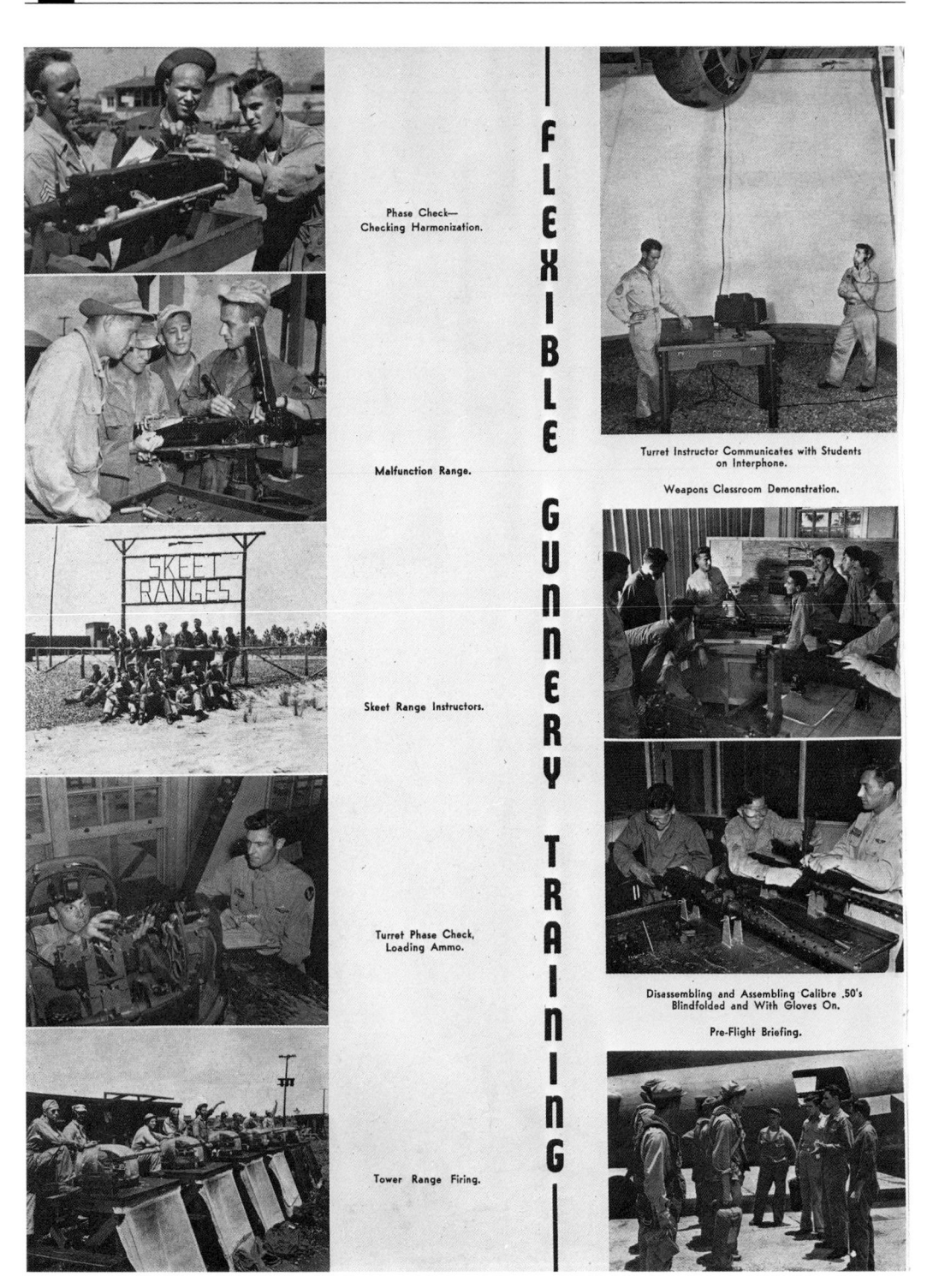

Phase Check—
Checking Harmonization.

Malfunction Range.

Skeet Range Instructors.

Turret Phase Check,
Loading Ammo.

Tower Range Firing.

FLEXIBLE GUNNERY TRAINING

Turret Instructor Communicates with Students
on Interphone.

Weapons Classroom Demonstration.

Disassembling and Assembling Calibre .50's
Blindfolded and With Gloves On.

Pre-Flight Briefing.

Multiple views of the World War II gunnery school at Tyndall Army Airfield in Panama City

At Governor Millard Caldwell's inauguration parade, marching soldiers provide a sober reminder that the war is still raging in Europe and Japan.

On April 12, President Roosevelt dies of a cerebral hemorrhage while serving in his fourth term of office. The nation grieves, and Vice President Harry Truman is sworn in as president.

On April 30, Adolf Hitler shoots himself in his Berlin bunker.

A 1943 or 1944 photograph of President Franklin Roosevelt aboard a train in Jacksonville. The President, who leads America through the Great Depression and World War II, dies on April 12, 1945, eighteen days before Hitler kills himself and three weeks before Germany surrenders.

On May 7, General Eisenhower accepts the unconditional surrender of Germany to the Allied forces. V-E celebrations (victory in Europe)

break out around the nation and state, while all understand that the war continues in the East.

On July 27, the Florida Supreme Court follows the U.S. Supreme Court decision in *Smith v. Allwright,* and strikes down the Florida Democratic Party's "white primary," designed to keep African Americans from holding office. In 1937, the Florida legislature had gotten rid of the state's poll tax that discouraged poor African Americans from voting, but the white primary had remained a significant obstacle. The percentage of Florida African Americans registered to vote will increase from 13 percent in 1946 to 32 percent in 1950. The percentage registered will be 51 percent in 1964 and, after the Voting Rights Act of 1965 passes, will increase to 64 percent in 1966.

On August 6, the United States drops an atomic bomb on Hiroshima, Japan, killing approximately 80,000 people. Three days later, after Japan refuses to surrender, a second bomb is dropped on Nagasaki, Japan, killing approximately 35,000 people. Paul Tibbets is pilot of Enola Gay (named after Tibbets' mother), the B-29 that drops the bomb on Hiroshima.

Paul Tibbets, pilot of the *Enola Gay,* grew up in Miami and is an alumnus of the University of Florida. His bombardier is Tom Ferebee of Orlando. Ferebee will later describe the "tremendous blinding light," from the explosion, which made it clear to him that this was no ordinary bomb.

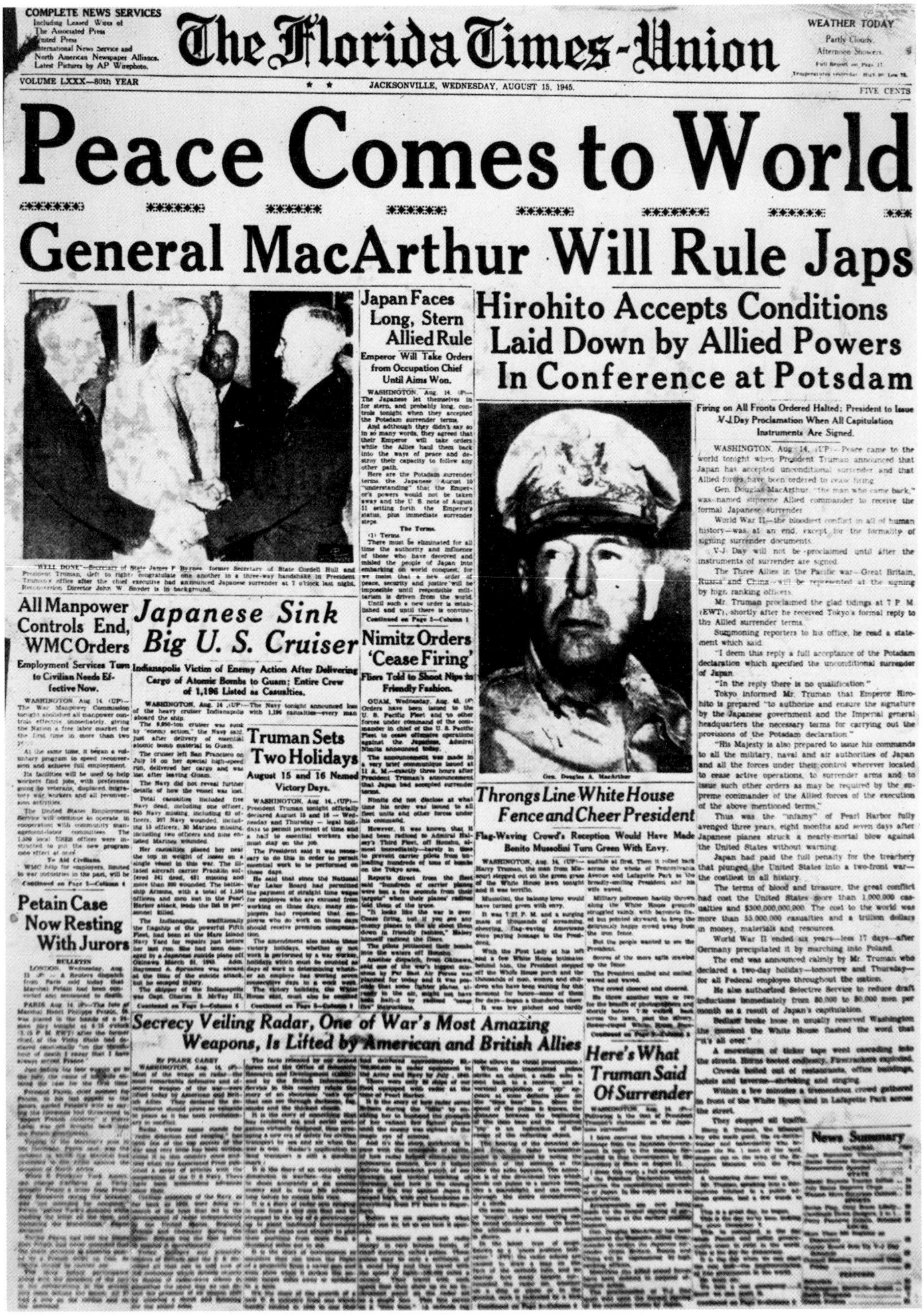

COMPLETE NEWS SERVICES Including Leased Wires of The Associated Press, United Press, International News Service and North American Newspaper Alliance. Latest Pictures by AP Wirephoto.

The Florida Times-Union

WEATHER TODAY Partly Cloudy. Afternoon Showers.

VOLUME LXXX—80th YEAR ★ ★ JACKSONVILLE, WEDNESDAY, AUGUST 15, 1945. FIVE CENTS

Peace Comes to World

General MacArthur Will Rule Japs

Hirohito Accepts Conditions Laid Down by Allied Powers In Conference at Potsdam

Firing on All Fronts Ordered Halted; President to Issue V-J Day Proclamation When All Capitulation Instruments Are Signed.

WASHINGTON, Aug. 14. (UP)—Peace came to the world tonight when President Truman announced that Japan has accepted unconditional surrender and that Allied forces have been ordered to cease firing.

Gen. Douglas MacArthur, "the man who came back," was named supreme Allied commander to receive the formal Japanese surrender.

World War II—the bloodiest conflict in all of human history—was at an end, except for the formality of signing surrender documents.

V-J Day will not be proclaimed until after the instruments of surrender are signed.

The Three Allies in the Pacific war—Great Britain, Russia and China—will be represented at the signing by high ranking officers.

Mr. Truman proclaimed the glad tidings at 7 P. M. (EWT), shortly after he received Tokyo's formal reply to the Allied surrender terms.

Summoning reporters to his office, he read a statement which said:

"I deem this reply a full acceptance of the Potsdam declaration which specified the unconditional surrender of Japan.

"In the reply there is no qualification."

Tokyo informed Mr. Truman that Emperor Hirohito is prepared "to authorize and ensure the signature by the Japanese government and the Imperial general headquarters the necessary terms for carrying out the provisions of the Potsdam declaration."

"His Majesty is also prepared to issue his commands to all the military, naval and air authorities of Japan and all the forces under their control wherever located to cease active operations, to surrender arms and to issue such other orders as may be required by the supreme commander of the Allied forces of the execution of the above mentioned terms."

Thus was the "infamy" of Pearl Harbor fully avenged three years, eight months and seven days after Japanese planes struck a nearly-mortal blow against the United States without warning.

Japan had paid the full penalty for the treachery that plunged the United States into a two-front war—the costliest in all history.

The terms of blood and treasure, the great conflict had cost the United States more than 1,000,000 casualties and $300,000,000,000. The cost to the world was more than 55,000,000 casualties and a trillion dollars in money, materials and resources.

World War II ended six years—less 17 days—after Germany precipitated it by marching into Poland.

The end was announced calmly by Mr. Truman who declared a two-day holiday—tomorrow and Thursday—for all Federal employes throughout the nation.

He also authorized Selective Service to reduce draft inductions immediately from 80,000 to 50,000 men per month as a result of Japan's capitulation.

Bedlam broke loose in usually reserved Washington the moment the White House flashed the word that "it's all over."

A snowstorm of ticker tape went cascading into the streets. Horns tooted endlessly. Firecrackers exploded.

Crowds boiled out of restaurants, office buildings, hotels and taverns—shrieking and singing.

Within a few minutes a tremendous crowd gathered in front of the White House and in Lafayette Park across the street.

They stopped all traffic.

"WELL DONE"—Secretary of State James F. Byrnes, former Secretary of State Cordell Hull and President Truman (left to right) congratulate one another in a three-way handshake in President Truman's office after the chief executive had announced Japanese surrender at 7 o'clock last night. Reconversion Director John W. Snyder is in background.

Gen. Douglas A. MacArthur

Japan Faces Long, Stern Allied Rule

Emperor Will Take Orders from Occupation Chief Until Aims Won.

All Manpower Controls End, WMC Orders

Employment Services Turn to Civilian Needs Effective Now.

Japanese Sink Big U. S. Cruiser

Indianapolis Victim of Enemy Action After Delivering Cargo of Atomic Bombs to Guam; Entire Crew of 1,196 Listed as Casualties.

Nimitz Orders 'Cease Firing'

Fliers Told to Shoot Nips in Friendly Fashion.

Truman Sets Two Holidays

August 15 and 16 Named Victory Days.

Thongs Line White House Fence and Cheer President

Flag-Waving Crowd's Reception Would Have Made Benito Mussolini Turn Green With Envy.

Petain Case Now Resting With Jurors

Secrecy Veiling Radar, One of War's Most Amazing Weapons, Is Lifted by American and British Allies

Here's What Truman Said Of Surrender

News Summary

Jacksonville's Florida Times-Union announces the end of a long and costly war

On August 14, the Japanese send a communication to the Allies announcing its surrender. World War II is over.

Flagler Street in downtown Miami breaks out in a victory celebration upon announcement that the Japanese have surrendered.

A marching band joins the celebration at the V-J Day parade in Tallahassee

On August 15, Jacksonville's *Florida Times Union* declares "Peace Comes to World," while the *Fort Lauderdale News and Evening Sentinel* reports on the city's victory celebration. Parades and celebrations take place in streets and parks throughout the state as Floridians contemplate the post-war years. The headline for the *Miami Herald* is succinct in type covering about one-third of the front page: WAR ENDS.

On September 2, General Douglas MacArthur and Admiral Chester Nimitz receive the formal surrender of Japan aboard the battleship Missouri *in Tokyo Bay. Over 290,000 Americans died in battle during World War II.*

On September 15, 1945, fire destroys blimps, airplanes, and hangars at Richmond Naval Air Station south of Miami.

On September 15, a catastrophic fire at Richmond Naval Air Station, south of Miami, destroys three large hangars, 366 airplanes, and 25 blimps.

On December 5, five United States Avenger torpedo bombers leave Ft. Lauderdale Naval Air Station for a training mission over the Atlantic. The group, designated Flight 19, apparently becomes disoriented and is lost at sea, with crews

Five United States Avenger torpedo bombers, like the one pictured here, are lost in the Bermuda Triangle on December 5, 1945.

totaling fourteen. During the massive search and rescue efforts that follow, a Martin Mariner PBM Seaplane, Training 49, also vanishes with its crew of thirteen. In 1964, in *Argosy* magazine, the term "Bermuda Triangle" will be introduced to define unexplained disappearances in the area bounded by Bermuda, Puerto Rico, and Ft. Lauderdale.

1946

After the war, thousands of veterans return to Florida as tourists and residents, sparking a major post-war house building and population boom.

Air-conditioning will spread in popularity as demonstrated by the Carrier Corporation's sales increase from $20 million in 1942, to $53 million in 1947, to $100 million in 1952. Air conditioning in Florida will begin to make its mark in Florida homes during this era, going from a rarity in 1950 to 18.3 percent of homes in 1960. Florida home construction and population explode. From 1940 to 1960, the census population goes from 1,897,414 to 4,951,560, a 161 percent increase in twenty years!

On March 5, Winston Churchill, in a speech delivered at Westminster College in Fulton, Missouri, alongside President Harry Truman, warns the world of the Soviet threat and proclaims that an "Iron Curtain" has been drawn across Europe. The Cold War has begun.

On March 17, Jackie Robinson steps on the field at City Island Ball Park in downtown Daytona Beach for a spring training game with the Montreal Royals, the Brooklyn Dodgers' AAA minor league baseball team. Having been signed by Dodgers president Branch Rickey, Robinson, who is the grandson of a slave, will become the first African American in

the twentieth century to play in a Major League Baseball game when he lines up for the Brooklyn Dodgers on April 15, 1947.

Daytona Beach's City Island Ball Park will be renamed Jackie Robinson Ball Park in 1990, in honor of the African American player who made his debut here with the Dodgers organization in 1946.

A circa 1950s photograph of cans of Minute Maid orange juice concentrate passing through a blast freeze tunnel set at -40 degrees Fahrenheit. In 1946, Minute Maid begins selling frozen orange juice, a product that greatly expands Florida's orange juice industry.

Also this year, Minute Maid begins to produce and sell frozen orange juice concentrate using a process developed under the leadership of the Florida Citrus Commission. The popularity of frozen concentrate will greatly expand Florida's orange industry—one billion gallons of orange juice will be consumed in the

United States by 1980. Florida groves produced 28.6 million boxes of oranges in the 1940–41 season; 67.3 million boxes in 1950–51; 142.3 million boxes in 1970–71; 151.5 million boxes in 1990–91; and 225 million boxes in 1999–2000. During the 1943–44 season, Florida's orange crop passed California's (which produced 75 percent of America's oranges in 1920) and will remain ahead going forward. The largest Florida citrus producers in 1950 will be Minute Maid, Snow Crop, Pasco Packing Company (Lykes Bros.), and Birds Eye (General Foods). In 1960, Coca Cola will acquire Minute Maid, with its three concentrate plants, 30,000 acres of groves, and headquarters in Orlando. Coca Cola later acquires Snow Crop, and in 1998 PepsiCo will buy Tropicana, a company that begins selling "Tropicana Pure Premium Orange Juice" in cartons in 1954, becoming a juice giant.

1947

In November, Marjory Stoneman Douglas, former *Miami Herald* columnist, publishes *The Everglades: River of Grass*, a description of the beauty and uniqueness of the land and a warning of the damage done. The Everglades is losing its deer, gators, panthers, orchids, palms, and other species to hunters, collectors, and, especially, due to the impact of drying out the land. The lack of water has stressed the food chain, encouraged invasive species, and fueled fires—one million acres burned in 1939 alone. Pineapple Press, a Sarasota publishing company, will publish the 70th anniversary edition in 2017, with an update detailing the ongoing challenges of the Everglades ecosystem.

On December 6, President Harry Truman dedicates Everglades National Park. The park had been proposed by the National Park Service in 1923 and had been autho-

An undated photograph of Marjory Stoneman Douglas, author of *The Everglades: River of Grass*

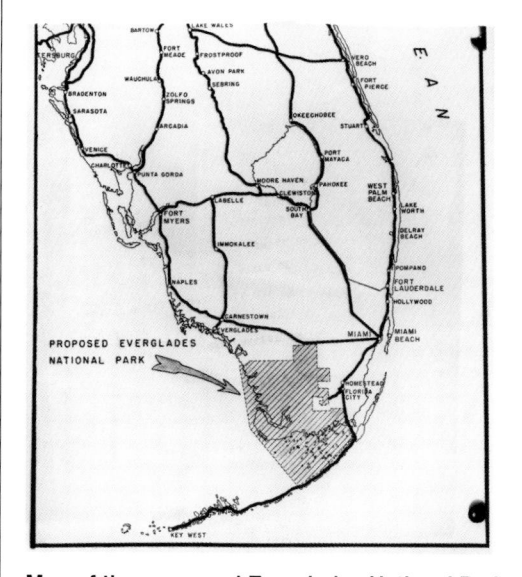

Map of the proposed Everglades National Park

rized by Congress in 1934, but it required a major political effort to accomplish. Among the efforts' many leaders were Florida Governor and U.S. Senator Spessard Holland and activist Ernest Coe. The 1.3-million-acre park is the nation's third largest, but excludes areas that Coe wanted included, such as Big Cypress and the Upper Keys. President Truman proclaims, "We have permanently safeguarded an irreplaceable primitive area."

Governor Caldwell and President Truman en route to Everglades park dedication

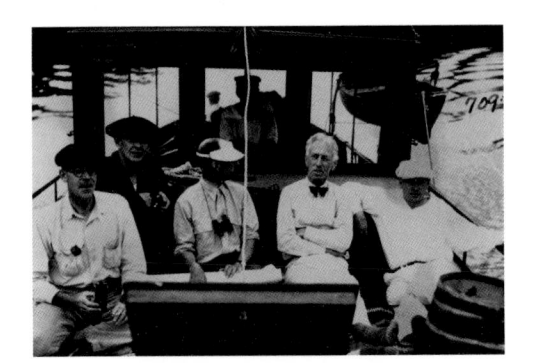

A 1929 boat ride with Ernest F. Coe (fourth from left with bow tie), fighter for the creation of the Everglades National Park

Also this year, as large numbers of veterans use the GI Bill to attend college, Florida State College for Women in Tallahassee becomes coeducational and is renamed Florida State University.

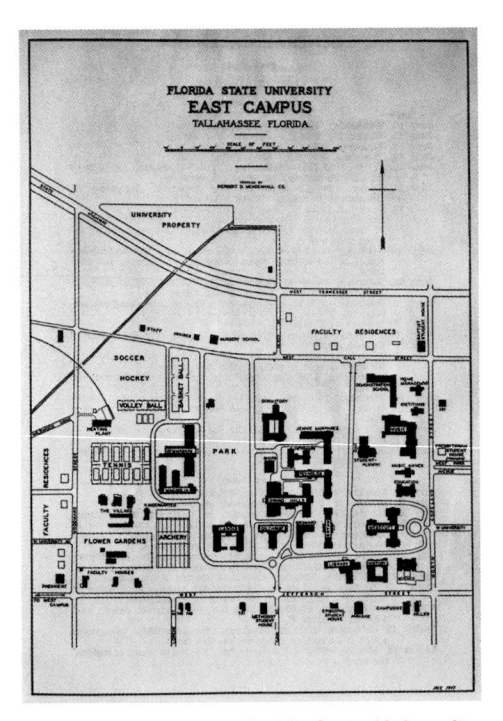

The main campus of Florida State University

President Truman, his wife, and his daughter visit what will become known as his "Little White House" at Naval Air Station Key West.

1948

On March 28, the Dade Broward Mosquito Control Division issues a report on the mosquito season: "From the mosquito control standpoint, it has been a bad year. We have probably been invaded by ten times the usual number of glades mosquitoes than we would expect in a normal year." Despite county expenditures of over $21,000 on DDT insecticide, mosquitoes and sand fleas continue to be an issue for southeast Florida. While the mosquitoes are not eradicated, infectious diseases are contained. Before the arrival of DDT, animals left in the open would sometimes die from over-exposure to mosquito bites. People wear long-sleeved dark clothing, even in the summer heat, and sometimes paint their screens with oil to catch no-see-ums and mosquitoes, wiping the screen and reapplying oil as the screens become covered in insects.

Mosquitoes are an ever-present hazard in early Florida development. Here, in 1903, a Florida East Coast Railway employee is attempting to control mosquitoes in Cape Sable, on the southwest tip of the Florida peninsula.

On May 3, in Shelley v. Kraemer, *the United States Supreme Court holds that state courts may not enforce restrictive covenants in deeds if such enforcement results in the violation of a potential purchaser's Fourteenth Amendment equal rights protections. The court strikes down an attempt by the Missouri Supreme Court to enforce a deed restriction that prohibited "people of the Negro or Mongolian Race" from owning property or living in a certain area.*

Examples of Florida deed restrictions include the Glenwood neighborhood in Clearwater, which prohibits conveyance "to people of African descent nor to any Jew or Hebrew," and similar restrictions at West Seminole Terrace in Seminole, Bella Vista in Safety Harbor, and others. The Memorial Cemetery in Seminole has restrictions prohibiting African American burial.

On May 6, Congress publishes the "Comprehensive Report on Central and Southern Florida Project for Flood Control and Other Purposes" (CSFP). The project follows a 1947 rain and hurricane season that brought one hundred inches of water to south Florida, flooding agricultural lands and east coast developments. The St. Lucie Canal and Hoover Dike kept Lake

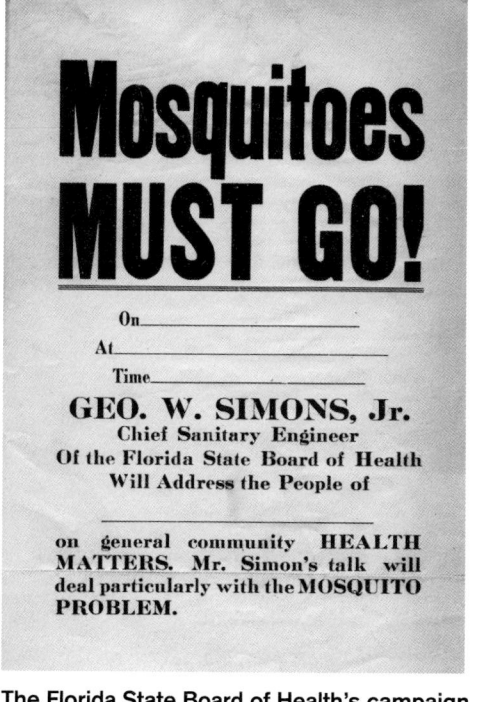

Mosquitoes MUST GO!

On_____

At_____

Time_____

GEO. W. SIMONS, Jr.
Chief Sanitary Engineer
Of the Florida State Board of Health
Will Address the People of

_____

on general community HEALTH MATTERS. Mr. Simon's talk will deal particularly with the MOSQUITO PROBLEM.

The Florida State Board of Health's campaign against mosquitoes

Okeechobee from overflowing, but the St. Lucie Canal also poured billions of gallons into the estuary at St. Lucie's mouth on the Atlantic, causing environmental damage.

The purpose of the CSFP is to control the water throughout the region and end the cycle of floods and droughts. It includes straightening out the Kissimmee River, a process started by Hamilton Disston in the nineteenth century, and building a series of levees and canals that separate the region into:

(1) cattle ranches north of Lake Okeechobee;
(2) the developments in southeast Florida;
(3) an agricultural area directly south of the lake; and
(4) water storage areas south of the agricultural area.

The water storage areas, larger than Rhode Island, are designed to provide water during droughts, absorb water during storms, and recharge the region's aquifer. During drought times, the Army Corps of Engineers will allocate the water among the populated areas, agricultural, and environmental interests. With the strong backing of Senator Spessard Holland, the project, which will take decades to construct, is approved by Congress. One part of the effort, to straighten the Kissimmee River (to be known as canal C-38), will cost $35 million, require five dams, and be completed in 1971.

On June 27, the Soviet Union cuts off traffic to West Berlin by rail or the autobahn. United States General Lucius Clay, backed by President Harry Truman, orders an air program to provide supplies to West Berlin. The "Berlin Airlift" will carry two million tons of supplies on 270,000 flights until May 12, 1949, when the Soviets cease the blockade.

1949

On January 4, Fuller Warren, a lawyer, legislator, and councilman from Jacksonville, becomes the thirtieth governor of Florida. Governor Warren pledges to make the roads safer: "We are going to stop the killing and crippling of people on the highways of Florida. We are going to stop much of it by eliminating roaming livestock from the roads of this state. We are going to stop more of it by eliminating drunken driving." He further confirms his opposition to a general sales tax (the legislature will pass a three-cent sales tax during his term), promises support for public schools and the citrus industry, and acknowledges the need to financially help the state's cities and towns: "I am acutely aware of the almost insolvent condition of many towns and cities."

On March 21, Florida's first television station signs on the air: WTVJ Channel 4 in Miami. In the early years of broadcasting, all of the networks (ABC, CBS, NBC, and DuMont) will provide programming for the station. Stations will expand throughout Florida. Jacksonville's WMBR

Miami's WTVJ becomes Florida's first television station on March 21, 1949, broadcasting from the Capitol Theater. News crew: George Thurston, Keith Leslie and Bill Tucker.

Florida Governor Fuller Warren makes a television appearance.

becomes Florida's second station on September 15, 1949. In 1953, five more cities add stations, including Ft. Lauderdale's WFTL, St. Petersburg's WSUN ("Why Stay Up North"), West Palm Beach's WIRK, Pensacola's WPFA, and Panama City's WJDM. In 1954, four more cities obtain television stations, including Ft. Myers' WINK, Orlando's WDBO, Tallahassee's WCTV, and Tampa's WFLA. Daytona Beach's WESH arrives in 1956 and Gainesville's WUFT is added in 1958. Television brings the world to Florida's living rooms.

On April 4, in Washington, D.C., the United States and eleven other nations sign an agreement to establish the North Atlantic Treaty Organization (NATO). The Cold War-era pact provides that an armed attack against any of the member countries "shall be considered an attack against them all."

On May 11, President Harry Truman signs legislation establishing the Joint Long Range Proving Ground to be built at the Banana River Naval Station on Cape Canaveral on Florida's east coast. It is later named Patrick Air Force Base after Air Force Major General Mason Patrick.

On September 23, President Truman announces that the Soviets have successfully

exploded an atomic device. U.S. scientists had believed that the Soviets were three years from developing the bomb.

On October 1, China "falls" to communism as Mao Tse-tung proclaims the People's Republic of China. A Soviet and communist China alliance, which will be signed in February 1950, increases Cold War tensions.

1950

By this year, Florida citrus production will exceed 100 million boxes for the first time. The citrus crop will surpass 200 million boxes by 1971. By 2010, there will be 8,000 citrus growers on 550,000 acres of land in Florida, generating over $9 billion in economic activity. The 2010 largest producing citrus counties will be, in order, Polk, Highlands, Hendry, DeSoto, Hardee, and St. Lucie. Florida's citrus industry adds frozen juice concentrate to its product offering.

On February 9, U.S. Senator Joseph McCarthy of Wisconsin announces to the Wheeling, West Virginia, Republican Women's Club that he has a list of 205 names of Communist Party members working in the U.S. State Department. McCarthy will become chairman for the Permanent Subcommittee on Investigations of the Senate Committee on Governmental Operations and will launch numerous attacks on alleged communists. The Senate will vote to censure him in December 1954 for his conduct.

On June 30, the State Department commits military and economic aid, including the use of U.S. troops, to South Korea. The action comes five days after communist North Korea invades South Korea.

On July 1, following through on Governor Warren's inaugural promise, the Florida Legislature's Fencing Law takes effect, banning cows, hogs, and other animals from Florida's public roads. In

1947 and 1948, there were 933 highway accidents in Florida involving animals; 257 people were injured and 24 people were killed.

On July 24, the first rocket is launched from Cape Canaveral Air Force Station, which started construction this year. The rocket is a 62-foot-long "bumper missile." The first stage V-2 climbs ten miles and successfully separates from the second stage, which travels another fifteen miles.

The Cape Canaveral location is chosen for several reasons. One factor is its proximity to the equator, which matters because the linear velocity of Earth's surface is greatest toward the equator. Another is that rockets can launch east along with the Earth's rotation. And the ocean is a safe downrange area in case of accidents. The National Aeronautics and Space Administration (NASA) will take over the facility in 1958. The aerospace industry will grow in the area that will become known as Florida's "Space Coast." The space race will have a profound impact on Brevard County over the next sixty years as the Space Coast grows along with America's space program. As one example, nearby Titusville's population nearly triples, from 2,220 in 1940, to 6,410 in 1960.

On September 5 and 6, a Category 3 hurricane strikes Cedar Key. It kills two, causes $33 million in damage, and drops almost 39 inches of rain on Yankeetown. Another Category 3 hurricane will strike Miami and Ft. Lauderdale next month, causing three deaths and $28 million in damage.

1951

On April 5, Julius and Ethel Rosenberg are sentenced to death by a federal court for revealing atomic weapon secrets to the Soviet Union. On June 19, 1953, they will become the first U.S. civilians to be put to death under the General Espionage Act of 1917. Julius Rosenberg was accused of receiving secret information from his brother-in-law, who was stationed near the atomic test site at Los Alamos, New Mexico, and passing on the information to Soviet contacts.

The first rocket is launched from Cape Canaveral on July 24, 1950. It is the beginning of a new era for Brevard County, Florida, America, and ultimately for mankind.

A 1958 photo of an Atlas missile launch at Cape Canaveral.

On April 11, President Truman relieves General Douglas MacArthur of command in the Korean War. MacArthur, a World War II legend, had repeatedly and publicly disagreed with the president on the conduct of the war. MacArthur will be cheered in a ticker-tape parade in New York City on April 20, one day after addressing both houses of Congress when he proclaims "Old soldiers never die, they just fade away."

Harry T. Moore, state secretary of the Florida NAACP, and his wife, Harriette, are fatally injured when a bomb explodes at their home on Christmas Day.

On December 25, Harry T. Moore and his wife Harriette are fatally injured at their home in Mims, five miles north of Titusville on Florida's Atlantic coast, in an attack carried out in response to Moore's civil rights activism. A bomb placed in the floor joists under their bed explodes, and both will die from their injuries. In 1952, the FBI will be brought in to investigate.

Moore is the Florida NAACP leader and founder of the Brevard County NAACP. Suspicion points to three Klan members, one of whom will kill himself the day after an FBI interview, but no arrests are made and the crime remains unsolved.

1952

Ready to start the 1961 race at Sebring

On March 15, the first "12 Hours of Sebring" automobile endurance race is held at a racetrack built on land that served as a United States Army Air Force training base during World War II. The winning drivers are Harry Gray and Larry Kulok driving a Frazer-Nash LeMans.

On November 1, the United States detonates a hydrogen bomb at Eniwetok Atoll. The development of the bomb, which carries an explosive power much greater than the atomic bomb, was approved by the president after the 1949 detonation of an atomic device by the Soviet Union.

On November 4, World War II General Dwight David Eisenhower is elected president and Richard M. Nixon is elected vice president with a campaign against "Korea, Communism and Corruption." Democratic Challenger Adlai Stevenson responds to the loss by commenting that he feels like the little boy who stubbed his toe in the dark: "He was too old to cry, but it hurt too much to laugh." Eisenhower is the first Republican elected to the presidency since Herbert Hoover in 1928.

1953

On January 6, Democrat Daniel T. McCarty becomes the thirty-first governor of Florida. A native of Ft. Pierce, Governor McCarty has been a cattle and citrus producer and is a decorated veteran of the 1944 D-Day invasion. Economic stability is a strong theme of his inaugural speech: "We depend primarily on three chief sources of income for our citizens in Florida—tourists, agriculture and industry. It will be the objective of this administration to foster, promote and develop these basic phases of our economy . . . Conservation and the development of our natural resources are essential . . ." Unfortunately, Governor McCarty will suffer a heart attack seven weeks after taking office and will die in September.

In March, Miami's Vizcaya opens to the public as the Dade County Art Museum. It will later be renamed Vizcaya Museum and Gardens. It is housed in the magnificent estate of the late industrialist James Deering. Deering had purchased the first 130 acres on Biscayne Bay (of Vizcaya's 180 total acres) from Mary

The remarkable Vizcaya Museum and Gardens on Biscayne Bay in Miami

Brickell in 1912. On September 10, 1987, President Ronald Reagan and Pope John Paul II will hold meetings at Vizcaya.

In May, the first Florida Folk Festival is held at the Stephen Foster Memorial in White Springs, about twelve miles northwest of Lake City and one hundred miles east of Tallahassee. This first year, the festival provides music, entertainment, and a St. Augustine pageant. The Memorial Day weekend festival will become

A large crowd enjoys a folk dance performance at the 1970 Florida Folk Festival in White Springs

A dancer from St. Augustine performing at the first Florida Folk Festival in White Springs. The festival continues today.

a popular annual event, and it continues today at the Stephen Foster Folk Culture Center State Park as a three-day celebration of the music, dance, stories, crafts, and food that make Florida unique. More than three hundred performers "give voice and meaning to Florida's heritage." It is one of the nation's oldest continuous folk festivals.

On July 27, the United Nations and North Korea sign an armistice agreement, ending the Korean War.

On September 28, Florida Governor McCarty dies, having suffered a heart attack in February. The state senate president, Charley E. Johns from Starke, becomes acting governor until a successor can be elected to finish the last two years of Governor McCarty's term. Governor Johns will support highway expansion and will end the toll on the overseas highway to Key West.

1954

On May 17, the United States Supreme Court hands down a landmark ruling in Brown v. Board of Education of Topeka. *The case holds that racial segregation in public schools is a violation of the Fourteenth Amendment. The court reverses its 1896 decision in* Plessy v. Ferguson *and holds that separate facilities are*

"inherently unequal." The next year the court will publish implementation guidelines requiring that desegregation be implemented "on a racially nondiscriminatory basis with all deliberate speed."

In response to the *Brown* decision, Florida U.S. Senator Spessard Holland calls it "revolutionary" and U.S. Senator George Smathers cautions: "It would be a mistake to rush into hasty decisions or to make inflammatory statements based on anger or resentment." Florida State Senator LeRoy Collins, a candidate for governor, responds: "I favor segregation in our public schools . . . It is part of Florida's custom and law. I will use all the lawful power of the governor's office to preserve this custom and law."

On September 6, at 10 A.M., the $22 million Sunshine Skyway Bridge opens from St. Petersburg to Manatee County, spanning 4.25 miles across Tampa Bay with a toll of $1.75 per car. The bridge reduces the overland trip from St. Petersburg to Bradenton by forty miles, although the Bee Line Ferry provided a shorter, direct route. By midnight of the first open day 15,000 cars will pass over the bridge, climbing a height equivalent to a fifteen-story building.

Acting Governor Charley E. Johns speaks at the 1954 dedication of the Sunshine Skyway linking St. Petersburg to Manatee County.

A second span of the Sunshine Skyway will be constructed in 1970.

Also this year, two Miami businessmen purchase the Insta-Burger King restaurant business that started in Jacksonville and move the business to Miami, rebranding it as Burger King. By 2015 it will have over 15,000 outlets in one hundred countries around the world.

1955

On January 4, Thomas LeRoy Collins, a lawyer and legislator from Tallahassee, is sworn into office as the thirty-third governor of Florida, having been elected to serve the last two years of deceased Governor McCarty's term. In his inaugural address, Governor Collins outlines the priorities of Florida to include "a program for clean, efficient, and economical government at all levels; for constitutional revision; for better educational facilities and opportunities; for improved labor, health, and welfare standards, for the conservation of our natural resources; for agricultural and industrial research and development; for highways adequate to meet proven needs; for effective highway safety; and for the proper promotion of Florida's tourist business." He speaks at length about the need for honest government.

On September 24, Fred Coppock and Captain W.B. Gray open the Miami Seaquarium on the Rickenbacker Causeway. It will become the longest operating oceanarium in the United States.

On December 1, forty-three-year-old Rosa Parks refuses to give up her seat toward the front of the Cleveland Avenue bus in Montgomery, Alabama. Her action defies a local law requiring African Americans to sit in the back of buses and results in her being jailed. A boycott follows her arrest and will continue until the city agrees to comply with the November 13, 1956, U.S. Supreme Court ruling, declaring segregation on such buses unconstitutional.

1956

On March 5, the Florida Supreme Court holds that Governor LeRoy Collins may run for reelection to a full four-year term because his 1954 election provided him

The Miami Seaquarium opens on September 24, 1955.

with only the final two years of deceased Governor McCarty's term. Since prior governors were subject to the consecutive term prohibition in the Florida Constitution, Governor Collins will become the first governor to serve consecutive terms when he takes office again in January of 1957.

Reverend C. K. Steele (center left) of Bethel Missionary Baptist Church, Reverend Dan Speed (center right), and Reverend A.C. Redd of St. James CME Church protest Tallahassee bus segregation by sitting in the middle instead of the back of the bus. This action ends the boycott started when two FAMU students are arrested for sitting beside a white woman. Tallahassee desegregates its buses.

On May 26, Florida A&M University (FAMU) students Wilhelmina Jakes and Carrie Patterson board a Tallahassee city bus and sit down in the front seat next to a white woman. The driver orders the girls to the back of the bus. When the students refuse, the driver drives to a nearby gas station, calls the police, and has the girls arrested. The arrest will trigger the Tallahassee bus boycott, the third of its kind in the nation. The African American community joins the boycott, led by the Inter-Civic Council and Bethel Baptist Pastor C.K. Steele. After seven months of the boycott, the city will agree to allow seating on buses

as first-come first-serve, and agrees to hire African American drivers.

On June 29, President Eisenhower signs the Federal Aid Highway Act, authorizing $33.5 billion to be spent on road construction over the next thirteen years. The federal highway budget for 1957 through 1959 will be $6.55 billion, $110 million of which will go to Florida. The total planned United States interstate system is 41,000 miles, 1,164 miles of which are planned for Florida to be completed over the next thirteen years at an estimated cost of $500 million.

Following several shows the previous week at Miami's Olympia Theater, on August 7, Elvis Presley is in St. Petersburg to perform at the Florida Theater. Over six thousand fans pay $1.25 or $1.50 to pack the hall at all three performances. Fire department emergency personnel treat six girls for overheating and fainting spells. The city's fire marshal exclaims: "I hope we never have anything like this again." Earlier in the year, in February, Presley had played in Jacksonville's Gator Bowl.

Governor LeRoy Collins addresses the opening convocation at the University of South Florida on September 26, 1960.

In December, the State Board of Education establishes the University of South Florida, the fourth state university in Florida, in Hillsborough County near Tampa. The campus will be built on a practice bombing range just north of World War II's Henderson Air Field.

On September 20, a federal district judge issues an order preventing Arkansas Governor Faubus from continuing to use Arkansas National Guard troops to block integration of Little Rock Central High School. After mobs gather outside the school, President Eisenhower orders ten thousand Arkansas National Guardsmen into federal service who, along with a thousand paratroopers, ensure the African American students safe passage.

1957
On January 8, Governor LeRoy Collins begins his second term as governor. Governor Collins describes the needs of the state to include improvements in highways, public schools, institutions of higher learning, correctional facilities, and institutional care for the mentally handicapped. He speaks at length to the integration issue, stating that "the average white person does not object to non-segregated seating in buses—any more than he objects to riding the same elevators with Negroes or patronizing the same stores." But the governor does object to "boycotts, ultimatums, and preemptory demands" and further argues caution in public schools: "I continue to say that our traditions and customs of segregation in the public schools can be expected to prevail for the foreseeable future."

On October 4, the USSR launches Sputnik, the first artificial satellite sent from earth. With the launch of Sputnik, Americans become highly concerned that the Soviet Union is leading the space race. Next year, congress will pass the National Aeronautics and Space Act in an effort to organize the nation's massive effort to get Americans into space.

Martin Marietta Corporation's electronics and guided missile plant in Orlando

On December 4, 1957, the Glenn L. Martin Company, later known as Martin Marietta, opens a defense industry manufacturing plant on 7,300 acres along Orange Blossom Trail in Orlando. Governor LeRoy Collins announces, "I declare this plant formally dedicated to the service of America." The plant will produce army field artillery missiles, navy air-to-surface missiles, and an electronic air defense control system. It is today's Lockheed Martin. Due to its proximity to Patrick Air Force Base, Cape Canaveral, Kennedy Space Center, and Port Canaveral, this area will attract other defense industry–related companies, providing a boost to the local economy.

1958
On January 31, at Florida's Cape Canaveral, the United States launches *Explorer 1*, its first satellite, into orbit. The space race heats up.

On June 5, after the federal courts rule that St. Petersburg may not exclude African Americans from using Spa Beach and Pool, eight blacks purchase tickets and use the pool. City Manager Ross Windom responds by closing the facility. After months of negative press and concern over impacts on tourism, on January 6, 1959, the city council will vote four to three to reopen Spa Beach and Pool, permitting use by all citizens.

On June 18, a federal court orders the University of Florida to allow qualified African Americans to enroll in its graduate schools. African American George H. Starke will enroll in the university's law school the following fall semester.

Also in September, Texas Instrument engineer Jack Kirby demonstrates the world's first integrated circuit, consisting of five electrical components on a wafer of germanium. In 1959, Robert Noyce, who will eventually become the founder of Intel, will develop a similar circuit made from silicon. The silicon-integrated circuit will become widely used in the developing computer industry.

On October 1, President Dwight D. Eisenhower organizes the National Aeronautics and Space Administration (NASA), more forcefully thrusting America into the effort to put a man in space.

NASA will significantly and positively change the Florida Space Coast.

1959

On January 7, the United States recognizes the Cuban Revolutionary Government of Premier Fidel Castro.

During the next thirty-five years over 800,000, Cubans will flee Castro's Cuba for the United States. Most will settle in Florida. The United States will embargo Cuban sugar and within five years the amount of acreage growing sugar south of Lake Okeechobee in the upper Everglades will increase fourfold to 223,000.

Racers along Daytona Beach, before the opening of the new speedway in 1959

The 1959 Daytona 500 race underway at the new speedway

On February 22, Lee Petty narrowly defeats Johnny Beauchamp in the inaugural Daytona 500 auto race at the new Daytona International Speedway. Forty-two thousand fans attend the race at the new speedway. Prior to the opening of the speedway, Daytona has been legendary for the land speed records set by racers on Daytona Beach.

The "Mystic Sheiks of Morocco" performing at Busch Gardens

On June 1, Anheuser-Busch, Inc., opens a brewery and gardens near Tampa. On opening day, one thousand people attend the attraction, which charges no admission fee and features a trained parrot and cockatoo show, a storybook land with dwarfs, free beer samples for adults, and a glimpse of a few African animals roaming a pasture. The gardens are built as a $500,000 aesthetic addition to the $20 million brewery and are today's Busch Gardens.

Chapter 7

Turbulent Times: 1960 through 1979

This is a period of intense change and turbulence.

At the beginning of the era, the Cold War heats up and the world finds itself on the brink of nuclear war over missiles heading from Russia toward Cuba. Throughout the United States, the civil rights movement grows, with sanitation worker marches, boycotts, sit-ins, and protests. In the Sunshine State, the protests take place on the streets of its cities as mayors and governors struggle to maintain peace and move Florida forward.

John Kennedy becomes the fourth president in American history to be assassinated, a few days after visiting Florida. Less than five years later, the nation's top civil rights leader and the slain president's brother, a presidential candidate, are also assassinated, shocking an already unsettled nation that is struggling through a period of social upheaval and an unpopular war in Vietnam. Again, grieving and unrest follow in Florida's towns and cities.

An NAACP march on March 27, 1964, in Tallahassee, calling for Congress to pass the Civil Rights bill, which will be signed into law the following July.

With the nation in turmoil, Republican and Democratic national conventions come to Miami Beach, along with protestors and the television world, thus presenting the city to the nation's living rooms. As America's involvement in Vietnam comes to a close, a scandal brews over a break-in of a political party headquarters at the Watergate, in Washington, D.C. The resulting cover-up and the discovery of other activities ultimately force an American president to resign rather than face removal from office, a first in American history. The later presidential pardon of the resigned president helps the nation turn a page, but it results in his successor losing the presidency to Jimmy Carter, a former Georgia governor and peanut farmer from Plains.

The Florida Space Coast becomes the focus of the world as America overtakes the Soviet Union in the space race. After one American successfully launches into space and another orbits the Earth, the nation sets a goal to launch the first man to land on the moon and return him safely to Earth. It succeeds before the end of the 1960s, with the ship commander calmly describing it as a "giant leap for mankind," which, of course, it is.

Florida dramatically expands its tourism industry as beach hotels flourish and Mickey Mouse arrives in Orlando. Retirees flock to the Sunshine State in record numbers. New universities are established. Professional sports teams begin to arrive, an indication of the growing prominence of Florida's urban centers. The era ends with a president who describes the nation as being stuck in a "malaise" and an upcoming presidential campaign that will determine whether the country and state can regain their footing.

> Throughout this book events in Florida are set in Roman (non-italics), and events outside Florida are set in *italics*.

Timeline

1960

In January, the Howard Frankland Bridge opens, spanning three miles and providing a second automobile link between St. Petersburg and Tampa. In 2010, it will be Florida's sixth longest bridge behind, in order:

1) the Seven Mile Bridge (from Marathon to Big Pine Key in the Florida Keys);
2) the Sunshine Skyway (4.1-mile bridge from St. Petersburg to Terra Ceia, by way of Bradenton);
3) the Mid-Bay Bridge (3.6-mile bridge from Miramar Beach to the mainland, east of Ft. Walton Beach);
4) the Garcon Point Bridge (3.5-mile bridge from Tiger Point to the mainland, east of Pensacola); and
5) the Henry H. Buckman Sr. Bridge (3.1-mile bridge spanning the St. Johns River in Jacksonville).

On February 1, four black college students are denied service at a Woolworth lunch counter in Greensboro, North Carolina, but they refuse to move. The lunch counter sit-ins will spread to cities throughout the South.

On March 2, in response to the nation's lunch counter demonstrations, the *St. Petersburg Evening Independent* proclaims that there must be considerable rejoicing in Moscow now, and "the Communist's plan to disrupt the United States through race disorders is having a measure of success in the current flurry of eating place incidents ... Should this irresponsible, Communist inspired move to disrupt business and disturb the peace of the community be brought to this city, it should be met with prompt police action and with quick application of such fines and penalties as the law provides."

Some 250 Florida A&M students march in protest when 27 of their fellow students are arrested during a lunch counter sit-in at McCrory's and Woolworth's in Tallahassee.

On March 12, 250 Florida A&M students take part in a protest march in Tallahassee. They are protesting the arrest of twenty-three of their classmates earlier in the day who took part in lunch counter sit-ins at McCrory's and Woolworth's department stores. All available police officers are called to duty.

On March 20, Florida Governor LeRoy Collins gives a speech in response to lunch counter sit-ins in the state's major cities and asserts that it is "unfair and morally wrong" not to allow African Americans to eat at lunch counters when they are otherwise invited to buy at the stores. Nevertheless, the governor acknowledges that the merchant "has a legal right to do this. But I still don't think he can square that right with moral, simple justice." Florida's Senate President Dewey Johnson responds that the governor's speech confirms Johnson's belief that Collins is a "strict integrationist."

In April, the Student Non-Violent Coordinating Committee (SNCC) is founded at Shaw University in Raleigh, North Carolina. SNCC uses direct, nonviolent actions to achieve civil rights reforms.

A circa 1890 photograph of the sugar mill in St. Cloud, in Osceola County, about ninety miles north of Lake Okeechobee

In July, fifty-four farmers charter the Sugar Cane Growers Cooperative with the goal of working together to harvest, mill, process, and market sugar. By joining forces, they hope to achieve more stability. Farmers located in the Glades Agricultural Area now farm over 400,000 acres. The first mill they build together in 1962 will operate 24 hours a day throughout the roughly 150-day harvest season. By 2016, the Florida sugar industry will employ a reported fourteen thousand people.

On September 26, the University of South Florida opens its first class of about two thousand students at its new campus near Tampa in Hillsborough County.

Problems caused by crowds of spring breakers descending on Fort Lauderdale each year will eventually get to be more than the city is willing to tolerate. By the late 1980s, Mayor Robert Dressler has had enough. He shows them the door on *Good Morning America*. Mayor Dressler is shown here (third from left) with his wife (between the two men) and friends.

On December 28, *Where the Boys Are* is released. The hit movie is about Midwestern college girls who spend spring break in Ft. Lauderdale. Florida beaches will become the focus of the nation's college students for spring break, from Ft. Lauderdale to Daytona Beach to Clearwater to Panama City. Three months after the movie's release, fifty thousand college students arrive in Ft. Lauderdale for spring break. By 1985, the city's spring break crowds exceed three hundred seventy thousand. The students' behavior concerns officials, and eventually Mayor Robert Dressler announces on ABC's *Good Morning America* that students are no longer welcome for spring break.

Spring break in Cocoa Beach about thirty years after the release of the film *Where the Boys Are*, about young people during spring break in Fort Lauderdale

A sugar cane mill used by Osceola Farms in Pahokee, southeast of Lake Okeechobee

Also this year, Cuban immigrant Alfonso Fanjul acquires the 4,000-acre Osceola Farms in Pahokee, on Lake Okeechobee's southeast shore. His family was a major sugar producer in Cuba, but he was forced to flee after Castro took control. Fanjul settles in Palm Beach, builds a mill, and grows sugar. After the United States embargoes Cuban sugar, Fanjul will expand his operations. After Fanjul dies in 1980, his sons, Alfonso Jr. and José Pepe, will continue to operate the business with the label Florida Crystals. By the end of the century, Florida Crystals will control 180,000 acres in Florida, south and east of Lake Okeechobee, in addition to farmland in the Dominican Republic. Together

Daytona Beach becomes known for fast cars and spring break

with U.S. Sugar, Florida Crystals will become known as "Big Sugar."

During the coming two decades, air conditioning will make its mark in Florida, and people will follow:

- Air-conditioned homes in Florida will increase from rare in 1950, to 18.3 percent in 1960, to 84 percent in 1980.
- A population boom follows the cool air, with the Florida census going from 4,951,560 in 1960 to 9,746,961 in 1980, an increase of 97 percent over twenty years.

1961

On January 3, Democrat C. Farris Bryant, a lawyer and legislator who was born on a Marion County farm, becomes the thirty-fourth governor of Florida. Governor Bryant's inaugural address stresses the need for unity in the state and discusses his philosophy rather than his agenda for the coming four years.

On April 12, Soviet cosmonaut Yuri Gagarin makes man's first orbital flight, once around the Earth, in 108 minutes at a speed of 17,700 miles per hour.

On April 24, President Kennedy acknowledges his responsibility for America's involvement in the failed effort, earlier this month, by 1,500 Cuban exiles to invade Cuba at the Bay of Pigs on the south coast of Cuba.

On May 1, a National Airlines passenger airplane flying from Marathon to Key West is hijacked to Cuba. The hijacker will be imprisoned in Cuba and then in the United States upon returning in 1975. On March 12, 1968, three Cubans hijack a DC-9 aircraft from Tampa to Cuba. During the coming years, dozens of commercial and private planes will be hijacked to Cuba. In response, the United States and Cuba will enter into an agreement to return or prosecute hijackers. In

1973, the United States will install metal detectors at its airports to screen passengers for weapons.

Astronaut Alan B. Shepard lifts off from Cape Canaveral on May 5, 1961, and becomes the first American in space.

On May 5, Alan Shepard blasts off from Cape Canaveral in the Mercury spacecraft that he names *Freedom 7.* He becomes the second human and first American to travel in space as the nation pushes to catch the Russians in the space race.

On May 25, President John F. Kennedy addresses a special joint session of the United States Congress and proclaims: "I believe this nation should commit itself to achieving the goal, before this decade is out, of landing a man on the moon and returning him safely to Earth." Kennedy's vision will be realized in July of 1969, over five years after his death.

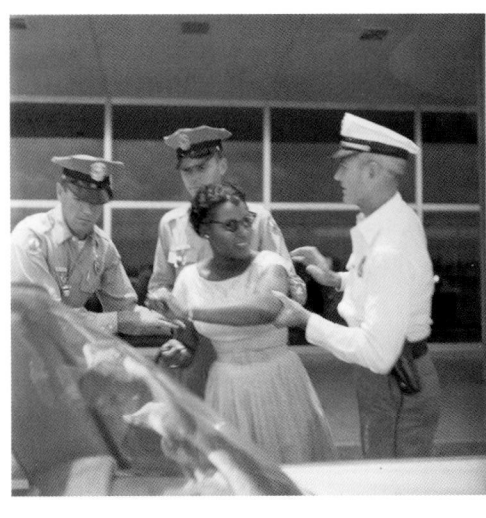

Priscilla Stephens is arrested at the Tallahassee Regional Airport on June 16, 1961, as the Freedom Riders "Tallahassee Ten" seek to be served at the segregated airport restaurant.

On June 16, Freedom Riders who challenged segregated interstate buses by traveling from Washington to Tallahassee are arrested for unlawful assembly when they try to obtain service at the segregated airport restaurant in Tallahassee. They will become known as the Tallahassee Ten.

On July 15, the Florida legislature authorizes a new university in Boca Raton. Florida Atlantic University will be built on the site of a World War II-era Army Air Force training facility.

A civil rights "wade-in" demonstration at a segregated Fort Lauderdale beach, led by officials from the Broward NAACP

On July 24, members of the Broward County branch of the NAACP lead a "wade in" protest at a segregated Ft. Lauderdale beach. Demonstrations will continue until a court order strikes down the city's segregated beaches ordinance.

On August 13, the East German army closes the border with West Berlin. Workers tear up streets and install barbed wire and fences around the three West-controlled sectors of West Berlin and along the border between East Berlin and West Berlin, while soldiers line the border with orders to shoot those attempting to defect. Later, concrete walls and mines will be added as Berlin families are split apart and East Berliners are no longer able to travel to friends and jobs in the West. The Berlin Wall becomes a stark symbol of the Cold War. Many will die attempting to enter West Berlin in the coming decades until 1989, when the wall begins to come down.

Also, during the summer, the first two African American students are permitted to enroll at St. Petersburg Junior College, Florida's oldest community college.

On September 8, Hurricane Donna strikes the middle Florida Keys as a Category 4 storm with sustained winds of 128 mph. It moves northwest, strikes the west coast of Florida near Naples and continues through the state in a northeast direction, exiting into the Atlantic on Florida's northeast coast. It will continue up the Atlantic striking North Carolina and the New England states. The storm will cause fifty deaths and $387 million in damage in the United States.

On October 26, President Kennedy sends correspondence to President Ngo Dinh Diem of South Vietnam, pledging assistance from America.

Astronaut John Glenn is welcomed back to earth in a Cocoa Beach parade on February 23, 1962. Vice President Lyndon Johnson is with Glenn.

1962

On January 11, the United States secretary of the interior officially recognizes the Miccosukee Tribe as an official tribe, separate from the Seminoles.

On February 20, after launching from Florida's Cape Canaveral, John Glenn orbits the Earth aboard Friendship 7. *The first American to orbit the Earth, he travels at over 17,000 miles per hour and splashes down in the Atlantic, east of the Bahamas.*

On October 1, following anti-integration riots, James Meredith becomes the first black student to attend the University of Mississippi. Two people are killed and twenty-eight marshals are wounded during the disturbances.

On October 14, United States reconnaissance photographs are taken that show missile sites in Cuba capable of launching missiles that can reach American soil. On October 22, President Kennedy orders a blockade preventing Russian ships from taking missiles to Cuba.

The world appears on the brink of global nuclear war until the Cuban Missile Crisis is resolved with Soviet Premier Nikita Krushchev agreeing to remove the missiles from Cuba on October 28.

Governor Farris Bryant (left), Sam Banks (center), chair of the Florida Citrus Commission, and Doyle E. Conner (right), Commissioner of Agriculture, inspecting damage to the crop in Polk County after the 1962 freeze devastates the citrus industry in central Florida. Growers will move south to plant their groves.

In December, a significant freeze strikes central Florida and damages 25 percent of the state's citrus crop. Lake Alfred, fifteen miles east of Lakeland in Polk County, is hit with a 12-degree temperature. As Florida struggles through the 1962 freeze, along with freezes that will follow in 1981, 1983, 1985, and 1989, Brazil passes Florida (in 1981) as the world's leading source of oranges. Citrus growers respond to the freezes by planting new groves farther south in the state. In 1950, Florida's leading citrus counties were Orange, Polk, and Lake—Orlando's county (Orange) and the counties immediately northwest and southwest. By 2000, the leading citrus counties will still include Polk but will largely shift south to St. Lucie, Indian River, DeSoto, Hardee, Highlands, and Hendry, counties that are around Lake Okeechobee, along with Collier—Naples' county on the southwest coast. As one example, 100,000 new acres will be planted in Hendry County (east of Ft. Myers and southwest of Lake Okeechobee) by 2000.

Governor Claude Kirk talking with retirees at a shuffleboard court in Fort Pierce. With their increasing numbers, retirees carry significant political weight and draw the attention of politicians in Florida and nationally.

Also this year, the first residents move into Sun City Center, a 12,000-acre retirement community twenty-five miles south of Tampa. Dubbed "the town too busy to retire," Sun City will have sixteen thousand retired residents by 2000. In 1968, Century Village in West Palm Beach will start the first retirement condominium on 685 acres, with units selling for $9,000. Retirement homes and communities will grow throughout Florida, the largest of which will be the Villages, twenty miles southeast of Ocala. By 2015, almost 115,000 people will live in the Villages, which will have its own newspaper, television station, radio station, and bank, along with 4.2 million square feet of commercial space. The Social Security Act of 1935 and the related increase in private employee pension plans provide Americans with income in their older years, enabling them to leave their home states and retire in sunny Florida. Some resulting statistics:

- The percentage of Florida residents over sixty-five will increase from 4.8 percent in 1930, to 11.2 percent in 1950, to 18.4 percent in 2000;
- By the early 1960s, one thousand retirees will move to Florida each week;
- By the 1990s, ten of the country's eleven "oldest" counties will be in Florida;
- In 2000, Clearwater will have America's highest percentage of residents over sixty-five (21.5 percent) and Venice, south of Sarasota, will have America's highest median age (68.8);
- Also in 2000, one-half of the 1.2 million Florida mobile home residents will be senior citizens;
- In the 1990s, the annual pension, Social Security, and other retirement income will bring $55 billion to the state, confirming retirement's place among Florida's other leading industries, such as tourism, agriculture, and construction.

1963

On February 12, Northwest Orient Flight 705, a Boeing 720, takes off from Miami International Airport en route to Portland via Chicago, Spokane, and Seattle. Shortly after take-off, the flight encounters a severe thunderstorm and crashes into the Everglades. Thirty-five passengers and eight crew members are killed in the accident.

On March 18, the United States Supreme Court issues an opinion in *Gideon v. Wainwright* involving a man convicted in a Panama City burglary. The court holds that accused individuals must be represented by an attorney, significantly altering the rights of those arrested.

Beginning April 3, large demonstrations take place in Birmingham, Alabama, protesting racial injustice. The demonstrations, led by Martin Luther King Jr., president of the Southern Christian Leadership Conference, result in the arrest of over one thousand protesters. Police dogs and fire hoses are used to control demonstrators. On May 11, an African American leader's home is bombed. President Kennedy sends in three thousand federal troops.

On May 26, the Sanibel Causeway opens. In 1904, a ferry began to run from Punta Rassa (southwest of Cape Coral and Ft. Myers) to Sanibel Island, and in 1926 the ferry expanded to transport cars. The ferry was operated by brothers George and Andrew Kinzie. Construction on the causeway cost $2.73 million. The bridge will lead to significant growth on the island, with the population increasing from three hundred in 1963 to fifteen hundred in 1972.

St. Petersburg Civil Rights leaders (l-r) Ralph James, Chester James Sr., and Reverend Chester James Jr., president of the Citizens Cooperative Committee and a leader in the movie theater stand-in protest. (Courtesy of Bertha James)

The *Yankee Clipper* ferrying people and automobiles to Sanibel Island. The couple in the middle are identified as honeymooners. Sanibel is a popular spot for honeymoons and family vacations.

African American students await their fate in a Tallahassee courtroom following a 1963 protest against segregated movie theaters. Future State Senator Arthenia Joyner sits among a crowd of her peers.

On May 31, 220 African American students face charges of contempt for demonstrating against segregated movie theaters in Tallahassee. The Congress on Racial Equality (known as CORE) supports the students. CORE was formed in 1942 to challenge segregation laws in the United States through nonviolent protest and civil disobedience.

On June 11, Governor Farris Bryant signs into law a bill to create a new state university near Orlando. Florida Technical University will open for classes on October 7, 1968, and will change its name to the University of Central Florida in 1978.

On June 17, the United States Supreme Court bars required Bible reading and recital of the Lord's Prayer in public schools. Pinellas County schools respond by replacing Bible reading and the Lord's Prayer with moral and patriotic exercises.

On June 21, the Florida Theater and State Theater in St. Petersburg are picketed by African Americans who are refused entry. The picketing is organized by the local Youth Council. On July 16, unrestricted admission of black patrons will begin at the Florida, State, Cameo, Playhouse, and Center Theaters.

On June 26, President John F. Kennedy travels to West Berlin to give a speech of support to the citizens of the West German city. During his address Kennedy speaks of the strength of freedom: "Freedom has many difficulties and democracy is not perfect. But we have never had to put a wall up to keep our people in, to prevent them from leaving us . . . When all are free, then we . . . can look forward to that day when this city will be joined as one . . . All free men, wherever they may live, are citizens of Berlin. And, therefore, as a free man, I take pride in the words 'Ich bin ein Berliner.'" Translation: "I am a Berliner."

On July 18, picketing and sit-in protests begin at St. Augustine's downtown lunch counters to protest segregation. As

President Kennedy and Senator George Smathers in Miami on November 18, 1963.

the city prepares for its four-hundred-year anniversary celebration in 1965, civil rights leaders seize the opportunity to protest segregation in the city. Civil rights leader Andrew Young calls St. Augustine an "intractably racist town."

On August 28, two hundred thousand march on Washington, D.C., in support of civil rights reforms. Martin Luther King Jr. proclaims, "I have a dream that one day this nation will rise up and live out the true meaning of its creed: 'We hold these truths to be self-evident, that all men are created equal.'"

On September 15, amid threats by segregationists, a bomb explodes in Birmingham's predominantly black 16th Street Baptist Church, killing four little girls attending Sunday school.

President John Kennedy in a motorcade in Tampa four days before his assassination (Courtesy of the Tampa Bay Times)

On November 18, 1963, President Kennedy speaks at fiftieth anniversary of the first commercial flight from St. Petersburg-Tampa airline, just four days before he is assassinated in Dallas.

On November 18, President John Kennedy appears before ten thousand people at Al Lopez Field in Tampa, celebrating the fiftieth anniversary of the St. Petersburg-Tampa Airboat line and talking business in an address before the Florida Chamber of Commerce. According to a *St. Petersburg Times* headline, the president's talk, which includes issues ranging from monopolies to deficits to inflation, wins respect but few converts. Kennedy is the first sitting United States president to visit the area. He visited Miami the same day.

On November 22, President John F. Kennedy is shot to death by Lee Harvey Oswald while riding in a motorcade in Dallas, Texas. As Vice President Lyndon Johnson is sworn in as president, the nation and state grieve the slain leader.

Florida schools, government offices, and many businesses will close the Monday following the assassination of President Kennedy in honor of the slain president, while churches and temples hold memorial services. President Johnson will rename the Cape Canaveral area "Cape Kennedy," but after local objections, the facility will become the Kennedy Space Center at Cape Canaveral.

On December 13, the Interstate Commerce Commission approves the merger of Seaboard Air Line Railroad (SAL) and the Atlantic Coast Line Railroad (ACL), both of which have lines and stations in Florida. The new railroad is to be known as the Seaboard Coast Line Railroad.

Also in December, legendary big-band leader and jazz musician Count Basie is refused service at the Tallahassee's Mecca restaurant across the street from the gate to Florida State University after he had played a concert at FSU. He joins a civil rights picket protest outside the restaurant.

Count Basie protesting segregation at the Mecca restaurant, across the street from Florida State University, after he is refused service

A construction barge on Cross Florida Barge Canal

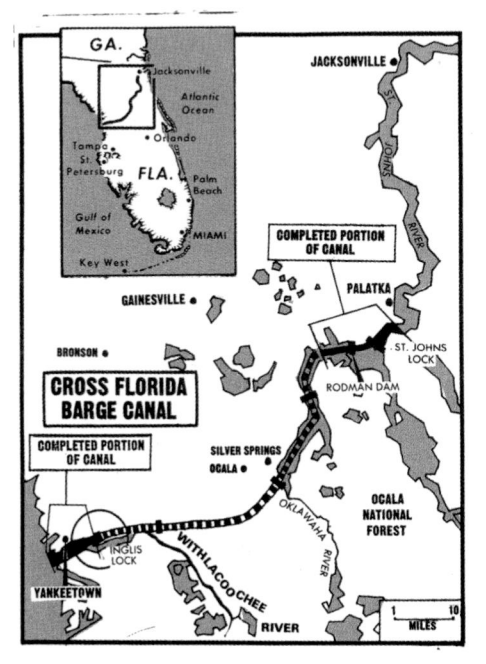

A map of the planned route for the Cross Florida Barge Canal

1964

On Thursday, February 27, President Lyndon Johnson pulls a switch to set off a dynamite explosion starting the construction of the Cross Florida Barge Canal, on the west side of the St. Johns River, south of Palatka. Proponents of the canal see it as an economic boon to Florida and an opportunity to better connect shipping in the Gulf of Mexico to the Atlantic seaboard and Europe. A canal crossing Florida had been proposed in 1826 and attempted in the 1930s. This version of the canal was authorized by Congress in 1942.

The canal will largely follow the route of the canal project scuttled in 1936, along the St. Johns River and Ocklawaha River, across a newly built canal to the Withlacoochee River, then to the Gulf of Mexico near Yankeetown. This time, however, in order to alleviate concerns from south Florida about saltwater contamination into the aquifer and harm to the water supply, the canal will use locks and dams and not be as deep. Nonetheless, opposition to the canal will build from environmentalists seeking to protect the Ocklawaha River.

Rickards High School students in class on September 3, 1967, the first day of desegregated schools in Tallahassee

On May 7, six African American parents in Pinellas County file suit objecting to the segregation policies of the Pinellas

County Schools. In *Leon Bradley, et al. v. Pinellas County Board of Public Instruction*, United States District Court Judge Joseph Lieb orders the county to submit a desegregation plan. In March 1965, Judge Lieb approves Pinellas County's desegregation plan, which calls for the immediate start of desegregation, the phasing out of African American Gibbs Junior College, and full desegregation by 1967–1968. During the desegregation era of 1967 to 1972, enrollment at private schools in the county will nearly double and will continue to increase in the years that follow, reaching over 14 percent of the total enrollment by 1981.

On May 29, a house rented for Dr. Martin Luther King Jr. in St. Augustine is sprayed with gunfire. Two days earlier, King tells a St. Augustine congregation that the city's segregation will end because "trouble don't last always."

On June 3, Edward H. White II becomes the first astronaut to walk in space, spending twenty minutes outside of his Gemini *spaceship. He will be awarded the Distinguished Service Medal, will be congratulated by President Johnson, and will get a ticker tape parade in Chicago. Newsmen camp outside the St. Petersburg Snell Isle home of White's parents during his historic flight. His father is General Edward White. On January 27, 1967, White, along with astronauts Virgil Grissom and Roger Chaffee, will be killed in a fire aboard their* Apollo I *spacecraft at Florida's Cape Canaveral.*

On June 11, civil rights leader Martin Luther King Jr. and seventeen other protesters are arrested for trespassing at St. Augustine's Monson Restaurant when they request service at the segregated establishment. Later this night, two hundred civil rights protesters will conduct a nighttime march in the city, circling the old slave market while counter-protesters jeer and throw firecrackers into the gathering. King will later describe St. Augustine as "the most lawless city I have ever been in." St. Augustine's active Ku Klux Klan chapter clashes regularly with protesters in the city.

On June 18, a St. Augustine grand jury calls for Martin Luther King Jr. and the Southern Christian Leadership Conference (SCLC) members to leave the city for one month in order to diffuse tensions, concluding that the protesters had disrupted "racial harmony." King calls the request immoral, saying that the city "never had peaceful race relations." On June 30, Florida Governor Farris Bryant will announce the formation of a biracial committee to address St. Augustine's racial issues.

Martin Luther King and Ralph Abernathy respond to press in St. Augustine

On July 3, the Civil Rights Act of 1964 is signed into law by President Lyndon Johnson. The act outlaws discrimination in public accommodations, establishes the Equal Opportunity Commission, provides voting safeguards, and authorizes the Department of Justice to file suits in support of school integration.

Referring to the Civil Rights Act of 1964, civil rights leader Andrew Young remarks, "It may be that we would not have had a Civil Rights Act without St. Augustine . . . if it hadn't provided a vivid reminder of the injustices the bill was designed to address."

On July 24, the final section of the Sunshine State Parkway, a toll-road turnpike running 265 miles from Miami to the 1-75 connection at Wildwood, is complete. The Florida State Turnpike Authority, which constructed the road, was created in 1953 by act of the Florida Legislature.

On August 7, the United States Senate passes the Gulf of Tonkin resolution authorizing the president to "take all necessary measures to repel any armed attack against the forces of the United States and to prevent future aggression." It is the basis for U.S. military expansion in Vietnam.

On August 27, Hurricane Cleo strikes Miami, the first hurricane to directly strike the city since 1950's Hurricane King, with winds of 105 mph and 135 mph gusts. The storm will sweep north, causing massive damage along the Florida Atlantic coast.

On September 11, the rock band the Beatles holds a press conference at the George Washington Hotel in Jacksonville. The band did not book rooms at the hotel due to its segregation policy, and they refuse to play at the Gator Bowl until they receive assurances that the audience will not be segregated by race at the concert.

The Beatles onstage at Jacksonville's Gator Bowl. They refuse to play until they receive assurance that the concert will not be segregated by race.

The Beatles (l-r, Paul McCartney, George Harrison, John Lennon, and Ringo Starr) at their September 11, 1964, news conference at the George Washington Hotel in Jacksonville

Mitzi, a bottle-nosed dolphin shown here leaping over a bar at Santini's Porpoise School in Marathon (Florida Keys), plays Flipper in the original 1963 movie *Flipper*. In the popular television series based in south Florida, Flipper is played by five female dolphins and one male dolphin.

On September 15, the first episode of the television series *Flipper* is broadcast on NBC. It will continue until April 15, 1967. The Flipper character is a bottlenose dolphin living in Coral Key Park and Marine Preserve (fictional) in south Florida. He is friends with Porter Ricks, Chief Warden, and his sons Sandy and Bud. It is filmed in Miami and Key Biscayne. Flipper has many adventures with the Ricks family protecting the park. The show exposes the nation in a positive way to the south Florida life as the characters interact with the ocean and its creatures.

President Lyndon Baines Johnson surveys Hurricane Dora damage in Jacksonville. To the left of the president are U.S. Senator George Smathers, Governor Farris Bryant, and Jacksonville Mayor Haydon Burns.

Also in September, Hurricane Dora hits Florida's Atlantic coast, striking St. Augustine with winds of 125 miles per hour and a twelve-foot storm tide. Jacksonville and Fernandina will also be hit with a ten-foot storm tide, and there is a great deal of flooding along the St. Johns River. Total damage is estimated at $250 million.

In October, construction is finished on a thirteen-mile stretch of Interstate 4 in Hillsborough County, leaving segments in St. Petersburg and Daytona Beach to be built before it will be complete from Interstate 95 near Daytona Beach to St. Petersburg. The Interstate 4 section going through downtown Orlando is designed to handle seventy thousand vehicles each day.

Also this year, the *Jackie Gleason Show* begins to broadcast from the Fillmore Theatre in Miami Beach. Each week the show is introduced with the words "from the sun and fun capital of the world," and Gleason ends the show proclaiming, "The Miami Beach audience is the greatest audience in the world."

Actor Jackie Gleason and President Gerald Ford play golf in Ft. Lauderdale.

1965

On February 13, President Johnson orders Operation Rolling Thunder, a bombing campaign against North Vietnam. American troop deployment in South Vietnam increases to 154,000.

On April 16, ground is broken for construction of the University of West Florida in Escambia County. The Florida legislature had originally authorized the university in 1955.

On July 1, opening ceremonies are held for the new Bay Campus of the University of South Florida at the former Maritime Service Training Base on Bayboro Harbor. USF pledges that "the entire resources" of the university are behind the campus. USF promises to start 250 freshman students next term and to provide graduate programs at the campus in business administration, engineering, and education. Oceanographic research will also be stressed. Today, the university is independently accredited as USF St. Petersburg.

On August 6, President Lyndon Johnson signs into law the Voting Rights Act of 1965, prohibiting states from using poll taxes, literacy tests, or similar methods of impeding voter registration for minorities.

Beginning August 12, the Watts area of Los Angeles erupts in race riots after police arrest an African American for drunk driving. Thirty-four are killed, more than one thousand are injured, and four thousand are arrested. Twenty thousand National Guardsmen are activated by Governor Edmund Brown to control the riots, which cause $40 million in property damage.

Maxwell Courtney accepts his diploma from FSU President John Champion, becoming the first African American student to graduate from Florida State University.

Also on August 12, Maxwell Courtney becomes the first African American to graduate from Florida State University.

On September 7, at night, Hurricane Betsy brushes Miami as a Category 3 storm heading south. In an attempt to avoid the approaching storm, the 441-foot freighter *Amaryllis* runs aground on Singer Island near Palm Beach. After many attempts to free the ship, the effort and ship will be abandoned by the owners. Years of abandonment, oil seepage, danger of coral reef damage, and police raids of teenage parties aboard the ship raise increased public concern about the nuisance. Finally,

on August 22, 1968, the *Amaryllis* is towed three-quarters of a mile out to sea and sunk in 85 feet of water to create an artificial reef.

The 441-foot freighter *Amaryllis* runs aground on Singer Island near Palm Beach while attempting to flee Hurricane Betsy.

Hurricane Betsy will strike Key Largo on the morning of September 8 and sweep through the Florida Keys into the Gulf of Mexico. The hurricane will make landfall on the Louisiana coast near Grand Isle, with wind gusts of 160 mph. The storm will cause $1.42 billion in damage. Fifty-three storm deaths will be reported in Louisiana and Mississippi.

On October 10, Cuban dictator Fidel Castro opens the Port of Camarioca for Cubans who want to leave for America. The port will remain open until November 15, and almost three thousand Cubans will flee. From September 28, 1965, through April 7, 1973, Freedom Flights will bring almost three hundred thousand Cubans to the United States. Large populations of Cubans will settle in Miami and a part of the city west of downtown will become known as "Little Havana." By 2014, 70 percent of the Miami population will be Hispanic and 54 percent will be Cuban.

Also this year, the state legislature establishes the Downtown Development

Authority for Ft. Lauderdale, an independent taxing district charged with the revitalization of the city's decaying downtown. The DDA is charged with creating a master plan and helping to fund building, green space, and transportation projects to revitalize the district. Ft. Lauderdale's DDA is similar to efforts in other large Florida cities that will advance during the coming decades. The suburbanization of America from post-World War II through the 1960s resulted in the decay of the country's central cities, including those in Florida, necessitating action. Over the next forty-five years, many of the Florida's big city downtowns will see a resurgence in employment and urban living.

1966

On September 2, the Miami Dolphins, the newest American Football League franchise, play their first game against the Oakland Raiders at the Orange Bowl. The Raiders beat the Dolphins 23-14. Miami will finish their first regular season with a record of 3-11. The team's first win will be a 24-7 victory over the Denver Broncos on October 16, 1966. The franchise was awarded in 1965 to lawyer Joe Robbie and actor Danny Thomas. The name "Dolphins" was selected in a contest that attracted almost twenty thousand entries, which included such proposed names as Missiles, Moons, Sharks, Mariners, and Suns.

1967

On January 3, Claude R. Kirk Jr., whose Jacksonville professions have included law, insurance, and investments, takes office as the thirty-sixth governor of Florida. He is Florida's first Republican governor since Marcellus L. Sterns took office in 1874 during Reconstruction. In his inaugural address, Governor Kirk promises a vig-

orous war on crime to be led by Miami security firm executive George Wackenhut. He also favors reapportionment to provide for a more representative legislature and uses his speech to call an early legislative session to revise the "antiquated constitution." He declares a war on slums; sets a goal for Florida to be number one in education; promises to fight air and water pollution; and outlines various efforts for economic development.

On June 11, at 6:25 P.M., Martin Chambers is shot in the back by a white police officer on Central Avenue near downtown Tampa. The nineteen-year-old black man had been running, with two others, from pursuing police officers who suspected the men of burglary at Tampa Photo Supply. Angry crowds gather in response to the shooting, and three days of rioting begin, with looting, trashing, and burning of buildings in the city's black business district. Five hundred Florida National Guard troops, 250 local law enforcement officers, and 235 Florida Highway Patrol troopers are called to duty. The Hillsborough State Attorney will later hold that the shooting of Chambers was justified, despite community protests.

In addition to Tampa, in the "long hot summer" of 1967, race riots break out in Cincinnati, Buffalo, Newark, Detroit, Milwaukee, and other American cities. Anger over the treatment of African Americans by police officers and the continuing demands for civil rights result in national tension.

On July 16, St. Petersburg's second "Love-In" draws about five hundred young people to Williams Park. According to the *St. Petersburg Times,* the hippie boys attending the Love-In wore long hair, tight pants, and a bandanna or "way-out" hat, while the hippie girls wore mini dresses or shorts with no shoes. Attendees carry signs saying, "Love means peace, not war"; "Be happy"; and "Free love for a free world." The Love-Ins are part of the "Summer of Love," which began in June at San Francisco's Monterey Pop Festival attended by fifty thousand.

On July 30, riots break out in West Palm Beach and Riviera Beach after an altercation between two African American men and local police attempting to make an arrest at the Blue Heron Bar. The police arrest forty-five people in connection with the riots, which cause an estimated $350,000 in damage to Mullins Lumber Yard.

Also on July 30, the worst race riot in American history ends in Detroit, leaving thirty-eight dead and over $500 million in damage.

On September 30, President Johnson signs a $70 billion defense appropriation. By June of next year the U.S. military presence in Vietnam will increase to 525,000.

Also this year, the Florida legislature passes the Government-in-the-Sunshine law providing for open government meetings. Led by Florida Governor Reubin Askew in 1976, voters will pass the Sunshine Amendment to the Florida constitution, providing for public officials to disclose their personal finances and campaign finances and providing limitations on post-public service lobbying. Together, these laws will be referred to as the "Sunshine Laws," which are in addition to the Public Records Law passed in 1909.

1968

Public school teachers on strike in Orlando

On February 16, Florida's public school teachers elect to stage the nation's first statewide walkout to begin on February 19. The circuit court will issue an order enjoining the Florida Education Association and National Education Association from counseling or coercing teachers to quit their jobs, but the unions remain defiant. Thousands of teachers who elect to join the effort resign from their jobs. The state's schools are kept open with non-striking teachers and new hires, and on March 8 the FEA agrees to send the remaining holdout teachers back to work.

On April 4, Civil Rights leader Martin Luther King Jr. is shot to death during the Memphis sanitation workers strike. Riots break out in more than one hundred cities across the nation in response to the killing.

Firefighters attempt to put out the blaze at a grocery store burned during a riot in Tallahassee following the assassination of Martin Luther King Jr. Travis Crow, 19, is inside the blaze, dying. His family owns the grocery store.

Following the assassination of Dr. King, police in Florida report rioting and the use of Molotov cocktails to burn businesses and residences in Pensacola, Tallahassee, Gainesville, Ft. Pierce, Pompano Beach, Tampa, and Jacksonville. Nineteen-year-old Travis Crow will die in Tallahassee when a firebomb is thrown into his family's grocery store. Governor Claude Kirk works with state law enforcement to develop a statewide strategy to respond to the violence.

On April 10, four hundred people attend a memorial observance at Jack Russell Stadium in Clearwater for Dr. Martin Luther King Jr. "Not just one man pulled the trigger," says Rev. Thomas Larkens.

On June 5, Robert Kennedy, candidate for president and brother of slain President John Kennedy, is shot after a California primary victory speech in a Los Angeles hotel. He will die the next day.

On August 5–8, the Republican National Convention is held at the Miami Beach Convention Center. Miami Beach will also be picked for both parties' conventions in 1972. Richard Nixon, who served as vice president with President

Eisenhower from 1953 to 1961, is nominated as the Republican's presidential candidate, and Maryland Governor Spiro T. Agnew is selected as Nixon's vice presidential running mate. Nixon was also the Republican's presidential nominee in 1960, but he lost the presidential race to John Kennedy. This year, Nixon will win in November. The new president will maintain a "Winter White House" in Miami's Key Biscayne, near the home of his longtime friend and confident, Florida banker and businessman Charles "Bebe" Robozo.

California Governor Ronald Reagan campaigning for the Republican presidential nomination in Fort Lauderdale. It will be twelve more years before he is elected to the White House.

Nixon supporters at the 1968 Republican National Convention in Miami Beach

On October 1, the governments of Jacksonville and Duval County officially merge to create the consolidated City of Jacksonville. The consolidation was approved by a voter referendum in 1967. Six prior referenda for annexation were rejected by voters outside the city limits between 1960 and 1965. This time, the movement toward consolidation follows many problems in the community, among them being funding challenges in the city limits, the indictment of multiple city officials, and the simultaneous disac-crediting of all fifteen of Duval County's public high schools. Expressed reasons for consolidation include lower taxes, increased economic development, unifica-tion of the community, and more effective administration. The resulting city limits cover 841 square miles, twenty times larger than the city's prior size, making it the largest city in land area in the world at this time. Four smaller cities in Duval remained autonomous, including Jacksonville Beach, Atlantic Beach, Neptune Beach, and Baldwin.

On October 18, Hurricane Gladys, with winds of eighty-five miles per hour, passes Florida's west coast forty miles offshore en route to a landing at Crystal River. It will also impact Cedar Key and northeast Florida. The storm will leave five dead and $6.7 million in damage.

Also in October, Interstate 75 is completed to a Tampa junction with Interstate 4, which continues southwest to St. Petersburg and is today known as 1-275. By 1999, I-75 will run from Michigan south to Naples, cross Florida along Alligator Alley, and connect with State Highway 826 in Miami.

On November 5, Florida voters adopt a new constitution that replaces the 1885 constitution. Among the most significant changes, the new constitution authorizes the establishment of home rule at both the city and county level, transferring signif-icant power from the legislature to local governments.

1969

On Sunday, July 20, at 10:56 P.M., Ameri-can astronaut Neil Armstrong becomes the first human to step onto the surface of the moon.

Apollo 11 lifts off from the Kennedy Space Center at Florida's Cape Canaveral, en route to the moon.

On July 24, 1969, separated by the Mobile Quarantine Facility window, President Richard Nixon greets the crew of Apollo 11 upon their return to Earth. Left to right: Neil Armstrong, Michael Collins, and Edwin Aldrin.

As his foot touches the moon he proclaims: "That's one small step for man, one giant leap for mankind."

Armstrong's ship, *Apollo 11,* lifted off from Florida's Kennedy Space Center with Armstrong as mission commander, astronaut Edwin Aldrin Jr., who will become the second man to walk on the moon, and astronaut Michael Collins, who orbits the moon in the command module. When the "Eagle" lunar module touches down earlier at 4:18 P.M. in the moon's Sea of Tranquility, Armstrong radios Mission Control in Houston that "The Eagle has landed."

On August 16, a four-day music festival begins in Bethel, New York, at the farm of Max Yasgur. The gathering known as "Woodstock" features many future rock legends including Jimi Hendrix, Jefferson Airplane, The Who, Credence Clearwater Revival, and Joan Baez and draws crowds estimated at three hundred thousand to seven hundred thousand.

On November 13, one hundred college students from Pinellas and Hillsborough Counties travel by train to antiwar protests in Washington, D.C. One hundred and sixty students from Florida Presbyterian College, today's Eckerd College, travel by automobile to the capital. The Florida Presbyterian students had planned to use student association funds to make the trip, but Pinellas Circuit Court Judge Robert Beach issues an injunction preventing use of the funds. Locally, Florida Presbyterian students plan two days of events beginning with a sunrise memorial service and including a roll call of Americans killed in Vietnam.

On November 15, 250,000 protestors attend the largest anti-war rally in American history, marching in Washington, D.C., from the Capitol Building to the Washington Monument. The number of American military personnel in Vietnam reaches a peak this year at 540,000 troops.

Astronauts Neil Armstrong and Buzz Aldrin plant an American flag on the moon after completing the first nonstop Florida-to-moon flight.

Also this year, a U.S. Department of Defense program called "Advanced Research Projects Agency Network" (ARPANET) is established to provide a secure communications network for the defense industry. The National Science Foundation (NSF) will take over the technology and expand the network to handle a broader user base and greater traffic. By the mid-1990s, the network, to be known as the "Internet," will serve more than twenty million users in more than one hundred countries. By 2010 that number will grow to 2.023 billion users worldwide.

1970

On January 1, President Richard Nixon declares that the 1970s will be the decade of the environment. He will later pledge to "repair the damage we have done to our air, our land, and our water." President Nixon will create the Environmental Protection Agency and will sign the Clean Air Act, the Endangered Species Act, and the National Environmental Policy Act.

On January 16, the Everglades Jetport Pact is entered into by the federal government, the state of Florida, and Dade County, effectively stopping the planned Everglades Jetport, which had been under construction in the Big Cypress region of the Everglades. The planned airport included six runways and a thousand-foot-wide transportation corridor linking both coasts with a new highway and monorail. It was to be the largest airport in the world, five times the size of JFK International. Significant concerns over the environmental impact of the airport were raised by Friends of the Everglades, Marjory Stoneman Douglas, and many others. Governor Claude Kirk opposes the project and President Richard Nixon kills the jetport after one runway is complete. The runway is now the Dade-Collier Training and Transition Airport, an aviation training facility located on the east end of the Big Cypress National Preserve.

A 1970 antiwar protest march by FSU students in Tallahassee

On February 13, the 691-foot Greek tanker *Delian Apollon* runs aground in Tampa Bay, about one mile south of the Gandy Bridge, triggering a major oil spill. The tanker, headed to Florida Power's Weedon Island plant, struck the sand in a heavy fog. St. Petersburg's beaches, seawalls, boats, and seabirds from Weedon Island to Pinellas Point will be affected by the oil spill, which causes damages initially estimated in the millions of dollars.

On April 18, five hundred Vietnam War protestors march in downtown St. Petersburg chanting "End the war." At a Straub Park rally, University of Florida Professor Robert Canning urges the demonstrators to "Smash the system." After the speech, Canning is arrested on charges of using obscene language for saying "g.. d..." during his talk. As police work to contain the crowd, which becomes "disorderly," a total of eleven protestors are arrested. Local and statewide anti-war groups at the rally include the Junta of Militant Organizations, the Community Liberation Movement, the Anti-war Coalition, People for Peace, the Malcolm X Community Liberation Front, Veterans for Peace, and "a few war-painted yippies."

On May 4, National Guardsmen fire on two hundred Vietnam War protesters at Kent State University in Ohio, killing four.

On May 11, reflecting a state and national trend, the Pinellas County School Board approves a more liberal student dress code allowing girls to wear slacks, walking shorts, and boots, and allowing boys to wear shorts, sandals, and shoes without socks. However, about two hundred boys at Northeast High and Boca Ciega High are warned to cut their hair. Most comply, but several are suspended for failure to get a trim.

This fall in Tallahassee, "Radical Jack" Lieberman teaches a noncredit course at Florida State University's Center for Participant Education. The course is entitled "How to make a revolution in the U.S.A." After a series of Lieberman-led protests and complaints from Florida legislators, FSU president Stanley Marshall will expel Lieberman from the university.

1971

On January 5, Democrat Reubin O. Askew, a lawyer and legislator from Pensacola, becomes the thirty-seventh governor of Florida. Governor Askew identifies the debate for the next four years to include "tax reform, education, preserving the balance of nature, transportation and government efficiency." He promises to fight for a corporate income tax and to oppose any increases in the "burdensome consumer taxes and property taxes on middle and low income families." With respect to higher education, the governor argues that the "current focus on campus unrest across the country should not distract from the tremendous progress Florida universities have made." He intends also to focus on environmental protection and economic growth, including "our two largest industries—tourism and agricultural."

On January 15, responding to concerns from environmentalists, the district court issues a temporary injunction halting construction of the Cross Florida Barge Canal, begun in 1964. Four days later, at the urging of former Florida Governor Claude Kirk, President Richard Nixon will sign an executive order suspending work on the canal, effectively killing the project. When the work stops, the canal is one-third complete at a cost of $74 million. In 1990 the canal route will be dedicated as a greenway. On November 28, 1990, President George H.W. Bush will sign a bill de-authorizing the canal and, in 1998, the 110-mile greenway will be renamed the Marjorie Harris Carr Cross Florida Greenway, in honor of the environmental activist who fought the canal project. The fate of the completed Kirkpatrick Dam and Rodman Reservoir along the canal route will be debated for years to come.

On April 14, 2,500 people attend a dedication ceremony led by Florida Governor Reubin Askew for the new $83 million Tampa International Airport.

On April 20, in Swann v. Charlotte-Mecklenburg Board of Education, *the United States Supreme Court rules that, when school authorities fail in their affirmative duty to create a unitary system in which racial discrimination is eliminated "root and branch," then the federal district courts have broad powers to fashion a remedy. In* Swann, *a case involving a school district encompassing Charlotte, North Carolina, the Supreme Court includes among such broad district court authority the power to force cross-district busing of students to create a unitary school system.*

On May 1, the national Railroad Passenger Corporation (Amtrak) is established with the mission of taking over much of America's passenger rail service. Passenger service to southwest Florida will be eliminated.

On May 3, seven thousand antiwar visitors are arrested in Washington, D.C., blocking an attempt to close down the Capitol.

On October 1, Walt Disney Resort near Orlando opens the Magic Kingdom theme park with magical lands, a Cinderella castle, and two hotels. Beginning in 1964, an unnamed developer had been acquiring millions of dollars of farmland southwest of Orlando. After speculation grew about the purchases, Disney confirmed on November 15, 1965, that the

magic was coming. It cost $400 million to build on 27,500 acres. The attraction, and others that follow, will fundamentally transform the Orlando region and tourism in Florida.

At a press conference on November 15, 1965, Walt Disney, Governor Haydon Burns, and Roy Disney announce that Disney World is coming to Florida. The theme park opened in October 1971.

1972

Leon County Sheriff Raymond Hamlin with student protesters at an anti-war march at Florida State University on May 11, 1972

On May 11, students at Florida State University in Tallahassee march in protest to the war in Vietnam.

On June 17, police officers arrest seven burglars who are breaking into the Democratic National Committee's headquarters at the Watergate apartment complex in Washington, D.C. The break-in will trigger a series of events that will lead to the resignation of President Richard Nixon, a first in U.S. history.

On June 19, Hurricane Agnes approaches the Florida Panhandle as a Category 1 storm, striking near Panama City. It continues through Georgia to the northeast, exiting into the Atlantic and again strikes land in the northeast United States. Agnes will cause 122 deaths and $2.1 billion in damage.

On July 10–13, the Democratic National Convention is held at the Miami Beach Convention Center. South Dakota Senator George McGovern is selected as the Democrats' presidential nominee and Missouri Senator Thomas Eagleton is selected for vice president.

On August 21–23, the Republican National Convention is held at the Miami Beach Convention Center, the same location as both the Democrats' July convention, and the 1968 Republican convention. President Richard Nixon receives his party's presidential nomination for the third time, the first two being in 1960 and 1968. The convention is targeted by an estimated three thousand protesters, mostly against the Vietnam War.

Governor Rubin Askew at the Democratic National Convention in Miami Beach

Anti-war protesters in Miami Beach rally against the Vietnam War at the 1972 Republican National Convention in Miami Beach.

On September 5, terrorists claiming to be a Palestinian guerrilla group called Black September kill two Israelis—a coach and an athlete—and take nine other Israeli coaches and athletes hostage at the Munich Olympics. The terrorists demand the release of two hundred Arab guerrillas jailed in Israel. By the end of the day the hostages, five of the terrorists, and one West German police officer will be dead after a failed rescue attempt.

Also in September, Miami's new Florida International University will open for upper-division students at the site of the former Tamiami Airport.

Also in the fall, the University of North Florida opens classes in Jacksonville as an upper-division university. The university will admit freshmen and sophomores in 1984.

On Friday, December 29, Eastern Airlines Flight 401, a Lockheed L-1011, takes off from New York's Kennedy Airport on the way to Miami. While approaching Miami International, the indicator that signals the landing gear has lowered fails to light. While the crew checks to see if the gear is down, the autopilot is accidently disengaged. The plane begins to descend over the Everglades. By the time the pilot recognizes the descent, it is too late and, just before midnight, the plane crashes into the swamp. After a harrowing rescue effort and many miraculous events, 75 people survive but 101 are killed, including the captain, first officer, a flight engineer, and two of the flight attendants.

1973

On January 14, the Miami Dolphins defeat the Washington Redskins 14 to 7 in Super Bowl VII at the Memorial Coliseum in Los Angeles. The Dolphins, at 17 and 0, become the first undefeated team in NFL history. During the Super Bowl game, Dolphin kicker Garo Yepremian's effort to handle a blocked field goal results in a Redskins touchdown runback that will become part of football folklore. The Dolphins will win their second Super Bowl championship next year, on January 13, 1974.

On March 7, Captain David S. Gray Jr. of Treasure Island in Pinellas County is among eighty American POWs released from North Vietnam to arrive at Maxwell Air Force Base in Montgomery, Alabama. His wife greets him with homemade chocolate chip cookies and Chivas Regal Scotch. Mrs. Gray traveled to Paris twice to seek information about prisoners in Vietnam and was active in the National League of Families of Prisoners of War.

On August 12, the last U.S. ground troops leave Vietnam.

On October 10, Vice President Spiro T. Agnew resigns from office after pleading no contest on a charge of income tax evasion. On December 6, Gerald R. Ford will be sworn in as vice president after his appointment by President Nixon and approval from Congress.

On October 17, Arab oil-producing nations ban oil shipments to the United States in response to U.S. support of Israel in its recent war with Egypt and Syria—the Yom Kippur War. Gasoline prices rise and shortages cause motorists to wait hours for a turn at the pumps. President Nixon warns of the worst energy crisis since World War II. The embargo will continue until March 1974.

On December 15, SeaWorld opens in Orlando, the third park in the SeaWorld chain, after San Diego and Aurora, Ohio. It features a mixture of animal exhibits and shows. Anheuser-Busch, which owns Busch Gardens in Tampa, will purchase the SeaWorld parks in 1989.

On December 28, President Richard Nixon signs the Endangered Species Act of 1973. The

Act protects various species of plants and animals facing extinction by limiting land development and man-made environmental hazards.

Among other species protected under the act are the American bald eagle and the American alligator. The latter had previously been listed as endangered in 1967 at a time when alligator hunting and habitat loss threatened their survival. The 1973 act prohibits alligator hunting. By 1987 the American alligator will recover to the point that it will be removed from the endangered species list. The U.S. Fish and Wildlife Service will continue to regulate the harvest and trade of alligators and, beginning in 1988, Florida will conduct limited annual alligator harvests.

Law enforcement officials with poached alligator hides. By the 1960s, hunting and habitat loss will threaten the species' survival. After protections are put in place, the alligator population will recover and, beginning in 1988, annual alligator harvests will be conducted.

Late in the year, MITS, an electronics firm, introduces the Altair 8800, a construction kit computer costing $399. It is the first broadly used personal computer. In 1977, Bill Gates will start Microsoft with the objective of developing a compiler for the Altair. By the end of the century, there will be over fifty million personal computers in use worldwide, and the success of Microsoft will make Bill Gates the wealthiest person in the United States. By 2008, more

than one billion personal computers will be in use worldwide.

1974

The Rowdies celebrate their second NASL Soccer Bowl championship at Al Lang Stadium in downtown St. Petersburg in 2012. (Courtesy of the Tampa Bay Rowdies)

In July, the Rowdies are founded, an American professional soccer team playing in Tampa with the North American Soccer League. The team will play its first season in 1975, and will move to downtown St. Petersburg in 2011. The Rowdies will win the NASL Soccer Bowl in 1975 and 2012. The Rowdies join NASL's Miami Toros, which started in 1972 and will become the Ft. Lauderdale Strikers in 1977.

On August 9, President Richard M. Nixon resigns the presidency under threat of impeachment for actions relating to the break-in at Democratic Party offices at the Watergate, in Washington, D.C. Vice President Gerald R. Ford is sworn in as president of the United States.

On September 8, President Gerald Ford grants an unconditional pardon to former President Richard M. Nixon for all federal crimes that he "committed or may have committed or taken part in" while in office. The action helps the nation turn a page on the Watergate scandal, but it will become a significant issue in Ford's attempt to retain the presidency in the

1976 election, which he will lose to Georgia governor and peanut farmer Jimmy Carter.

President Gerald Ford pardons former President Richard Nixon on September 8, 1974. Here, Ford meets with Egypt's President Anwar Sadat in November 1975 at the Deerwood Country Club in Jacksonville.

On October 11, President Gerald Ford establishes the Big Cypress National Preserve in south Florida. The 728,000-acre preserve, approximately the size of the state of Delaware, is located about thirty miles east of Naples. It is west of the Everglades Wildlife Management Area, east of the Picayune Strand State Forest, and north of the Everglades National Park. About one-third of the preserve is covered with cypress trees, although the old, giant bald cypress trees are gone. In the 1920–1950 era, hundreds of millions of board feet of pine timber and cypress were logged out. The movement to create the preserve follows the failed 1968 effort to create the Everglades Jetport on the Big Cypress property.

1975

Governor Reubin Askew with presidential candidate Jimmy Carter at a 1976 event in Jacksonville

On January 7, Governor Reubin Askew becomes the first Florida governor to be sworn into office for a second consecutive four-year term, thanks to the changes in the 1968 Florida constitution that eliminated the prohibition against successive terms and permits a governor to succeed himself if he has not completed six years of office. The focus of Governor Askew's second inaugural address is on the economy: "[P]ain and poverty still linger in the cities and in the countryside . . . Unemployment lines are longer. Prices are higher. And hopes are fewer." He acknowledges the need to address the state's large budget deficit but rules out gambling taxes as a solution: "Simple answers, such as those offered by supporters of legalized casino gambling, are no answers at all. The social and economic costs of such an enterprise would far outweigh any possible benefits."

On April 30, South Vietnam surrenders to communist forces, ending the war in Vietnam in which over 56,000 Americans died.

Joseph Hatchett is appointed by Governor Reubin Askew to be the first African American Florida Supreme Court justice.

The former Fort Harrison Hotel in downtown Clearwater becomes part of the headquarters complex of the Church of Scientology.

1976

The marquee at Tampa Stadium announces the October 17 game against Seattle and the October 24 game against Miami during the inaugural season of the Tampa Bay Buccaneers.

On September 2, Governor Askew appoints Joseph Woodrow Hatchett as Florida's first African American supreme court justice. Hatchett grew up in Clearwater's south Greenwood area.

On October 27, Clearwater's Fort Harrison Hotel is purchased by Southern Land Sales and Development Corp. for $2.3 million. A few days later, the former Bank of Clearwater building is purchased by the corporation for $550,000. In January 1976, it will be announced that L. Ron Hubbard's Church of Scientology controls Southern Land Sales and Development Corp. and thus owns the properties. The group will move the organization's worldwide headquarters to Clearwater. The Scientologists will eventually own a dozen properties in Pinellas and employ more than six hundred staff members. Their presence will grow into the next century.

On September 12, the Tampa Bay Buccaneers play their first National Football League regular season game, losing to the Houston Oilers. The Bucs will go 0–14 their first season and will lose a National Football League record twenty-six consecutive games before winning their first game against the New Orleans Saints on December 11, 1977.

1977

On January 19, temperatures in south Florida fall to the low 30s and in the early morning it snows in Miami and as far south as Homestead. Although snow flurries hit windshields and settle a bit, it is not enough to measure so it is designated "a trace of snow."

In June, Jacksonville Mayor Hans Tanzler celebrates the completion of the St. Johns River cleanup effort by skiing along the river with Cypress Gardens performers. The aggressive cleanup includes, among other actions, significant upgrades to the sewage system. In 1968, industrial and agricultural pollution, toxic chemicals, and fifteen million gallons per day of untreated sewage flowed from seventy-seven untreated outfalls into the river.

1978

On January 15, two coeds from St. Petersburg are beaten to death in the Chi Omega sorority house at Florida State University. The attack is a national and local tragedy. Serial killer Ted Bundy will be arrested one month later and will be executed at Starke prison on January 24, 1989. Before he dies, Bundy confesses to thirty-one murders in nine states.

Serial killer Ted Bundy after his arrest

The electric chair at the Starke prison, about twenty-five miles northeast of Gainesville. The note accompanying the photograph reads: "This is a file photo of Florida's electric chair at Florida State Prison at Starke, Fla. Murderer Theodore Bundy is scheduled to be executed Wednesday morning." Notice the witness chairs in the background.

On May 2, the *Phosphor Conveyor*, a large phosphate ship that regularly docks at the Port of Tampa, loses power and appears heading for a collision course with the Sunshine Skyway Bridge. The ship pilot slows down by using the ship's anchors. The vessel stops forty feet short of the bridge. A *St. Petersburg Times* article calls the possibility of a ship hitting the bridge a "problem nobody ever thought of."

On June 28, the United States Supreme Court rules that Allan Bakke, a white male, had been the victim of reverse discrimination by the University of California at Davis Medical School.

1979

On January 2, Democrat D. Robert "Bob" Graham, a lawyer and legislator who has worked in his family's cattle and real estate businesses in the Miami area, becomes the thirty-eighth governor of Florida. In his inaugural speech, Governor Graham describes the hopes and dreams of Floridians whom he met while doing workdays around the state during his campaign—oil riggers in Jay, fishermen in Apalachicola, tomato pickers in Collier County, Palatka paper mill workers, Cuban sandwich makers in Ybor City, and others. He calls on Floridians to become involved personally in the government and "in all the rich and varied life of Florida."

On March 26, in Washington, D.C., President Anwar el-Sadat of Egypt and Prime Minister Menachem Begin of Israel sign a landmark peace treaty for the Mideast.

On November 4, a mob of Iranian students seize the United States Embassy in Teheran, taking ninety hostages. The final hostages will not be released until January 20, 1981, after President Ronald Reagan is sworn into office.

On December 14, the Seminole Tribe of Florida opens a bingo hall at their

Jimmy Carter campaigns for Bob Graham for Florida governor. Graham is elected the state's thirty-eighth governor and takes office in January 1979.

reservation near Hollywood, Florida. The high-stakes game violates state law and the state moves to close it down. Eventually, on October 5, 1981 the United States Fifth Circuit Court of Appeals, in *Seminole Tribe of Florida v. Butterworth*, rules that Florida cannot regulate the high-stakes bingo hall on the Seminole reservation. The decision paves the way for expansion of gambling on reservation land.

> **❝** *The future doesn't belong to the fainthearted; it belongs to the brave. The Challenger crew was pulling us into the future, and we'll continue to follow them.* **❞**
>
> **President Ronald Reagan, after the explosion of America's space shuttle after it lifted off from Florida's Cape Canaveral**

Chapter 8

Hope and Growth: 1980 through 2010

The era begins with Republican Ronald Reagan, former governor of California, running for president on a campaign of hope and confidence in the nation. He compares America to a shining city on a hill. After winning he sets out to accomplish that goal, emerging as a strong adversary of the Soviet Union and communism—a focus that ultimately results in Cold War victory and the tumbling of the Berlin Wall.

The Information Age goes into full swing as personal computing merges with the Internet, a combination of inventions that will reshape the world and increase the rapidity of change forever.

America's first Space Shuttle, *Columbia*, lifts off the launch pad at Cape Canaveral on April 12, 1981. A new era begins.

NASA and the Florida Space Coast shift focus to a reusable space shuttle program, an effort that experiences both triumph and tragedy. Mickey Mouse significantly expands his footprint in central Florida and other theme parks follow, further shifting and expanding the center of gravity for the Florida tourism industry. New state universities are established and existing universities grow in size and prominence. More professional sports teams come to the state in Miami, St. Petersburg, Orlando, Jacksonville, and Tampa, while IndyCar professional auto racing arrives on the streets of downtown St. Petersburg.

At the turn of the millennium, America becomes embroiled in one of the most controversial elections in United States history, and Florida is the center of the political world. After Florida recounts, hanging chads, military ballots, and court cases, former president George H.W. Bush's eldest son becomes President George W. Bush.

The new president's brother, Florida governor Jeb Bush, advances an aggressive effort to improve education and expand the state's economic base, especially in the technology and research fields. Governor Bush receives high marks nationally for his steady response to a dramatic period of hurricane activity, and he advances an ambitious plan to restore the environmental condition of the Everglades.

On September 11, 2001, terrorists kill thousands in New York, Washington, D.C., and Pennsylvania, launching the United States into a war with a global terrorists, one that will be vigorously prosecuted by the new president.

Toward the end of this era, Lehman Brothers investment firm files for bankruptcy protection, the most significant indicator of a financial collapse that will send Florida, the United States, and the world into the greatest economic downturn since the Great Depression. The Great Recession, as it will be labeled, results from a federal policy encouraging massive real estate lending to borrowers who are ultimately unable to pay their debt and the securitization of the resulting "subprime mortgages" in a manner that will drag the stock market down as real estate values

> Throughout this book events in Florida are set in Roman (non-italics), and events outside Florida are set in *italics*.

plummet. Despite the national downturn, the state's population will almost double during this era.

In 2009, America will inaugurate President Barak Obama. The former United States Senator is the first African American elected to the highest office in the nation.

The era, and this look at Florida's past, closes with the nation in economic uncertainty—but with a state whose people have always had confidence that its natural and individual assets will ultimately result in a return to prosperity and sunshine once again. Newly elected Governor Rick Scott echoes that confidence predicting that the coming years will be "the most exciting time in our history."

Timeline

1980

Salvage workers lift the Coast Guard buoy tender *Blackthorn* off the bottom of Tampa Bay. The ship sank in less than five minutes after colliding with the *Capricorn*. (Courtesy of the Tampa Bay Times)

On the night of January 28, the Coast Guard buoy tender *Blackthorn* is heading back to its home port in Galveston, Texas, after a four-month overhaul in Tampa. The *Capricorn*, a 605-foot tanker, is carrying 150,000 barrels of oil from St. Croix to a power-generating plant on Weedon Island in north St. Petersburg.

The *Blackthorn* sails under the Skyway Bridge heading out to the Gulf, while the *Capricorn* steers toward the Skyway. As the two ships proceed forward they collide near the bridge. One of the *Capricorn's* two 13,500-pound anchors cuts into the *Blackthorn*, tearing the ship open on the port side. The buoy tender is dragged by the anchor, then capsizes and sinks in almost fifty feet of water. Twenty-three seamen aboard the *Blackthorn* die in the tragedy. The *Capricorn* sustains only minor damage. The channel will be closed for three weeks, and Blackthorn Memorial Park will be established two miles from the location of the collision on the north side of the Skyway.

On February 2, the United States Olympic hockey team defeats Finland 4–2 and wins the gold medal. The U.S. team had earlier upset Russia in a "David and Goliath" matchup.

On February 16, the 720-foot oil carrier *Jonna Dan* slams into one of the main piers supporting the steel superstructure of the southbound span of the Sunshine Skyway Bridge. Damage to the bridge appears minor, but the Florida Department of Transportation concedes that if the ship had dealt the pier a direct, hard blow it would have toppled the bridge. On February 19, the *St. Petersburg Times*, in an editorial recounting several close calls involving the Skyway, urges Governor Graham to order immediate DOT studies on how to protect the bridge from ship traffic.

The *El Dorado* arrives in Key West with Cuban refugees during the Mariel boatlift.

Between April and September, almost 125,000 "Marielitos" from Cuba's Mariel Harbor arrive in Florida after crossing the Florida Straits in a flotilla of boats.

On May 9, the Liberia–registered freighter *Summit Venture* is heading north into Tampa Bay in order to pick up phosphate rock bound for Korea. The weather deteriorates rapidly and causes visibility to drop to zero. At 7:34 A.M. the

The site of the Sunshine Skyway Bridge disaster shortly after the *Summit Venture* strikes the southbound span, collapsing the bridge and killing thirty-five people in the southbound lanes. (Courtesy of the Tampa Bay Times)

ship crashes into a support column of the southbound span of the Sunshine Skyway Bridge. "Mayday" is radioed to Coast Guard Base St. Petersburg. Portions of the bridge collapse, plunging vehicles into the bay, including a Greyhound bus bound for Miami. Thirty-five people die, including all twenty-six on board the bus. One driver survives when his truck lands on the freighter before bouncing into the bay.

Richard Hornbuckle's car rests where it skidded to a stop 14 inches from the edge of the collapsed Sunshine Skyway Bridge. (Courtesy of the Tampa Bay Times)

Rioting occurs in Miami after a Tampa jury finds four Miami policemen not guilty in the beating death of a black businessman.

The National Guard is called up in response to the 1980 Miami riots.

On May 18, three days of riots break out in the Overton and Liberty City sections of Miami after four white police officers are tried for manslaughter and acquitted by an all-white Tampa jury in the December 17, 1979, beating and subsequent death of 33-year-old Arthur McDuffie, a black salesman and former Marine. State Attorney Janet Reno, future U.S. attorney general, prosecuted the case. McDuffie had been subdued by the officers following a high-speed car chase. Five thousand people protest the decision and the protest turns violent. Florida Governor Bob Graham will order five hundred National Guard troops into action. By the end of the three days of riots, 18 people will die, 350 will be injured, and 600 people will be arrested. Property damage will be estimated at more than $100 million. The Norton Tire Company building on Northwest 27th Avenue will continue to burn for six days. In 1981, Dade County will pay McDuffie's family a settlement of $1.1 million after they file a civil lawsuit.

On November 1, Seaboard Coast Line merges with the Chessie System to become CSX Corporation, the nation's largest railroad system, with 27,000 route miles. It will serve twenty-two states and employ seventy thousand. During a December 1985 restructure, 1,500 miles of slightly used lines will be sold or abandoned.

1981

Paula Hawkins will represent Florida in the United States Senate from January 1, 1981, to January 3, 1987.

On January 1, Paula Hawkins takes office in the United States Senate. She is the first woman elected in Florida to serve in the Senate.

On January 20, minutes after President Ronald Reagan is sworn into office, fifty-two Americans being held hostage in Iran are released from captivity. The hostages had been held for 444 days, since a mob of students stormed the American embassy on November 4, 1979.

On March 27, at 3 P.M., a five-story condominium construction project known as Harbour Cay in Cocoa Beach collapses as the top floor is being poured. A massive rescue effort begins with assistance from the Kennedy Space Center, Brevard Correctional Institute, Patrick Air Force Base, local rescue workers, and volunteers. By the time the rescue effort is halted, near midnight on March 29, eleven workers are dead and many are injured.

On March 30, President Reagan is shot and seriously wounded by John W. Hinckley Jr. while leaving the Washington Hilton Hotel.

The Space Shuttle *Discovery* riding piggyback on a 747. It makes a detour on its trip from Texas to Cape Canaveral to do a low flyover of the Florida Capitol.

On April 12, America's first space shuttle, *Columbia*, takes off at Cape Canaveral from Pad 39A, with astronauts John Young and Bob Crippen. After a 54 1/2-hour mission testing the shuttle's systems, the crew will land on a runway at Edwards Air Force Base in California.

On May 8, a massive sinkhole opens up in Winter Park near the corner of Denning Drive and Fairbanks Avenue. The hole will grow to 320 feet wide and 90 feet deep, consuming large portions of the road and a local municipal pool. The hole is now a small lake.

1982

This year, the Florida legislature will adopt a single-member district system for electing its members, rejecting the former at-large (multi-member) system that has had the impact of preventing minority voters from pooling their votes in concentrated districts to elect minorities to the legislature. The number of African Americans elected to

the Florida legislature will increase from three out of 160 in 1977 to twelve in 1982.

On March 10, the Salvador Dali Museum holds a grand opening in St. Petersburg at Bayboro Harbor. The collection of ninety-six oil paintings, two hundred drawings, and more than a thousand graphics and sculptures by the Spanish surrealist is considered the largest gathering of works of Salvador Dali in the world. Reynolds and Eleanor Morse, friends of the artist for over forty years, donated the collection.

In June, the Seminole Bingo Hall in Tampa opens at capacity with 1,300 bingo players. The site of the hall is the new Seminole Tribe Reservation on I-4 and Orient Road, an 8.5-acre parcel purchased in 1981 for $185,000. The reservation was

The massive 1981 sinkhole in Winter Park

created after archaeologists found a cemetery with bones on a construction site for the planned Fort Brooke parking garage in downtown Tampa. The skeletons were from a mixture of white settlers and Seminoles. The site was the prior location of the Fort Brooke military encampment, which was in operation during the Seminole Wars. The Seminole Tribe and city officials agreed that the Orient Road parcel would be purchased for the Seminoles and that the remains would be moved to a "shrine and cultural museum" on the site. The U.S. Department of the Interior designated the site with separate nation status and it became a Seminole Tribe Reservation. Under earlier court decisions this designation allows for high-wage bingo at the site. Future court rulings and congressional action will allow casino gambling on the reservation.

On July 26, the Orlando-area Central Florida Research Park welcomes its first tenant, the American Electroplaters Society. The park is a cooperative effort between the University of Central Florida and the Orange County Research and Development Commission. It will become the home to defense, aerospace, and other industries with about ten thousand employees.

On October 1, Disney opens its second Florida theme park near Orlando. It is called EPCOT—Experimental Prototype Community of Tomorrow. It is a futuristic park including Future World showcasing tomorrow and the World Showcase featuring pavilions from around the world. Disney will add to its theme park offering with Disney MGM Studios in 1989 and Animal Kingdom in 1998. By 2010, 16.97 million people will visit the Magic Kingdom, 10.83 million will visit EPCOT, while Animal Kingdom and the renamed

Hollywood Studios (formerly MGM) will each draw just under 10 million visitors that year. Among the many non-Disney tourist attractions that will come to the Orlando area, Universal Studios will arrive in June of 1990, providing visitors with movie-themed rides.

On November 17, President Ronald Reagan addresses members of the South Florida Task Force in Homestead, south of Miami, on fighting the growth in crime, increase in violence, and gang killings tied to the illegal drug trade. The president proclaims that the goal of the federal/state/local partnership in relation to the drug industry is "to end their profits, imprison their members, and cripple their organizations." The development and widespread use of the convenient "crack" cocaine has struck a new blow in south Florida and the nation in the ongoing battle against the illegal drug trade.

1983

In January, Governor Bob Graham begins his second term of office. He calls Florida a "land of dreamers" and asserts that the "goals of economic development, education, environmental protection and responsive social services must all intersect in our path to progress . . . The next chapter of Florida's economic future will be written in its classrooms." Finally, Governor Graham calls for preservation of the state's natural resources: "Today it is the unrestrained growth of our population that threatens the survival of the magical qualities of land and sea that have attracted so many of us here." Governor Graham will leave office early to begin his eighteen-year career in the United States Senate, and the final three days of the governor's term will be served by his Lieutenant Governor, Wayne Mixon.

Crew members for the June 8, 1983, Space Shuttle *Challenger* launch from Cape Canaveral include the first American woman in space, Sally K. Ride, along with (l-r) John McCreary Fabian, Robert Crippen, Norman Thagard, and Frederick Hamilton "Rick" Hauck. Ride Sally Ride!

On June 8, the Space Shuttle *Challenger* launches from Florida's Kennedy Space Center at Cape Canaveral. The mission will continue until a June 24 landing. Its crew will include Sally K. Ride, the first American woman to fly in space.

In August, Florida Governor Bob Graham announces "Save the Everglades," an effort of land acquisition, partial natural flow restoration, and Kissimmee River de-channelization. The program results from a growing realization that the various south Florida flood control and water supply measures, including work completed under the Central and Southern Florida Project, have caused significant damage to the natural ecosystem running from Kissimmee through Lake Okeechobee to the Everglades and to Florida Bay. The channelized Kissimmee River, now called Canal C-38, has become a waterway dumping the waste from cattle ranches and groves north of the Lake Okeechobee into the lake and ultimately into south Florida's wetlands.

Agricultural runoff flows into the water conservation area, then to the Everglades, causing harm to estuaries, plant life, animal species, and water quality. Phosphorus runoff is feeding invasive cattails, which choke out sawgrass, fish, birds, and the River of Grass itself. The cost of partially restoring the historic filtering flow of the Kissimmee River, only part of Graham's program, is estimated at $500 million. The challenge of south Florida is achieving the sometimes inconsistent objectives of (1) providing adequate water supply for populated areas, ecosystems, and agricultural interests; (2) protecting against flooding; and (3) protecting ecosystems from harmful runoff. Successful progress will be made on the Kissimmee River, but significant problems will continue fifteen years from now, when a new ambitious cleanup plan will be unveiled by Governor Jeb Bush.

1984

On January 2, the University of Miami Hurricanes defeat the Nebraska Cornhuskers 31–30 in Miami's Orange Bowl. The Hurricanes, led by quarterback Bernie Kosar, win their first college football national championship for the 1983 season. The win comes when Nebraska, previously ranked number one in the nation, goes for two points to win the game on an extra point conversion instead of kicking for one point to tie the game. The attempt fails and Miami wins. Miami will go on to win football championships in 1987, 1989, 1991, and 2001.

Passengers boarding the Miami's Metrorail, which opens in 1984

In May, Miami Metrorail opens. It is an elevated rail system, the only urban transit rail in Florida.

On September 16, the hit television show *Miami Vice* broadcasts its first show. Starring Don Johnson and Philip Michael Thomas as two Metro-Dade police detectives, the popular program will run through the 1989 season and will regularly show beautiful scenes of the fast-paced, glitzy city.

On December 19, in *McMillan v. Escambia County, Florida*, a consolidated case brought against the City of Pensacola and Escambia County, the Federal Circuit Court of Appeals holds that the method of electing the Pensacola city council and Pensacola-area school board and county commission violates the Voting Rights Act of 1965 because it is discriminatory. In the past, many Florida counties elect these bodies, as well as their county representation to the Florida legislature, on an "at-large" basis, effectively keeping minority voters from consolidating their votes to choose a minority representative. From the initial *McMillan* appellate decision in 1981 through 1991, twenty-four county commissions and eighteen school boards in Florida will change from at-large to single-member or mixed systems, resulting in Florida having twenty-eight

black county commissioners and thirty-six black school board members, most due to the new district voting systems.

1985

Smoke in the distance from the 1985 Florida forest fires west of Daytona

May 12 is dubbed "Black Friday" by the State Division of Forestry, referring to the almost nine thousand forest fires burning almost 350,000 acres in Florida, destroying two hundred structures around the state. One hundred thirty homes are destroyed in Flagler County, on Florida's Atlantic coast north of Daytona Beach.

In late August, Hurricane Elena stalls 55 miles off Florida's west coast, pummeling the coast for days with 100 mph winds, high tides, and heavy rains. Almost one million people are evacuated.

Governor Bob Graham appoints Rosemary Barkett as the first woman to serve as a justice on the Florida Supreme Court.

On October 14, Rosemary Barkett becomes the first woman to take a seat on the Florida Supreme Court, having been appointed by Florida Governor Bob Graham.

1986

A photograph taken on January 28, 1986, at 11:39:17.361 A.M., showing the explosion of the Space Shuttle *Challenger* after liftoff from the Kennedy Space Center at Cape Canaveral

On January 28, the Space Shuttle *Challenger* lifts off from the Kennedy Space Center in Cape Canaveral and explodes seventy-three seconds into its flight, killing its seven crew members, including Christa McAuliffe, a school teacher selected to be part of the mission. President Reagan addresses the nation, saying: "We will never forget them, nor the last time we saw them, this morning, as they . . . waved goodbye and slipped the surly bonds of Earth to touch the face of God." The explosion will be attributed to a failed O-ring seal in its right rocket booster. The shuttle fleet will be grounded for almost three years.

On February 14, Valentine's Day, distressed Park Bank of Florida is sold by federal regulators to Chase Manhattan Corp. of New York for $441 million. The failure of St. Petersburg's Park Bank is the largest bank collapse in Florida history to date and the largest in the nation since 1983. It is a prelude to the upcoming financial institutions collapse of the next few years.

1987

Bob Martinez, former mayor of Tampa, is sworn in as Florida's fortieth governor on January 6, 1987.

On January 6, Bob Martinez, a former educator and mayor of Tampa, becomes the fortieth governor of Florida. He is Florida's second Republican governor since reconstruction and America's first elected Hispanic governor. During his inaugural address, Governor Martinez recites the daily increases in needs from Florida's rapid growth: "Each day, we need another 130,000 gallons of potable water . . . there is another 111,000 gallons of wastewater . . . we need two more miles of highway, three more jail beds, two more police officers, two more classrooms, and two more teachers . . . During the last eight years, this kind of growth resulted in a 168 percent increase in spending by state government, from $6.2 billion in 1979 to

$16.5 billion in 1987." The new governor urges restraint: "We must return to the basics—public safety, public education, public health and public works—and we must do those things well."

On February 25, the United States Supreme Court, in California v. Cabazon Band of Mission Indians, *rules that California cannot apply state gambling laws on the Indian reservations unless Congress expressly consents, and that Congress has not done so. In 1988, Congress will respond by passing the Indian Gaming Regulatory Act to establish the rules for gambling on Indian reservations. The act divides gambling into three classes, the first two classes covering traditional Indian gaming, social gaming for small prizes, bingo, and card games not played against the house. Class III gaming includes games commonly played at casinos, such as slot machines, blackjack, craps, roulette, and others. In order to provide Class III gambling at reservations, among other requirements, the tribe and the applicable state must enter into a negotiated compact that is approved by the secretary of the interior.*

By 1997, Florida's Seminole Tribe will have casinos in Tampa, Hollywood, Immokalee, and Brighton.

On March 5, 2007, the Seminole Tribe will purchase the Hard Rock International franchise. At the time it will be the largest purchase ever by a Native American tribe. In 2015 one report will estimate annual Seminole gambling revenue at $2.2 billion.

On April 23, Governor Bob Martinez signs into law a broad expansion of the Florida sales and use tax on services. The intent of the law, which takes effect July 1, is to broaden the base of Florida tax receipts by assessing the growing service industries. After the services tax takes effect, advertising and media special interests launch a massive campaign for its repeal. Advertisers mount boycotts against

the state as newspaper editorial boards and electronic media rail against its implementation, some claiming an infringement on free speech. Responding to the pressure, the legislature will repeal the tax during a December special session, a move supported by the governor, and will increase the state sales tax from five to six cents.

Pedestrians cross the new Sunshine Skyway Bridge on its 1987 opening. (Courtesy of the Tampa Bay Times)

On April 30, after five years of construction, the new $240 million Sunshine Skyway Bridge, spanning 4.14 miles from St. Petersburg to Manatee County, opens to the public. The old bridge will be converted into fishing piers.

On June 12, President Ronald Reagan gives a speech to tens of thousands of people, and to the world, at West Berlin's Brandenburg Gate by the Berlin Wall. President Reagan welcomes the Soviet Union's progress toward openness and calls for them to send a clear message that real change toward liberty has come: "There is one sign the Soviets can make that would be unmistakable, that would advance dramatically the cause of freedom and peace. General Secretary Gorbachev, if you seek peace, if you seek prosperity for the Soviet Union and Eastern Europe, if you seek liberalization, come here to this gate. Mr. Gorbachev, open this gate. Mr. Gorbachev, tear down this wall!"

On September 30, after seventeen years of effort, the Florida Department of Transportation completes Interstate 275 from the Howard Frankland Bridge to the Sunshine Skyway.

On October 19, the New York Stock Exchange's Dow Jones industrial average plunges 508 points, the worst one-day drop in its history. As the real estate industry weakens, the nation's savings and loan industry is facing a crisis.

1988

On January 12, Florida's lottery begins with the "millionaire" instant lottery game.

Smokestacks at the St. Regis Paper Company plant in Jacksonville. Before the Jacksonville City Council's 1988 anti-odor ordinance, travelers through Jacksonville would often smell the strong odor emitted by the paper mills.

In March, the Jacksonville City Council passes an anti-odor ordinance with fines up to $10,000 per offense. The ordinance is aimed at eliminating the smell in the city's air caused by local paper and chemical companies. The ordinance will result in an improvement to the scent of the city's air.

On July 25, Congress deliberates on the final version of legislation to create the Resolution Trust Corporation, or RTC. The RTC is being formed in response to the nationwide crisis in America's savings and loan industry involving "600 or more dead or dying savings and loan associations." By the time the RTC closes its doors in 1995, it will have confiscated more than $400 billion in assets from 747 failed institutions. The savings and loan industry collapse, one of the worst financial crises in American history, will cost taxpayers over $200 billion in losses.

Eleven Florida savings and loans will be among the casualties of the industry collapse, including Florida Federal Savings and Loan, an institution chartered in 1933 that was formerly one of America's largest savings and loans.

On November 5, the Miami Heat plays their first game for the new National Basketball Association franchise, losing to the Los Angeles Clippers 111-91. The Heat will lose its first seventeen games before beating the Clippers 89-88 on December 14.

1989

On November 3, East Germany's communist leader Egon Krenz lifts restrictions on East Germans crossing to the West and thousands flee through Czechoslovakia to West Germany. On November 9, East Germany will declare its borders open, and a bulldozer will crash a hole through the Berlin Wall at Potsdamer Platz. By December 22, the Brandenburg Gate, symbol of the divided Germany, will reopen. To many historians, the crumbling of the Berlin Wall symbolizes the end of the Cold War.

On November 4, the Orlando Magic play their first game of the new National Basketball Association's expansion franchise, losing to the New Jersey Jets 111–106 in Orlando. They will complete the first season with a record of 18–64.

1990

On August 26, police discover the bodies of two University of Florida coeds who had been stabbed to death in their apartment. Later that night police will find another female stabbed to death in her off-campus duplex. The next day two more students, a man and woman, will be found stabbed to death in their apartment. Gainesville, the college town, goes into a state of high alert. After DNA tests confirm his guilt, Danny Rolling will confess to the crimes on the eve of his trial in 1994. He blames abuse by his father for his crimes. He will be put to death by lethal injection on Wednesday, October 25, 2006.

1991

On January 8, Democrat Lawton M. Chiles Jr., a lawyer and legislator from Lakeland, becomes the forty-first governor of Florida. Governor Chiles had served for eighteen years in the United States Senate before running for governor. Having defeated Bob Martinez following the Republican governor's support of and then repeal of the state services tax, the new governor discusses the state's budget problems and the need for change during his inaugural address: "I know we need tax reform. I know our sales tax is too narrowly based, and in many ways it is unfair and inequitable. I doubt our present tax situation can generate enough revenue to take care of Florida's needs."

On January 17, the United States, along with a coalition of nations, goes to war against Iraq in Operation Desert Storm. Iraq had previously invaded neighboring Kuwait. By February 28, President George H.W. Bush will announce, "Kuwait is liberated."

1992

In April, south-central Los Angeles erupts into three days of race riots after four white police officers are acquitted in the beating of black motorist Rodney King. The riots leave thirty-seven dead, over 1,500 injured, and $600 million in property damage.

On August 24, Hurricane Andrew strikes Homestead, Florida, forty miles south of Miami, as a Category 5 storm, with a 17-foot storm surge and peak gusts of 164 mph. It will cross the southern point of Florida exiting into the Gulf of Mexico, eventually striking the Louisiana coast. Almost 50,000 homes in the Miami area are destroyed and another estimated 108,000 homes are damaged. The storm causes at least twenty-six deaths and $26.5 billion of damage in the United States. During the recovery period, Broward County becomes the base of operations for supplies to send to Dade and Monroe Counties, which are devastated. After Hurricane Andrew, Florida's building code will be overhauled to require buildings to be built with greater resilience to the massive tropical storms.

1993

Janet Reno taking the oath as Dade County State Attorney in 1978. President Bill Clinton will appoint her Attorney General of the United States in 1993, the first woman to hold that office.

On March 11, Janet Reno, the Miami prosecutor appointed by President Bill Clinton to serve as United States Attorney General, is unanimously confirmed by the Senate. She is America's first female attorney general. Reno, who was educated at Harvard Law, responds: "I hope I do the women of America proud."

On April 5, the Florida Marlins (today's Miami Marlins) defeat the Dodgers in the first game of the Major League expansion team's history.

On August 10, more than 328,000 gallons of oil are spilled after two ocean-going barges and a freighter collide in the shipping channel near Fort DeSoto, off St. Petersburg. Oil washes ashore over southern Pinellas beaches. Cleanup work will continue for over a year.

1994

President George H. W. Bush with legendary Florida State University coach Bobby Bowden, who wins the 1993 college football national championship

Charlie Ward, quarterback of the FSU national champions and 1993 Heisman trophy winner

On January 7, Florida State University's Seminole football team, led by Coach Bobby Bowden, defeats the Nebraska Cornhuskers 18–16 in Miami's Orange Bowl. By beating Nebraska, the "Noles" win their first Division 1A football national championship, being named number one in both the Associated Press and USA Today/CNN polls. Seminole quarterback Charlie Ward is the 1993 Heisman trophy winner.

On January 17, an earthquake rocks Los Angeles in the early morning, measuring 6.6 on the Richter Scale, killing thirty-four and causing $7 billion in damage.

In May, Governor Lawton Chiles signs the Everglades Forever Act, a law endorsed by President Clinton, designed to reduce phosphorus levels in the Everglades through the development of 40,000 acres of filtering marshes, at a cost of $700 million, part coming from the sugar growers. Within ten years phosphorus levels will be reduced from 200 to 30 parts per billion, and the spread of cattails will be reduced, but the phosphorus levels will remain above the 10 ppb environmental goal and cattails will continue to spread. By the end of the decade, the Everglades ecosystem will still be seen as being in critical condition.

On August 5, anti-government demonstrations break out in Havana. Castro blames the disturbances on United States immigration policies and encourages Cubans to leave if they desire. In one month, more than thirty-five thousand refugees will leave, many on poorly made rafts, bound for the United States. President Clinton directs the Coast Guard to intercept the rafts and orders refugees sent to Guantanamo and Panama. After weeks of chaos, a migration accord is reached. Detained Cubans are allowed into the United States and Cuba closes its beaches to rafters.

On November 8, Republicans win control of both houses of the United States Congress for the first time in forty years.

On November 15, Hurricane Gordon moves across the Straits of Florida heading for the Florida Keys. By 2 P.M. on November 16, the storm's center crosses into Florida on the southwest coast near Ft. Myers, downgraded to a tropical storm. It crosses the state and exits into the Atlantic just north of Vero Beach. Although estimates vary, the death toll from the storm in Haiti likely exceeds one thousand. In Florida, eight die from the storm and it causes $335 million in damage. Of that amount,

$275 million includes agricultural losses to Florida tropical and winter vegetable crops, largely in Miami-Dade and Collier Counties.

1995

Florida Governor Lawton Chiles and his wife, Rhea

President Bill Clinton addresses a joint session of the Florida legislature in Tallahassee on March 30, 1995.

On January 3, Governor Lawton Chiles is sworn into office for his second term, having narrowly defeated Jeb Bush, son of former president George H.W. Bush, last November 8. Governor Chiles, in his second inaugural speech, acknowledges that he has pondered the unhappy mood of his citizens: "I have never seen the anger, the distrust, the cynicism toward government and its leaders." He discusses the need to restore some level of confidence in the government so that people will work with their leaders.

On April 19, domestic terrorist Timothy McVeigh detonates a large truck bomb in front of the Murrah Federal Building in Oklahoma City, killing 168 men, women, and children and injuring 500 others. It is the deadliest act of domestic terrorism in American history.

On August 18, a new National Football League expansion team, the Jacksonville Jaguars, play their first preseason game against the St. Louis Rams. They will finish with a 4–12 record season their first year, and will make it to the playoffs in their second season.

1996

In March, the bodies of dead manatees begin washing up on Florida's beaches around Charlotte Harbor. As the number of dead manatees increases, the Florida Marine Research Institute (FMRI) temporarily relocates a lab to Sanibel. By May, the Department of Environmental Protection will declare the episode over, and in July, FMRI will attribute the deaths to a bio-toxin consumed by manatees in sea grasses they ate during a red tide. One hundred fifty-one manatee deaths are attributed to the incident.

Manatees at the Miami Seaquarium attraction. More than 150 manatee die around Charlotte Harbor in 1996.

A view of Everglades Holiday Park, where a fisherman witnesses ValuJet 592 plunge into the Everglades on May 11, 1996

On May 11, a fisherman in Holiday Park, Everglades, calls 911. About twenty-five miles northwest of Miami International Airport, just west of Highway 27, he reports to the dispatcher: "I am fishing at Everglades Holiday Park and a large jet aircraft has just crashed out here." ValueJet 592 had departed Miami ten minutes earlier, bound for Atlanta. A fire began in the cargo department, then spread throughout the cabin. Disabled, the plane plunged into the Everglades, pointing nearly straight down, shattering on impact and leaving a shallow crater. All 110 aboard are dead, including 2 pilots, 3 flight attendants, and 105 passengers.

On July 27, a terrorist bomb kills two and leaves more than one hundred injured at the Atlanta Olympic Games.

On October 20, the Tampa Bay Lightning professional hockey team defeats Wayne Gretzky and the New York Rangers 5–2 before 20,543 fans in Tampa's newly opened Ice Palace, having moved from St. Petersburg's ThunderDome.

On October 24, two white police officers stop eighteen-year-old African American TyRon Lewis at the intersection of Sixteenth Street and Eighteenth Avenue South in St. Petersburg. When, according to the officer, the car lurches forward into the officer who is standing in front of the car, he fires his gun into the car, killing Lewis. Widespread riots and twenty-eight fires erupt in the city's south-central area, resulting in substantial damage. A state of emergency is declared and two hundred National Guard troops are called out. A second riot will occur on November 14 after a grand jury chooses not to indict the officer.

1997

On January 2, the University of Florida Gators football team wins its first Division 1A national championship by defeating previously top-ranked Florida State 52–20 in New Orleans' Sugar Bowl. FSU had defeated the Gators 24–21 in the season's final regular season game last November 30.

On August 25, the state of Florida enters into a settlement with the tobacco industry after a three-year battle led by Governor Lawton Chiles, which included a 1994 Florida legislative act strengthening the state's legal position. Florida had sued the industry, seeking both punitive damages and damages to the state for tax money spent on treating sick, uninsured smokers. Under the terms of the settlement, the industry will pay the state $11.3 billion; $1 billion within a year and the balance over twenty-five years. The industry also agrees to remove its billboards in the state within six months, starting with those close to schools; to cease placing cigarettes in vending machines where children have access; to remove outdoor advertising in sports venues and mass transit; and to acknowledge that nicotine is addictive and that cigarettes kill people. The state will receive its first installment of $775 million on September 15, 1997.

Also in August, the first classes are held at the new Florida Gulf Coast University in Ft. Myers. It had been established in 1991.

On October 26, the Florida Marlins (today's Miami Marlins) defeat the Cleveland Indians 3–2 in eleven innings in the seventh game to win the Major League Baseball World Series. The game winning walk-off home run is hit by shortstop Alex Gonzalez.

1998

Devastating tornadoes sweep through central Florida in February 1998, killing forty-two and destroying the Hyde Park Mobile Home Community in Orange County

During the night of Sunday, February 22 and the early hours of February 23, multiple tornadoes rip through central Florida, in Orange, Osceola, Seminole, and Volusia Counties. Before the storm is over, 260 people are injured, 42 are killed, and 3,600 homes are destroyed. The damage is estimated at almost $37 million. Governor Lawton Chiles visits the area Monday and calls the disaster "Andrew revisited." President Bill Clinton will tour the damage on Wednesday.

On March 30, the state of Florida puts Judy Buenoano to death in the electric chair at Starke. She had fatally poisoned her Air Force husband with arsenic in 1971 and drowned her paralyzed son. She had been dubbed the "Black Widow" by prosecutors, who said she used the insurance money she received from her victims' deaths to buy a new car and a diamond ring. It is the first execution in Florida of a woman since 1848, and Buenoano is the first woman to die in the electric chair. In 1848, a slave named Celia had been hanged after she killed her former master.

On March 31, Major League Baseball's Tampa Bay Devil Rays (today's "Rays") of the American League open their new franchise in St. Petersburg's Thunder-Dome, renamed Tropicana Field, with a game against the Detroit Tigers. The Rays lose 11–6 before 45,369 fans.

In June and July, after a prolonged drought, wildfires spread through central Florida. They destroy 126 homes, burn around 500,000 acres, and cause damage in estimates ranging from $400 million to $600 million.

On August 16, Florida's St. Joe Co. (formerly St. Joe Paper Company) closes and sells the Port St. Joe paper mill. In 1999, it will sell a portion of its north Florida land. In 2013, the company, a public corporation since 1990, will sell more than 380,000 acres of its remaining timber and rural land, holding a remaining 184,000 acres, much of it in northwest Florida, as it focuses on its real estate development mission. By 2006, one report will show the company being worth an estimated $4.5

billion, up from $56 million at the time of founder Alfred duPont's death in 1935. DuPont's brother-in-law, Ed Ball, was a leader in that development from before duPont's death until Ball's death in 1981.

On November 3, by a vote of more than 55 percent, Florida voters approve Amendment 8 to the state constitution. The measure dramatically changes the Florida cabinet, eliminating the cabinet posts of secretary of state and education commissioner as elected positions and merging the positions of state treasurer and state comptroller. The resulting cabinet members—the attorney general, chief financial officer, and agricultural commissioner—will attend regular cabinet meetings with the governor. The prior cabinet membership was established as a post-Civil War reform measure in the constitution of 1868.

Also on November 3, Florida voters elect Jeb Bush, son of former President George Bush, as governor. For the first time since Reconstruction, Florida Republicans control the governorship and both chambers of the state legislature.

Governor Lawton Chiles dies of a heart attack on December 12, 1998, less than four weeks prior to the end of his term. Here, in Florida's Old Capitol, Rhea Chiles places flowers on the casket of her late husband.

On December 12, twenty-four days before the end of his term, Governor Lawton

Chiles dies of a heart attack while exercising in the governor's mansion gymnasium. Lieutenant Governor Buddy MacKay becomes the forty-second governor of Florida, serving out the remainder of Governor Chiles' term. Lieutenant Governor MacKay had been defeated in November by Jeb Bush in the election to succeed Governor Chiles.

On December 19, the House of Representatives impeaches President Bill Clinton for perjury and obstruction of justice relating to an Oval Office affair which the president had with a White House intern. Clinton is the second impeached president in United States history.

1999

On January 5, John Ellis "Jeb" Bush, a Miami real estate developer, son of former President George H.W. Bush, and brother of future president George W. Bush, becomes the forty-third governor of Florida. Governor Bush's inaugural address is a personal message: "Faith, family, friends. These are what's best. These will endure. We should trust in these more than we trust in government . . . Government will be unencumbered to make a true differ-

Jeb Bush is sworn in as Florida's forty-third governor by Florida Supreme Court Chief Justice Major B. Harding. Governor Bush's wife, Columba (with the black hat), is by his side. His father, former President George H.W. Bush, is seen behind Justice Harding, and his brother, future president George W. Bush, is behind him looking on.

Governor Jeb Bush will hold Cabinet meetings around the state of Florida. Above is the governor before a cabinet meeting at St. Petersburg City Hall, with Mayor Rick Baker and the mayor's family - wife Joyce and children Julann and Jacob.

ence where it is most needed and where it can be most effective: Education, public safety, public works, and the protection of the frailest and weakest among us." The new governor makes it clear that public education will be his major focus: "We can see that children learn a year's worth of knowledge in a year's worth of time, and work with an unbridled determination to ensure that no child in our education system is left behind."

Also on March 29, the Dow Jones Industrial Average, the index of blue chip U.S. companies, closes above 10,000 (10,006.78) for the first time in history.

The flag corps at the Orlando Naval Training Center in 1970. The base closes in 1999.

Orlando Mayor Glenda Hood launches an aggressive economic development effort to reuse the Naval Training Center in Orlando. She is the first woman and youngest person to serve as the city's mayor. She is shown here in her later role as Florida Secretary of State under Governor Jeb Bush.

On April 30, the Naval Training Center in Orlando closes as part of the federal military base cutbacks and closures under the Base Realignment and Closure program known as BRAC. Cecil Field in Jacksonville will also close this year on September 30 under the BRAC program. Orlando Mayor Glenda Hood will lead an aggressive reuse plan for the center that will later by hailed by the Florida Chamber as "the most ambitious economic development project in the city's history." Hood is the first woman and youngest person elected mayor of Orlando.

On May 27, Governor Jeb Bush vetoes a massive $313 million from the budget presented by the Florida legislature, following up on his promise for a "turkey-free" budget. The governor explains: "What ultimately goes to fund a special project comes straight from the dinner tables of working-class families, the desks of schoolchildren, and the savings of our elderly."

On October 26, the United States Supreme Court enters a stay halting further executions in Florida until they decide whether electrocution in Florida is cruel and unusual punishment under the United States Constitution. The stay follows Florida's 1997 execution of Pedro Medina, whose mask burst into flames as he was put to death. In a special session held in January 2000, the Florida legislature will name lethal injection as a legal method of execution.

2000

On January 1, at 12:01 A.M., the world celebrates the dawning of the third millennium.

On January 4, the Florida State Seminoles defeat Virginia Tech 46–29 in New Orleans' Sugar Bowl to win the college football national championship for the second time. Florida State completes the season with a perfect 12-0 record and becomes the first college football team in NCAA history to be continuously ranked number one in the nation from the preseason to the bowl games.

On February 23, just after 7 A.M., murderer Terry Melvin Sims is given a lethal dose of chemicals, putting him to death for the fatal shooting of a sheriff's deputy in Longwood, outside of Orlando, on December 19, 1977. He is declared dead at 7:10 A.M. by a prison doctor. It is the first execution by lethal injection in Florida history, and the first by any manner other than electrocution in more than seventy-two years.

From March to December, the Dow Jones Internet Index will drop by more than 72 percent, reflecting a bursting of the "dot-com bubble," the frenzied increase in the new

Internet-related company stock prices. The event triggers a national economic downturn.

On March 7, an estimated ten thousand people protest at the steps of the Florida Capitol in opposition to Governor Bush's "One Florida"—an effort to increase college and other opportunities for minorities while eliminating racial quotas. While Jesse Jackson leads the protestors, Governor Bush responds that the people of Florida "want their governor to be focused … in the fight against discrimination." Ten years from now, on December 14, 2009, the *St. Petersburg Times* will write an article conceding that "A decade after Gov. Jeb Bush announced his controversial plan to end race-based university admissions, the number of minority students statewide has risen, according to a Times/Herald review of enrollment figures."

Protesters against the One Florida plan holding a candlelight vigil in Tallahassee

On April 22, under orders from United States Attorney General Janet Reno and a federal magistrate, six-year-old Elián González is seized from his relatives in Miami and, on June 28, will return to live with his father in Cuba. In November 1999, Elián had fled Cuba on a small aluminum boat with fourteen people, including his mother. Ten of the refugees, including Elián's mother, died on the trip. The court battles and conflict between Elián's Miami and Cuban relatives draw national attention and heated feelings.

John Delaney, the mayor of Jacksonville who proposes an aggressive effort to drive the city's economy and improve its infrastructure. He later becomes the president of the University of North Florida.

On September 5, Jacksonville voters approve a one-half-cent sales tax increase to fund the $2.2 billion Better Jacksonville Plan, aggressively promoted by Mayor John Delaney. The programs to be funded with the revenue include road and transportation improvements, a new library, arena, a baseball park, a courthouse, and others.

On October 27, the CityPlace urban center opens on Okeechobee Boulevard in downtown West Palm Beach. It is a large, $375 million lifestyle center with shopping, restaurants, movies, and residential components.

On November 7, the presidential election is held between Democrat Al Gore, the sitting vice president, and Republican George W. Bush, governor of Texas and son of former president George H.W. Bush. By late in the evening, it becomes clear that the national election is so close that Florida's twenty-five electoral votes will decide the election. Florida's vote remains close throughout the night. Although Gore concedes at about 3 A.M. on November 8, he later retracts his concession when Bush's margin of victory in Florida is estimated at about eighteen hundred votes, close enough to trigger an automatic recount.

On November 8, Florida counties begin to recount the votes in the presidential election. A lawsuit is filed, claiming voter confusion over the "butterfly ballot" used in Palm Beach County.

On November 9, Al Gore's campaign requests manual recounts in Palm Beach, Miami-Dade, Volusia, and Broward Counties. Bush's campaign will sue to stop the manual recounts. Over the coming weeks, the campaigns will engage in debates statewide at county elections offices, along with state and federal lawsuits on multiple issues relating to the election counts. Manual recounts, absentee ballots, overseas ballots, military ballots, and punch card ballots with "hanging chads" will all be at issue.

Florida Secretary of State Katherine Harris, who certifies the presidential election results and declares George W. Bush Florida's winner

On November 26, Florida Secretary of State Katherine Harris certifies the election results, declaring George W. Bush Florida's winner. Gore's campaign contests Harris' certification.

Lawyers for George Bush and Al Gore leave a hearing before the Florida Supreme Court. The state court's decision to order a statewide manual recount will be overruled by the United States Supreme Court, leaving the Florida elections results standing, meaning a win for Bush.

Reporters from throughout the nation descend on Tallahassee during the presidential election controversy in Florida.

On December 8, in a 4-3 decision, the Florida Supreme Court orders a statewide manual recount of votes to begin, a victory for Gore's challenge.

On December 11, President Clinton signs into law the $7.8 billion Comprehen-

sive Everglades Restoration Plan (CERP) to restore the Florida Everglades. The plan, to be funded half each by Florida and the federal government, involves sixty-nine endangered species and twenty national parks and refuges, and is considered the largest environmental restoration project in world history. CERP includes (1) the storage of one trillion gallons of water to supply populated areas, agricultural lands, and ecosystems through large reservoirs and aquifer storage wells; (2) an underground barrier to keep water from flowing out the eastern Everglades toward the populated southeast coast; and (3) more filtering marshlands to lower the ecosystem's phosphorus content. Florida Governor Jeb Bush, a key leader and supporter of the federal-state partnership, calls the effort "the restoration treasure for our country."

On December 12, the United States Supreme Court, in *Gore v. Bush*, issues a 5–4 decision reversing the Florida Supreme Court and holding that the Florida manual recounts cannot be conducted. The decision effectively ends Al Gore's legal challenge.

On December 13, Al Gore concedes the presidential election to George W. Bush. The final Florida vote is 2,912,790 for Bush and 2,912,253 for Gore—a margin of 537 Florida voters who decide the presidency of the United States.

2001

On January 16, President Clinton, four days before the end of his term, rejects a proposed major commercial airport in Homestead. The airport had been planned for a location between Biscayne Bay and the Everglades National Park. The decision follows a five-year conflict between environmental and economic interests in south Florida.

On March 29, 2001, with Dale Earnhardt's widow and legislators looking on, Governor Jeb Bush signs the "Earnhardt Family Protection Act" in Tallahassee, giving family members access to autopsy photos, videos, and audio, but banning others from access without a court order. The legendary race driver died in a crash at Daytona on February 18, 2001.

On February 18, NASCAR legend Dale Earnhardt dies from injuries sustained in a crash at the Daytona 500.

President George W. Bush and Governor Jeb Bush announce the financing for the Everglades cleanup on June 4, 2001.

On June 4, at an Everglades National Park press conference, President George W. Bush and Florida Governor Jeb Bush announce the president's commitment to budget $219 million to fund the Everglades comprehensive clean up.

On September 10, President George W. Bush spends the night at the Colony Beach and Tennis Resort on Longboat Key, near Sarasota. He is scheduled to leave the Colony the next day at 8:30 A.M. to drive to Emma E. Booker Elementary School in Sarasota, where he will read to students.

On the day of the 9/11 terrorists attack, the president's brother is Florida's governor. The flag over the state capitol is flown at half-mast, and a large flag is draped over the front of the Old Capitol in honor of those lost. The nation and world are at war.

On Tuesday, September 11, nineteen suicide terrorists sponsored by the international terrorist organization al Qaeda, led by Osama bin Laden, board four commercial jets.

It will later be learned that at least fifteen of the nineteen terrorists lived in Florida for a time prior to the attack, and three of the terrorist pilots trained at two flight training schools in Venice, Florida, about twenty miles south of Sarasota.

The planes depart Newark, Boston and Washington, D.C., with significant fuel loads for their cross-country flights to Los Angeles and San Francisco. The terrorists, some trained as pilots, kill flight crew members, passengers, and flight attendants with box cutters and seize control of the planes.

At 8:46 A.M. the terrorists crash American Airlines Flight 11 into New York City's World Trade Center North Tower.

At 9:03 A.M. United Airlines Flight 175 strikes the World Trade Center South Tower.

At 9:37 A.M American Airlines Flight 77 crashes into the Pentagon in Washington, D.C..

At 9:59 A.M, the South Tower collapses.

At 10:00 A.M, after President Bush makes an early exit from Sarasota's Booker Elementary, Air Force One with the president on board takes off "like a rocket" from the Sarasota–Bradenton airport.

At 10:03 A.M., United Airlines Flight 93 crashes into the ground near Shanksville, Pennsylvania. It will later be believed that Flight 93 was bound to Washington, D.C., for an attack on the Capitol Building or White House, but that the terrorists, upon being overtaken by passengers, flew the plane into the ground.

At 10:28 A.M., the North Tower collapses.

Excluding the terrorists, 2,996 die, including passengers, office workers, Pentagon personnel, foreigners from over ninety countries, and hundreds of New York City firefighters and police officers. Many jump to their deaths, trapped in the burning towers. All commercial aircraft in the United States are ordered by federal officials to land at the nearest airports, and commercial traffic ceases in the skies over the United States. New York City Mayor Rudy Giuliani promises, "We will rebuild!"

The September 11 attack will drive an economic downturn in the United States and Florida, led with the decline in the airline industry as some fear flying.

On September 20, President Bush addresses a joint session of the United States Congress to outline the nation's response to the now-declared War on Terrorism. President Bush calls upon the Taliban government in Afghanistan to close the terrorists' camps in the country and turn over the al Qaeda leaders or, alternatively, "share their fate." Under the Bush doctrine, the president declares that the United States will not distinguish between terrorists and those countries that harbor them. Congress will pass, and the president will sign, the Homeland Security Act and the USA Patriot Act to protect the nation's security and track down terrorists. There will not be another successful terrorist attack in the United States under President Bush's watch through the end of his term on January 20, 2009.

Also on September 20, a letter containing suspicious powder is mailed with a St. Petersburg postmark to anchor newsman Tom Brokaw at NBC News. Other letters from the city will follow, sent to the *New York Times* and *St. Petersburg Times*. Brokaw's assistant will develop a "skin form of anthrax," although federal law enforcement authorities will later report that none of the envelopes tested positive for anthrax.

On October 5, Bob Stevens, employee of American Media in Boca Raton, dies at a hospital, a victim of inhaled anthrax. On October 8, anthrax will be found at the offices of American Media, publisher of the *National Enquirer*. In the coming days, employees at CBS and NBC will test positive for anthrax, along with a New Jersey postal worker and the child of an ABC affiliate employee. By late November, five people will be dead from anthrax poisoning and the FBI will be searching for the person sending letters containing anthrax to media outlets and politicians. National concern is raised and governments and businesses put procedures in place to safely open mail. On July 29, 2008, Bruce Ivins will commit suicide while the FBI is targeting him as the prime suspect in the attack. Ivins is a former government scientist.

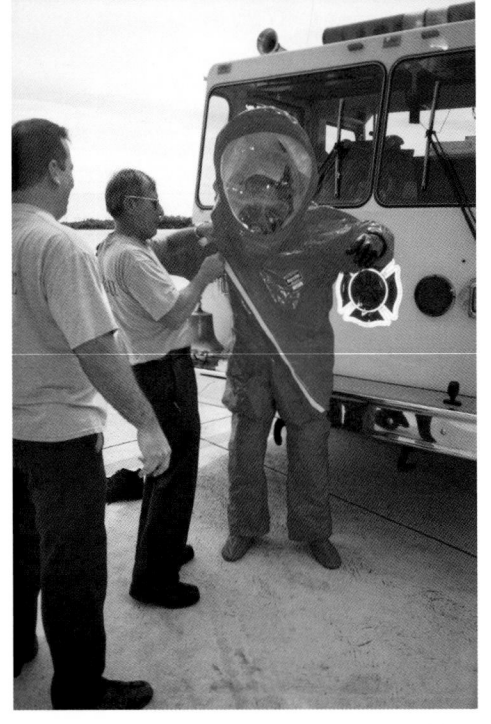

An October 19, 2001 photo of Key West Fire Department Battalion Chief Steve putting on a hazmat suit to inspect a package fitting the profile for Anthrax.

On October 7, the United States begins "Operation Enduring Freedom" in response to the September 11 terrorist attacks. The purpose of the military operation in Afghanistan is to destroy al Qaeda and remove the Taliban regime, which had failed to respond to President Bush's September 20 ultimatum. On October 9, 2004, the people of Afghanistan will hold a democratic election, choosing Hamid Karzai as its president. The people of Afghanistan will elect its National Assembly in 2005.

2002

On May 29, at the White House, President George W. Bush makes an unprecedented commitment to Florida Governor Jeb Bush for the protection of Florida's beaches and the Everglades from oil and gas drilling. The president agrees to buy back existing privately owned and previously leased rights to oil and gas interests. The action extinguishes the rights of oil interests in the Destin Dome off Pensacola and in the Big Cypress National Preserve, the Florida Panther National Wildlife Refuge, and the Ten Thousand Island National Wildlife Refuge in the greater Everglades ecosystem.

On November 5, 71 percent of Florida voters approve a constitutional amendment limiting indoor smoking. The amendment, along with a 2003 legislative amendment to the 1985 Florida Indoor Clean Air Act, prohibits smoking in indoor workplaces, including restaurants, but allows limited exceptions for stand-alone bars and tobacco shops. The law will go into effect on July 1, 2003.

2003

On January 7, Governor Jeb Bush begins his second term of office, the first Republican to be reelected as governor of Florida. In his second inaugural address he reiterates his first term theme of faith, family, and friends and outlines the tragic statistics of a failure in community values: "Each year, in Florida, 80,000 children are born without a father in the home . . .there are 85,000 abortions . . . 80,000 marriages are dissolved. Sadly, today, almost 50,000 children are in the custody of the state and hundreds of thousands more aren't receiving the child support they are due. . . Government can never fill the hollowness of the human heart . . . It can only be filled by another human heart." Governor Bush recites the successes of his first term, including the dramatic drop in violent crime resulting from tougher penalties for those who illegally use guns; increases in support for the developmentally disabled; and a historic Everglades cleanup effort. The governor cites as his most important achievement the "A+ plan," creating a school system that is accountable to the parents and students for academic success: "How is it possible that we tolerated a bureaucracy that was indifferent to the success or failure of a child? We will never, never, never go back!"

On January 26, the Tampa Bay Buccaneers defeat the Oakland Raiders 48–21 in Super Bowl XXXVII, at San Diego, California, to win the National Football League championship.

On February 1, the Space Shuttle Co-lumbia explodes on re-entry over Texas, killing its seven crew members. The disaster will be attributed to lost foam insulation that broke off from an external tank and struck the left wing.

One of many hurricane briefings in 2004, with: (l-r) Lieutenant Governor Toni Jennings, FEMA federal coordinating officer Bill Carwile, Florida Emergency Management Director Craig Fugate, and Governor Jeb Bush. Jennings is Florida's first woman lieutenant governor.

On March 3, Governor Jeb Bush appoints former Florida senate president Toni Jennings to be Florida's first woman

lieutenant governor. Two hours before the announcement, Frank Brogan resigns the lieutenant governor position in order to take the job as president of Florida Atlantic University in Boca Raton. Jennings runs a construction business in Orlando.

On March 20, Operation Iraqi Freedom begins. A coalition of international forces led by the United States invades Iraq. The invasion follows the persistent failure of Iraqi's Saddam Hussein to comply with United Nations resolutions and sanctions that followed the 1991 war with Iraq—a war caused by Hussein's invasion of Kuwait. By December 2003, Hussein will be captured. He will later be tried by the Iraqi government and executed for crimes against humanity. By May 1, 2003, the major combat operations will be complete with the defeat of the Iraqi armed forces; however, terrorist activities will escalate and continue in the country for much of the decade. While concern over Hussein's past use and possible current development of weapons of mass destruction is identified as one rationale for the invasion, the weapons will not be located at the time the major combat operations are completed.

On October 25, the Florida Marlins defeat the New York Yankees 2–0 in the sixth game, to win their second Major League Baseball World Series title. In both series the Marlins entered the playoffs as a wild card team.

2004

On June 7, Ruslan Fedotenko's two goals lead the Tampa Bay Lightning to a 2–1 victory over the Calgary Flames at the St. Pete Times Forum in the seventh and final game of the Stanley Cup finals. It is the first Stanley Cup victory for a Florida team.

Hurricane Charley leaves a path of destruction, striking Punta Gorda as a Category 4 hurricane.

On August 13 (Friday the 13th) at about 1 P.M., Hurricane Charley turns to the east while heading north through the Gulf of Mexico and is now heading directly toward Punta Gorda. The storm had been forecast to hit near Tampa Bay but took a sharp, unexpected turn three hours before the projected landfall. Charley makes landfall at 3:45 P.M., just north of Captiva Island on Florida's southwest coast, with maximum winds near 150 mph, a powerful Category 4 storm. The eye of the storm will strike Punta Gorda, devastating the city, along with nearby Port Charlotte. The storm continues northeast inland, passing near Orlando before exiting back into the Atlantic near Daytona Beach, still at hurricane strength. The impact of Charley in the United States includes ten deaths and an estimated $15 billion in damage, the second costliest hurricane in

U.S. history. It is the first of four major hurricanes that will impact Florida this year.

On September 5, Hurricane Frances makes landfall from the Atlantic just after midnight near Stuart, about forty miles north of West Palm Beach. The storm strikes the coast at 105 mph, a Category 2 hurricane, and crosses the Florida Peninsula, exiting into the northeast Gulf of Mexico north of Tampa Bay. It will make landfall again in the Florida Panhandle and cut through the southeast United States. The storm takes seven lives and causes an estimated $8 billion in damage.

Florida Governor Jeb Bush listens to Florida Division of Emergency Director Craig Fugate during an August Tallahassee media briefing on Hurricane Charley. Governor Bush receives high praise for his handling of eight hurricanes in 2004 and 2005.

The incredible force of Hurricane Ivan's punch hit Navarre Pier in Navarre Beach, Florida, about twenty miles east of Pensacola, on September 16, 2004.

On September 16, Hurricane Ivan makes landfall near Gulf Shores, Alabama, about thirty miles west of Pensacola. It strikes the coast at 120 mph, a Category 3 hurricane, moves northeast through the southeast United States, exiting into the Atlantic Ocean, then moving south and crossing south Florida as a weakened storm. Ivan causes twenty-five deaths and an estimated $14.2 billion in damage in the United States.

On September 26, Hurricane Jeanne lands near Stuart at about the same location where Hurricane Frances struck three weeks ago. It arrives as a Category 3 storm

with 120 mph winds. The hurricane moves west and crosses the center of the state, then turns north near St. Petersburg-Tampa and goes up the Florida west coast, entering Georgia, weakening to a tropical depression. Storm damage in the United States is estimated at $6.9 billion. An estimated one hundred die in Florida during the storms that ravage the state this year.

Senators Bill Nelson (l) and Mel Martinez. Martinez is Florida's first Cuban-born United States senator. (Courtesy of the Tampa Bay Times)

On November 2, Republican Mel Martinez narrowly defeats Democrat Betty Castor to win Florida's United States Senate seat. Martinez, the former United States housing secretary, is America's first Cuban-American United States senator.

2005

On March 31, Terri Schiavo dies in hospice care in Pinellas Park. On March 18, her husband, Michael Schiavo, succeeded in his efforts to disconnect her from life support. Terri Schiavo had suffered a cardiac arrest in her St. Petersburg apartment on February 20, 1990, and had been diagnosed as being in a persistent vegetative state. After Michael Schiavo initially petitioned to have Terri's feeding tube removed in 1998, the case drew national attention as the governor, Florida

Legislature, and United State Congress attempted to intervene to prevent removal of the feeding tubes. Multiple federal and state legislative and court actions preceded the ultimate court decision to allow Terri Schiavo to die.

Dan Wheldon (center) wins the first IndyCar street race in St. Petersburg. He goes on to win the Indianapolis 500 that year. (Courtesy of the Tampa Bay Times)

On April 3, new St. Petersburg resident Dan Wheldon wins the inaugural Honda Grand Prix of St. Petersburg (today's Firestone Grand Prix of St. Petersburg). Racing legend Michael Andretti is among the group—also including Kevin Savoree, Kim Green, and Barry Green—who had been lobbied by Mayor Rick Baker to bring racing's top-level IndyCar series to the city. Baker had been an open wheel IndyCar fan since his childhood days in Indianapolis. The 180-mile, 100-lap race is run on the streets of downtown, with the straightaway being an Albert Whitted Airport runway. Wheldon will go on to win this year's Indianapolis 500 in May.

On July 10, Hurricane Dennis makes landfall as a Category 3 storm at Navarre Beach, about twenty-five miles west of Pensacola. Dennis causes three deaths and $31.7 million in damage in the United States.

On August 25, Hurricane Katrina makes landfall near the Miami Dade-Broward County line and moves southwest across southern Florida, exiting into the Gulf of Mexico near Florida's most southwestern point.

Hurricane Katrina will strengthen and move to the northwest, striking the Louisiana coast near New Orleans as a Category 3 hurricane with 125 mph winds. It is a catastrophic storm, causing over $75 billion in damage, the costliest United States hurricane on record. With a storm surge in excess of twenty-five feet and critical levee failures, the flooding in New Orleans and surrounding areas is epic. It will be the deadliest American hurricane since the 1928 Florida hurricane, leaving more than one thousand people dead in Louisiana, two hundred in Mississippi, and seven in Florida.

On October 24, Hurricane Wilma strikes Florida at Cape Romano, about twenty miles west of the Everglades on the southwest point of the state, as a Category 3 hurricane. It crosses southern Florida and exits into the Atlantic Ocean north of Palm Beach as a Category 2 hurricane, after causing five deaths and $16.8 billion in damage in Florida.

At the end of the 2005 hurricane season, Governor Jeb Bush provides an assessment of the challenges for Florida, which experienced "eight hurricanes and four tropical storms, $100 billion of insured losses and billions of dollars of uninsured losses over 17 months" in 2004 and 2005.

2006

On April 3, the Florida Gators defeat the UCLA Bruins 73-57 in the last game of the Final Four to win the NCAA men's basketball championship for the first time in the school's history. The Gators will win their second basketball national championship in 2007 with a win in the finals over the Ohio State Buckeyes, 84-75.

On May 22, seven Miami men are indicted for participating in a plot to blow up the Sears Tower in Chicago. The FBI describes the group as "a homegrown terrorist cell." They lived in a one-story warehouse in Miami's Liberty City section in a neighborhood described by the *New York Times* as "a struggling neighborhood of Haitian immigrants."

Also in December, the Florida Green Building Coalition names St. Petersburg the first "Green City" to be so designated in Florida. The extensive evaluation process analyzes water conservation and reuse programs, energy conservation, alternative energy use, recycling, tree planting, open space creation, pedestrian and bicycle transportation, and many other elements of the city's green city efforts.

2007

On January 2, Republican Charles J. "Charlie" Crist Jr., a lawyer, legislator, and Florida attorney general from St. Petersburg becomes the forty-fourth governor of Florida. Governor Crist defines Florida's common vision to include meaningful, secure work, affordable, accessible health care, a good home on a safe street, world-class schools, clean rivers and beautiful beaches.

On January 8, the Florida Gators defeat the Ohio State Buckeyes 41-14 in Arizona to win the college football national championship for the second time.

On April 5, the Florida Executive Clemency board votes 3–1 to let most felons regain their voting rights after prison. Florida has an estimated 950,000 ex-offenders who cannot vote. Before the vote, most felons had to apply and go through a process to have their voting rights restored.

Certain categories, including murders and sexual predators, still must apply.

On November 30, the *Wall Street Journal* reports that the national sub-prime-mortgage crises may be spreading into government funds after the State of Florida freezes withdrawals from a $15 billion state-run fund administered by Florida's State Board of Administration. Before the state froze withdrawals, local governments and school districts had removed $10 billion from the fund over two weeks. The fund's investment portfolio includes about $2.3 billion tied to subprime mortgages.

In the future, one author will describe the coming financial collapse as the result of "Years of reckless decisions by everyone from unqualified home buyers to profit-hungry investment banks . . . and [those in] Congress who helped shield Fannie Mae and Freddie Mac as they binged on unsustainable mortgages." The collapse of real estate values will trigger a loss of nearly $6.7 trillion in home equity nationwide between 2006 and 2011.

Florida's unemployment rate will rise from 3.5 percent in January of 2007 to 11.2 percent in January of 2010 as the real estate and economic crisis deepens and Florida sees increases in home foreclosures and closed businesses. Between November 2005 and 2006 alone, the Florida Association of Realtors reports that the median price for a Florida home fell by over $60,000.

2008

On January 29, Florida voters approve Amendment 1, a change to the state constitution, with a vote of 64 percent. Amendment 1 doubles the homestead exemption to $50,000, and does not apply to school taxes, so the state budget is not impacted in the same manner as city and county budgets. The amendment also allows portability for homeowners to transfer their "Save our Homes" tax breaks. The amendment is expected to cut taxes to local government by billions of dollars.

On June 24, Florida Governor Charlie Crist signs an agreement to purchase United States Sugar Corporation for $1.75 billion. The state plans to use the company's land south of the Everglades to restore a portion of the Everglades' natural flow and support the environment of the watershed area. The sale is not funded and, ultimately, the South Florida Water Management District will pay $197 million in 2010 to purchase 26,800 acres from U.S. Sugar and retain a ten-year option to buy the additional 153,200 acres.

On June 30, in the midst of a deepening collapse in the mortgage industry, President Bush signs a law giving the administration temporary authority to offer an unlimited line of credit to Fannie Mae and Freddie Mac. The U.S. government will seize control of the federally backed mortgage companies on September 7.

On September 15, Lehman Brothers, a financial institution holding over $600 billion in assets, files for Chapter 11 bankruptcy protection. It is the largest bankruptcy filing in United States history and it is a reflection and indicator of the collapse of the American financial industry brought about by heavy leverage and high exposure to the faltering housing market, especially subprime mortgage instruments. With the announcement, the Dow Jones Industrial Average falls by over 500 points. Among the iconic financial institutions going through the crises are AIG, Bear Stearns, and Merrill Lynch. The United States and world enter a prolonged period of economic distress that will come to be known as "The Great Recession."

On September 29, the United States House of Representatives votes 228 to 205 to defeat

the Troubled Asset Relief Program (TARP) proposed by President Bush. The intent of the program is for the U.S. government to allocate $700 billion to purchase assets and equity from financial institutions to strengthen the financial sector. Immediately after the vote the Dow Jones falls 777 points, the largest single-day point loss in its history. One analyst describes the situation as "a classic moment of financial meltdown."

On October 3, Congress votes again on the TARP bailout funding. This time it passes with some modifications and President Bush signs the act into law.

St. Petersburg's "Second Time Arounders" marching band in the world-famous Macy's Thanksgiving Day Parade in New York City on November 27, 2008 (Courtesy of City of St. Petersburg)

On November 27, St. Petersburg's "Awesome Original Second Time Arounders," at about 500 members, is the largest marching band in today's Macy's Thanksgiving Day Parade. The band, that plays "Let the Sun Shine In" at New York City's Herald Square, is a group of adults that formerly played in their high school or college bands.

2009

Tim Tebow, quarterback of the University of Florida national champions and the 2007 Heisman trophy winner, signs an autograph for State Representative Michelle Rehwinkel at the governor's mansion.

On January 8, the Florida Gators defeat the Oklahoma Sooners 24–14 at Dolphin Stadium near Miami to win their third college football national championship. Tim Tebow, 2007 Heisman award winner and University of Florida quarterback, is the offensive most valuable player of the game.

SPECIAL INAUGURATION EDITION | 6 PAGES OF COVERAGE INSIDE

Promoting democracy since 1905

TALLAHASSEE DEMOCRAT

Wednesday, January 21, 2009 — Tallahassee.com — 75 Cents

'HOPE OVER FEAR'

MILLIONS CHEER AS 44th PRESIDENT TAKES CHARGE

"With hope and virtue, let us brave once more the icy currents, and endure what storms may come."
— President Obama

Front page of the *Tallahassee Democrat* of January 21, 2009, featuring the swearing-in of President Barack Obama, the nation's first African American president

On January 20, Barak Obama is sworn into office as the forty-fourth president of the United States. He is the first African American to hold the post. As President Obama takes the oath, he places his hand on the Bible that Abraham Lincoln used when he took the oath in 1861. The new president carried Florida with 51 percent of the vote.

On May 13, initial reports are that nine people are killed when a boat overfilled with illegally smuggled Haitian migrants capsizes off Florida, about fifteen miles off Boynton Beach on Florida's Atlantic coast. Sixteen have been rescued, but the boat may have held up to thirty people when it left Bimini in the Bahamas.

On September 3, the United States Treasury Department formally removes almost all U.S. restrictions on families visiting relatives in Cuba, along with restrictions on money being sent by families in America to relatives in Cuba. President Obama announced in April that the change was coming.

Bobby Bowden, shown here celebrating Florida State's second football national championship, announces his retirement in 2009.

On December 1, legendary Florida State University head football coach Bobby Bowden announces that he will retire after the team's bowl game this season. At eighty years old, he is the second-winningest major-college football coach in America. He brought the Seminoles two national championships and two Heisman Trophy winners.

2010

The census taken this year will reveal that Florida's population has grown from 9,746,961 in 1980 to 18,801,310 in 2010, an increase of 9,054,359 people, or 93 percent. In other words, the number of people who became new residents of Florida between the late 1970s and 2010

is equal to the population to which the Florida population had grown during the 12,000 preceding years.

In February, President Obama releases his budget for NASA. The Constellation program designed to return to the moon is cancelled, signaling an end to the United States manned space program. Economic uncertainty looms over the Florida Space Coast.

On March 23, President Barak Obama signs into law the Patient Protection and Affordable Care Act in the East Room of the White House. The law, commonly referred to as Obamacare, is a sweeping and controversial social reform of the nation's health care system.

At a briefing at the State Emergency Operations Center on June 21, 2010, Florida Department of Environmental Protection Secretary Michael Sole points to a map of the Panhandle areas impacted by oil sheen, "tar balls," and mats of oil from the Deepwater Horizon disaster.

On April 20, an explosion occurs on the Deepwater Horizon oil rig, located in the Gulf of Mexico about forty miles off the coast of Louisiana. The oil company BP leases the rig, which becomes engulfed with fire and sinks on April 22. Eleven workers are killed and seventeen injured. Oil from the well, located on the seabed 5,000 feet below the surface, gushes into the water. After many attempts to stop the flow, a "capping stack" will be installed on July 12, slowing the leak. By then, an estimated

4.9 million barrels (206 million gallons) of oil will have escaped into the Gulf of Mexico. By September 19, a "bottom kill" procedure fills the well with cement and the well will be declared sealed. A massive effort is undertaken to clean the oil spill, which has catastrophic impacts on the Gulf environment, and on the fishing and tourist industries along the Gulf coast, including Florida. BP will set aside a $20 billion compensation fund for those impacted.

BP pledges $500 million over ten years for research on the impacts of the spill, with Florida Institute of Oceanography at the Port of St. Petersburg taking a central role for marine research in the state. Claims for losses to Florida businesses and governments impacted by the spill will continue for years to come.

On May 23, the Northwest Beaches International Airport opens eighteen miles northwest of Panama City. It replaces the former Panama City Airport. The St. Joe Company donated the land for the airport.

On May 24, work begins on the Port of Miami tunnel, a project designed to move cargo and cruise ship passenger traffic from the port, under Biscayne Bay, and directly to MacArthur Causeway and I-375 without going through the streets of downtown Miami. The tunnel will open on August 3, 2014, at a reported cost of almost $650 million. It will be reported to remove 80 percent of the port-bound cargo trucks from the streets of downtown Miami.

On November 2, Rick Scott becomes the third consecutive Republican to win election as Florida's governor, defeating Democratic state chief financial officer Alex Sink. With over one million Floridians unemployed, Scott campaigns on the promise to support the private sector in their efforts to create more jobs. In his inaugural address he will decry the "axis of unemployment," including taxation, regulation, and litigation. He pledges to reduce each, recruit new businesses, and "support home-grown success in our own backyard." In the midst of the Great Recession, he reminds the state that "[a]fter adversity, Floridians always come back stronger . . . we have what we need to make the next four years the most exciting time in our history." He will conclude with the theme that drove his campaign and will define his coming two terms in office: *"Let's get to work!"*

With his wife Ann to his right, Governor Rick Scott delivers his inaugural address on the steps of the Old Capitol in Tallahassee on January 4, 2011. "Let's get to work!"

View of the Shark River Valley in the Everglades National Park. Debate over the best way to restore the River of Grass will continue through the second decade of the 21st Century.

Epilogue
Beyond 2010

The challenge of any history book, especially a timeline history that attempts to cover the recent past, is that history continues to be made every day. Even as this book is being printed, events take place that could be included. The benefit of a timeline is that it can be easily updated. I have chosen the 2010 decade-end as the end date for this book, but other events continue to occur in Florida and the world.

In 2011, the Space Shuttle *Atlantis* lifts off from Cape Canaveral for the last time—both for that shuttle and America's shuttle program. The shuttles program's end, coupled with the earlier decision to step back from the nation's manned space program, causes economic uncertainty along Florida's Space Coast.

Sadly, violence and mass murder, become too commonplace: A gunman at Connecticut's Sandy Hook Elementary School in 2012; terrorist bombers at the 2013 Boston Marathon; a gunman at Orlando's Pulse nightclub in 2016; a 2016 rooftop gunman in Dallas who targets police officers on the ground, and the 2017 massacre in Las Vegas by a lone gunman shooting down at a concert venue from a hotel room high above the ground—the deadliest mass shooting in modern US history.

In Sanford, the 2012 fatal shooting of Trayvon Martin raises questions about race and justice, a topic to be debated nationally during the decade and reflected by the emerging "Black Lives Matter" movement.

After the 2004 and 2005 busy hurricane seasons, the Florida storm seasons remain quiet for eleven years until two hurricanes in 2016—Hermine and Matthew—provide a reminder that Floridians must stay wary. And September of 2017 brought Hurricane Irma, one of the most powerful hurricanes in history, that swept through the Keys then entered the mainland at Marco Island. It proceeded to roll north, and because it was so wide it impacted virtually the entire state from Miami to the panhandle. It is thought to be the largest evacuation in state history, causing many deaths, massive damage, and power outages throughout Florida.

In 2016, as algae from Lake Okeechobee flows into the St. Lucie River and along the Treasure Coast shoreline, debate rages on the coasts and in Tallahassee over the solutions to restoring the Lake Kissimmee and Everglades ecosystems. Politicians argue over education, the state's budget, and the expansion of medical care for the needy.

As the decade progresses, Florida's economic recovery surpasses the nation's, as Governor Rick Scott continues to focus on his "Let's get to work" job creation campaign. Many of the state's downtowns prosper, and Florida's tourism and housing industries thrive.

President Barack Obama is re-elected in 2012. War in the Mideast rages on, and the terrorist group ISIS expands territory and its violent reach.

In 2017, New York businessman Donald Trump, a seemingly unlikely candidate, is sworn in as the forty-fifth president of the United States. Trump defeated former Secretary of State Hillary Clinton in the November election and won Florida by over one hundred thousand votes. Protests break out by those who sought the election of Clinton even as President Trump takes the oath of office. In Florida, Palm Beach's Mar-a-Lago estate becomes a retreat away from Washington for the new president.

The details of these and other post-2010 events are for a later edition of this book. They are a reminder that time marches on.

Appendix

Florida Population through 2010 U.S. Census (except 1513)

Year	Population
1513	350,000*
1830	34,730
1840	54,477
1850	87,445
1860	140,424
1870	187,748
1880	269,493
1890	391,422
1900	528,542
1910	752,619
1920	968,470
1930	1,468,211
1940	1,897,414
1950	2,771,305
1960	4,951,560
1970	6,789,443
1980	9,746,961
1990	12,938,071
2000	15,982,824
2010	18,801,310

*Estimated native population upon arrival of Ponce de Leon.

Population of Florida's Largest Cities 2010 Ten-year Census

City	Population
Jacksonville:	821,784
Miami:	399,457
Tampa:	335,709
St. Petersburg:	244,769
Orlando:	238,300
Hialeah	224,669
Tallahassee	181,376
Ft. Lauderdale	165,521

Population of Florida's Largest Counties (Largest city in county) 2010 Ten-year Census

County (Largest city)	Population
Miami-Dade (Miami)	2,496,435
Broward (Ft. Lauderdale)	1,748,066
Palm Beach (West Palm Beach)	1,320,134
Hillsborough (Tampa)	1,229,226
Orange (Orlando)	1,145,956
Pinellas (St. Petersburg)	916,542
Duval (Jacksonville)	864,263
Lee (Cape Coral/Ft. Myers)	618,754

Acknowledgments

Researching and writing this book has been a journey of over fifteen years. Arguably it started even earlier when I was researching the history of St. Petersburg for my first book, *Mangroves to Major League*, a history of St. Petersburg, which was published in 2000.

I am thankful to all who have helped me on this journey.

First, as with everything in my life, I am thankful to God and his son, Jesus, who has taught me and given me life.

My family—Joyce, Julann, and Jacob—have been my greatest source of joy. My mother, Irene, remains my close mentor, and my brothers and their families are among my life's greatest blessings. My father, Russ Baker, passed away many years ago, but he still remains an influence in my life. My brothers and I have decided that the photo in this book of a WWII boxer at Jacksonville Naval Air Training Center may have been my dad. He boxed there and at 6'6" towered over many of his competitors, like the tall boxer in the photo.

Outside my mom and dad, the greatest mentor in my life has been John Galbraith, who has advised and supported many of my journeys, including this one.

Kathleen Shanahan, former Orlando Mayor Glenda Hood, Eric Eikenberg, and Tim Nickens provided advice and comments after reviewing the book and were kind enough to write endorsements of the book on the back cover.

Others who have assisted me by reviewing drafts and making comments on this book include my wife Joyce, my mom, my children Jacob and Julann, Rob Kapusta, Greg Holden, Jim MacDougald, Debbie Aleksander, former Jacksonville Mayor John Delaney, and Beth Herendeen. Jeb Bush has played a special role in every book I have written, including this one, and has been a close friend and mentor for many years. Bill Edwards, who has done much to develop the city of St. Petersburg, has helped me and this book project in many ways.

Brigitta Shoupe, an incredibly talented and hard-working graduate student at USF St. Petersburg, provided an enormous amount of assistance for this book at a time when it was sorely needed. I simply could not have crossed the finish line without her help.

June and David Cussen at Pineapple Press believed in this project and committed their considerable talents to its success. Ken Park provided an incredible cover design.

Finally, Dr. Gary Mormino, one of the great minds in Florida history, read transcript drafts and provided great comments and suggestions—he was enormously helpful. It is rare act of humility and generosity when an academician of such impressive credentials and standing is willing to assist a non-professional history-lover in an effort such as this book with the purpose of sharing our state's great history with those who may not otherwise be exposed to it. Gary is such a person, and he is a good friend.

Bibliography

Books, Articles, and Other Publications

"Judah P. Benjamin Confederate Memorial at Gamble Plantation – Ellenton, Florida. https://www.
   floridamemory.com/items/show/66832.

2011 Polo Season Economic Impact Report. Palm Beach: PROFILE Marketing Research. 2011.

500 Nations.com. "Brief History of Indian Casinos." http://500nations.com/news/Indian_Casinos/history.asp.

About Jacksonville. "A Rich & Vibrant History." http://www.coj.net/about-jacksonville/history.

Addeo, Alicia, and Bart Moore. "Crossbows to Bombers: The Military History of Mullet Key." *Tampa Bay
   History* 12, no. 1 (Spring/Summer 1990): 4-18.

Agency for Toxic Substances and Disease Registry. *Public Health Assessment for Former St. Joe Forest Products Site*.
   U.S. Department of Health and Human Services, Public Health Service. January 6, 2006.

Alanez, Tonya. "Homelessness in Fort Lauderdale: A City's Tortured History." *Sun Sentinel*, November 16,
   2014.

Allen, Kevin. "Tampa Bay Fends Off Calgary, Wins First Stanley Cup." *USA Today,* June 7, 2004.

Altman, Howard. "Report: MacDill's Economic Impact Jumps in Tampa Area." *Tampa Bay Online*, October
   14, 2015.

Amade, Charles W. "The Tampa Bay Area from the Aborigines to the Spanish." *Tampa Bay History* 1 (Spring/
   Summer 1979): 5-16.

American FactFinder. U.S. Census Bureau, 2010.

American Oil & Gas Historical Society. "First Florida Oil Well." http://aoghs.org/petroleum-pioneers/first-
   florida-oil-well/.

American Society of Sugar Cane Technologists, Executive Committee, Florida Division. "Sugarcane and the
   Everglades: A Good Relationship Science Can Improve." *Journal of the American Society of Sugar Cane
   Technologists,* 17 (1997): 9-12. http://www.assct.org/florida/flenviron.htm.

Appel, Adrianne. "Florida Counties Try to Contain Phosphate Mines." *New York Times,* August 4, 2007.

Archer, Patrick. "The History of the Cattle Industry in Florida." FLA VIP. July 14, 2015. http://flavip.com/
   history-cattle-industry-florida/.

Arnold, Laurence, and Brendan Coffey. H. Gary Morse, Billionaire Behind Florida's Villages, Dies at 77."
   Bloomberg.com, October 30, 2014.

Arsenault, Raymond. "The End of the Long Hot Summer: The Air Conditioner and Southern Culture." *Journal
   of Southern History* 50 (November 1984): 598-627.

Arsenault, Raymond. *St. Petersburg and the Florida Dream, 1888-1950*. Norfolk, VA: The Donning Company,
   1988.

Artman, L.P., Jr. *History of Key West*. Self-published, 1969.

Aumann, Mark. *Daytona Beach Morning Journal*, February 26, 1961.

Bacon, Eve. *Oakland, The Early Years*. Chuluota, FL: Mickler House, 1974.

Ballingrud, David. "Anthrax Letter From St. Petersburg Contains Reference to OKC Bombing." *St. Petersburg
   Times,* October 13, 2001.

Ballotpedia. "Florida Restructuring the State Cabinet, Amendment 8 (1998)." https://ballotpedia.org/
   Florida_Restructuring_the_State_Cabinet,_Amendment_8_(1998).

Barron Collier Companies website. 2016. http://www.barroncollier.com/Default.aspx?id=11.

Bartlett, Marguerite Blocker. *Vignettes of My Early Life*. Unpublished manuscript, 1978.*Beach Post,* March 2,
   2016.

Berry-Caban, Cristobal S. "DDT and Silent Spring: Fifty Years After." *Journal of Military and Veterans' Health* 19,
   no. 4 (October 2011).

Bertelli, Brad, and Jerry Wilkinson. *Images of America: Islamorada*. Charleston, SC: Arcadia Publishing, 2014.

Bethell, John A. *Pinellas: A Brief History of the Lower Point*. St. Petersburg, FL: Independent Press, 1914.
   Reprinted as *Bethell's History of Point Pinellas*. St. Petersburg: Great Outdoors Publishing Company, 1962.

Bicentennial History Book Committee. *Largo . . . Then 'til*. Largo, FL: Largo Historical Society (undated).

Bickel, Karl A. *The Mangrove Coast: The Story of the West Coast of Florida,* 4th ed. Sarasota, FL: Omni Print
   Media, Inc., 1989.

Blackman, E.V. 1921. *Miami and Dade County, Florida: Its Settlement, Progress and Achievement*. Washington, DC:
   V. Rainbolt.

Blake, Eric S., Chris Landsea, and Ethan J. Gibney. *The Deadliest, Costliest, and Most Intense United States Tropical Cyclones from 1851 to 2010 (and Other Frequently Requested Hurricane Facts).* NOAA Technical Memorandum NWS NHC-6. Miami: National Weather Service, National Hurricane Center, 2011.

Bohn, Lauren. "A Brief History of Spring Break." *Time,* March 30, 2009.

Bolin, Lois. "Stories from the News about Hurricane Donna, 49 Years Ago." *Florida Weekly,* September 10, 2009.

Bothwell, Dick. *Sunrise 200: A Lively Look at St. Petersburg's Past.* St. Petersburg: Times Publishing Company, 1975.

Bramson, Seth H. *The Greatest Railroad Story Ever Told: Henry Flagler & the Florida East Coast Railway's Key West Extension.* Charleston, SC: The History Press, 2011.

Brevard County Historical Commission. Historic Brevard Landmark Guide." Cocoa, FL: Brevard County Tourism Development Council, 2012.

Brevard County. "Historical Commission History Summary." Accessed August 20, 2016. http://www. brevardcounty.us/HistoricalCommission/HistorySummary.

Broughton, Ashley. "'Let Me Sleep,' Anthrax Suspect Wrote Before Suicide." CNN. New York, NY: Cable News Network, January 6, 2009.

Broward County Transit Division. *Fact Sheet.* Fort Lauderdale: Broward County Commission, 2015.

Buckley, James. *Street Railways of St. Petersburg, Florida.* Forty Fort, PA: Harold E. Cox, 1983.

Buker, George E. *Blockaders, Refugees & Contrabands.* Tuscaloosa Al.: The University of Alabama Press, 1993.

Bull, Roger. 2013. "St. Joe Selling Most of Its Florida Land for $565 Million." Jacksonville.com, updated November 8, 2013. http://jacksonville.com/business/2013-11-07/story/st-joe-selling-most-its-florida-land-565-million#.

Burnett, Gene M. *Florida's Past: People and Events That Shaped the State, Vol. 1.* Sarasota, FL: Pineapple Press, 1996.

Burnett, Gene M. *Florida's Past: People and Events That Shaped the State, Vol. 3.* Sarasota, FL: Pineapple, Press, 1996.

Burnett, Gene M.*Florida's Past: People and Events That Shaped the State, Vol. 2.* Sarasota, FL: Pineapple, Press, 1997.

Burrage, Gregg. "I-4 Connector, the Elevated Highway Linking I-4, Selmon (Crosstown) Expressway, Is Open to Commuters." Tampa Bay: ABC Action News, January 6, 2014.

Busbee, Jay. 2012. "Blood and Sand: The Hell-raising Story of Racing at Daytona Beach." Yahoo Sports, February 21, 2012.

Buzzacco-Foerster, Jenna, and Katy Torralbas. "Hurricane Donna's Destruction Still Vivid 50 Years Later to Naples Old-timers." *Naples Daily News,* September 10, 2010.

Cabeza De Vaca, Alvar Nunez. *Chronicle of the Narvaez Expedition.* New York: Penguin Classics, 2002.

Camp, Paul Eugen, and Olin King. "St. Petersburg's First Public School." *Tampa Bay History,* 7/1 (Spring/Summer 1985): 76-82.

Cave, Damien, and Don Van Natta Jr. "Deal to Save Everglades May Help Sugar Firm." *New York Times,* March 7, 2010.

CensusViewer.com. "Brandon, Florida Population: Census 2010 and 2000 Interactive Map, Demographics, Statistics, Quick Facts," 2011. http://censusviewer.com/city/FL/Brandon.

Central Florida Research Park. "About Us." Accessed September 6, 2016. http://www.cfrp.org/home/about.

Chardy, Alfonso. "Decades after Conception, Miami Has a Port Tunnel." *Miami-Herald,* May 17, 2014.

Cherbonneaux, Mattie Lou. *Mamaw's Memoirs.* St. Petersburg: Privately printed, 1979.

Chestnut, Cathy. "Big Cypress National Preserve Makes Big History: The Big 4-0." *Fort Myers News-Press,* February 17, 2014.

City of St. Petersburg Comprehensive Annual Financial Report, 1994-95.

Clark, James C. "Underwater Lots! Swamp Cities! $10 Down! Welcome to Florida, The Land of Sunshine, Surf and Scams." *Orlando Sentinel,* October 28, 1990.

Clark, James C. *A Concise History of Florida.* Charleston, SC: The History Press, 2014.

Clearwater, Florida. The School Board of Pinellas County. (Undated).

Clements, Patricia Lasche. *A Legacy of Leadership: Florida Governors and Their Inaugural Speeches.* Tallahassee, FL: Sentry Press, 2005.

Coles, Dr. David J., and David Gregory. *Florida World War II Heritage Trail.* A Florida Heritage Publication. Tallahassee, FL: Florida Department of State, Division of Historical Resources, 2004.

Coles, Dr. David J., Frederick P. Gaske, and David Stanford Gregory. Florida Civil War Heritage Trail. Tallahassee, FL: Florida Department of State, Division of Historical Resources, 2015.

Collier County Museums. "One Man's Vision: Barron Gift Collier." http://www.colliermuseums.com/history/barron_collier.

Collier Resources Company. "History of Oil Exploration & Development." http://www.collierresources.com/history-of-oil-exploration-development.

CollierCountyMuseums.com. "One Man's Vision: Barron Gift Collier." http:///www.colliermuseums.com/history/barron_collier.

Company-Histories.com. "Florida Crystals Inc." http://www.company-histories.com/Florida-Crystals-Inc-Company-History.html.

Congressional Record. Twenty-Seventh Congress, Session II. "An Act to provide for the armed occupation and settlement of the unsettled part of the peninsula of East Florida." August 4, 1842.

Cook, David. "LBJ Sets Off Dynamite Charge to State Canal Construction." *Ocala Star Banner*, March 19, 2006.

Cooper, Dennis R. *The People Machine.* Tampa, Florida: Hillsboro Printing Company, 1971.

Costin, Leonard, ed. "A Brief History of the Port of Port St. Joe." Port St. Joe Authority. http://www.portofportstjoe.com/port-history.cfm.

Costrini, Patricia Perez, ed. *A Tradition of Excellence Pinellas, County Schools: 1912-1987.* Clearwater: Pinellas County School Board, 1987.

Covington, James W. *The Seminoles of Florida.* Gainesville, FL: University Press of Florida, 1993.

Crawford, William G. Jr. 1997. "A History of Florida's East Coast Canal: The Atlantic Intracoastal Waterway from Jacksonville to Miami." *Broward Legacy*, Summer/Fall, 1997: 2-9.

Crist, Charlie. 2007. "Restoration of Felons' Civil Rights Speaking Points, 2007, Series 2068." Florida Memory. https://www.floridamemory.com/exhibits/floridahighlights/crist/.

Crooks, James B. 1998. "Jacksonville's Consolidation Mayor: Hans G. Tanzler Jr." *Florida Historical Quarterly* 80, no. 2 (Fall 2001): 198-224.

Curry, Christopher. 2003. "Villages' Founder Dies at 93." *Ocala Star Banner*, December 24, 2003.

D'Antonio, Patricia, and Jean C. Whelan. "Moments When Time Stood Still." *American Journal of Nursing* 104, no. 11 (November 2004): 67.

Danielson, Richard. "40 years in the Making, New Section of Tampa's Riverwalk Set to Open." *Tampa Bay Times*, March 27, 2015.

Daubert, Peggy, and Patty Keohane. *Treasure Island, Florida: A History.* Bicentennial Commission of Treasure Island,, 1976.

Davis, Enoch. *On the Bethel Trail.* St. Petersburg: Valkyrie Press, 1979.

Davis, Enoch. *Toward the Promised Land.* St. Petersburg: Economy Printing, 1984.

Davis, F. A. *Facts and Suggestions For Persons Forced to Seek Permanent or Temporary Homes on the Pinellas Peninsula.* Philadelphia: The F.A. Davis Co., 1896.

Davis, Jack E. "The Spirits of St. Petersburg: The Struggle for Local Prohibition, 1892-1919." *Tampa Bay History* 10 (Spring/Summer 1988): 19-33.

Davis, Jack E. "The Spirits of St. Petersburg: The Struggle for Local Prohibition, 1892-1919." *Tampa Bay History* 10 (Spring/Summer 1988): 19-33.

de Quesada, A.M. Jr., and Vincent Luisi. *Images of America: Pinellas County.* Charleston, S.C.: Arcadia Publishing, 1999.

De Quesada, Alejandro M. *A History of Florida Forts: Florida's Lonely Outposts.* Charleston, SC: History Press, 2006.

Deese, Alma Wynelle. *St. Petersburg Now and Then.* Charlston, S.C.: Arcadia Publishing, 1999.

DeYoung, Karen. "U.S. Removes Almost All Restrictions on Family Visits to Cuba." *Washington Post,* September 4, 2009.

DK Publishing. *Chronicle of America,* updated ed. New York: DK Publishing, Inc., 1997.

Douglas, Marjory Stoneman. *The Everglades: River of Grass.* Sarasota FL: Pineapple Press, 1947.

Douglas, W. Lovett. *History of Dunedin.* St. Petersburg: Great Outdoors Publishing Co., 1965.

Douthat, Bill. "Review Finds Ballots Mangled Many Ways." *Palm Beach Post*, November 29, 2000: 1A.

Dovell, J.E. "Origin of the Everglades Drainage District." In "A History of the Everglades of Florida," by J.E. Dovell. PhD thesis, University of North Carolina, 1947.

Ducassi, Daniel. "Unredacted Deposition Reveals $2.2B in Seminole Gambling Revenue Last Year." *Politico Florida,* May 13, 2016.

Dunn, Hampton. *Yesterday's St. Petersburg*. Miami: E.A. Seemann Publishing, Inc., 1973.

Dunn, Hampton. *Wish You Were Here*. St. Petersburg: Byron Kennedy and Company, 1981.

Dunn, Hampton. *Yesterday's Clearwater*. Miami: E.A. Seemann Publishing, Inc., 1973.

Dyckman, Martin A. *Floridian of His Century: The Courage of Governor Leroy Collins*. Gainesville, FL: University Press of Florida, 2006.

Eberson, Frederick, Ph.D., M.D. *Early Medical History of Pinellas Peninsula: A Quadricentennial Epoch*. St. Petersburg: Valkyrie Press, 1972.

Edwards, Wynette. *Images of America: Orlando and Orange County*. Charleston, SC: Arcadia Publishing, 2001.

Eisman, Alberta. "Thomas Edison's Florida." *New York Times*, June 24, 1990.

Encyclopaedia Britannica. "Potter Palmer." https://www.britannica.com/biography/Potter-Palmer.

Encyclopaedia Britannica. Vol. 15, 1911.

Encyclopaedia Britannica." "Bertha Honoré Palmer." https://www.britannica.com/biography/Bertha-Honore-Palmer.

Ensley, Gerald. "The Ride to Equality Started 60 Years Ago." *Tallahassee Democrat*, May 23, 2016.

Everglades Online. http://www.evergladesonline.com/history-big-cypress.htm.

Famell, Cheryl. "Dawn of the Automobile Age: A Photo Essay." *Tampa Bay History* 7/1 (Spring/Summer 1985): 42-43.

Federal Aviation Administration. "Lessons Learned From Transport Airplane Accidents, Eastern Airlines Flight 401, Lockheed Model L-1011, N310EA" Accessed September 28, 2016. http://lessonslearned.faa.gov/ll_main.cfm?TabID=3&LLID=8&LLTypeID=2

Federal Writers' Project. *Planning Your Vacation in Florida Miami and Dade County*. Northport, NY: Bacon, Percy & Daggett, 1941.

Fenlon, Paul E. "The Florida, Atlantic and Gulf Central Railroad: The Railroad in Jacksonville." *Florida Historical Quarterly* 32, 1953.

Fenlon, Paul E."The Florida, Atlantic and Gulf Central Railroad: The Railroad in Jacksonville." *The Florida Historical Quarterly* 32, no.2 (1953): 71-80.

Fewkes, J. Walter. *Preliminary Archaeological Explorations at Weeden Island, Florida*. Washington DC: Smithsonian Institution, 1924.

Florida A & M University, Florida State University. "College of Engineering: About the College." https://www.eng.fsu.edu/about/.

Florida Anti-Mosquito Association. "Proceedings of the Nineteenth Annual Meeting, Florida Anti-Mosquito Association." Clearwater, FL, 1948. Ft. Pierce, 47-51.

Florida Chamber of Commerce. "Glenda Hood." http://www.flchamber.com/team-members/glenda-hood/.

Florida Citrus Mutual. "Citrus Industry History." http://flcitrusmutual.com/citrus-101/citrushistory.aspx.

Florida Department of Health. "Florida Clean Indoor Air Act." http://www.floridahealth.gov/environmental-health/indoor-air-quality/indoor-air-act/index.html..

Florida Department of State, Museum of Florida History. "The Knott House Museum." http://www.museumoffloridahistory.com/about/sites/.

Florida Department of Transportation. "I-4 Ultimate Improvement Project, Overview." http://i4ultimate.com/project-info/overview/.

Florida Division of Historical Resources. "Florida Spanish Colonial Heritage Trail." Tallahassee, FL: Visit Florida, 2009.

Florida Division of Recreation and Parks. "Florida Folk Festival." Department of Environmental Protection, 2017. https://www.floridastateparks.org/folkfest.

Florida Geological Survey. "Florida's Minerals: Making Modern Life Possible." November 10. http://www.dep.state.fl.us/geology/geologictopics/minerals.htm.

Florida Historical Quarterly. "Florida Frontiers, Florida Cattle." June 10, 2014. https://myfloridahistory.org/frontiers/article/20.

Florida History Internet Center. "Florida in the 1920's: The Great Florida Land Boom." http://www.floridahistory.org/landbook.htm.

Florida Industrial and Phosphate Research Institute. "The Phosphate Industry and Florida's Economy." 2017. http://www.fipr.state.fl.us/about-us/phosphate-primer/the-phosphate-industry-and-floridas-economy/.

Florida Industrial and Phosphate Research Institute. Introduction. 2017. http://www.fipr.state.fl.us.

Florida Irish Heritage Center. "Frank & Ivy Stranahan — Founders of Fort Lauderdale." May 23, 2010. https://floridairishheritagecenter.wordpress.com/2010/05/23/frank-ivy-stranahan-founders-of-fort-lauderdale/.

Florida Legislature Office of Economic and Demographic Research. *Florida's Economic Future and the Impact of Aging*. Tallahassee, FL: Senate Committee on Children, Families, and Elder Affairs.

Florida Memory Blog. "Tallahassee CORE Flier (July 1963)." February 26, 2014. https://www.floridamemory.com/blog/2014/02/26/tallahassee-core/.

Florida Memory Blog. "When the Dam Breaks...." September 12, 2014. https://www.floridamemory.com/blog/2014/09/12/when-the-dam-breaks/.

Florida Museum of Natural History. "Florida Naturalists: John James Audubon." *http://www.flmnh.ufl.edu/naturalists/audubon01.htm*.

Florida State Racing Commission. *Fourth Annual Report of the Florida State Racing Commission*. Miami: The Franklin Press, 1935.

Florida State University. "History." https://www.fsu.edu/about/history.html.

Florida's Native American Heritage Trail. Tallahassee, FL: Florida Heritage, 2000.

Flynt, Wayne. "The Cross-Florida Canal and the Politics of Interest-Group Democracy." Florida Historical Quarterly 87, no. 1 (Summer 2008): 1-15.

Foley, Bill. "Out with the 'Old' Bridge, in with the Acosta." *Florida Times Union*, August 17, 1999.

Foner, Eric, and John A. Garraty, eds. *The Reader's Companion to American History*. Boston: Houghton Mifflin Company, 1991.

Foner, Eric. *A Short History of Reconstruction*. New York: Harper & Row, 1990.

Fort Lauderdale Daily News. December 1, 1930: A6.

Fox News. "90-Year-Old Among First Charged Under Fort Lauderdale's Strict Rules Against Feeding Homeless." November 4, 2014.

Frazer, Lynne Howard. *Images of America Naples*. Charleston, SC: Arcadia

Freed, David. "The Wrong Man." *The Atlantic*, May 2010.

Freeman, Douglas Southall. *R.E. Lee: A Biography*, Vol. 1. New York: Charles Scribner's Sons, 1947.

Friends of the Riverwalk. 2016. "A Brief History of the Riverwalk." http://www.thetampariverwalk.com/about/history.aspx.

Fuller, Walter P. *St. Petersburg And Its People*. St. Petersburg, FL: Great Outdoors Publishing Co., 1972.

Fuller, Walter P. *This Was Florida's Boom*. St. Petersburg, FL: Times Publishing Company, 1954.

FundingUniverse.com. "St. Joe Paper Company, Company History." http://www.fundinguniverse.com/company-histories/st-joe-paper-company-history/.

Gallagher, Charles R. "The Catholic Church, Martin Luther King Jr. and the March in St. Augustine." *Florida Historical Quarterly* (Fall 2004).

Gannon, Michael. *Florida: A Short History*. Gainesville, FL: University Press of Florida, 1993

Gannon, Michael. *The New History of Florida*. Gainesville, FL: University Press of Florida, 1996.

Gillis, Susan, and Betty Whatley Cobb, eds. *Broward County History: A Timeline*. Fort Lauderdale, FL: Florida Humanities Council, 2015.

Gillis, Susan. "Getting the Bugs Out: Fort Lauderdale Pest Control." *Broward Legacy*, 1-3, 2009.

Goodnough, Abby. "Hard Times Are Plaguing Flight Schools in Florida." *New York Times,* September 14, 2003.

Gould, Rita Slaght. *Pioneer St. Petersburg: Life In and Around 1888*. St. Petersburg, FL: Page Creations, 1987.

Greater Fort Myers Chamber of Commerce. "History of Fort Myers." https://fortmyers.org/live-in-fort-myers/history-of-fort-myers/.

Grismer, Karl H. *History of St. Petersburg, Historical and Biographical*. St. Petersburg, FL: Tourist News Publishing Company, 1924.

Grismer, Karl H. *Seeing St. Petersburg*. St. Petersburg, FL: Tourist News Publishing Company, 1925.

Grismer, Karl H. *The Story of St. Petersburg*. St. Petersburg, FL: P.K. Smith and Company, 1948.

Grun, Bernard. *The Timetables of History*. New York: Simon and Schuster, 1979.

Grunwald, Michael. *The Swamp: The Everglades, Florida, and the Politics of Paradise*. New York,: Simon and Schuster, 2006.

Gulf Coast International Properties. "Naples History." http://www.gcipnaples-portroyal.com/naples-history/.

Gulfport Historical Society. *Our Story of Gulfport, Florida*. Gulfport, FL: Gulfport Historical Society, 1985.

Gunderson, James. "The History of Lakeside Inn." Southern LivingLakeside Inn menu.

Harris, Robert C. "The Seven McMullen Brothers of Pinellas County." *Tampa Bay History* 1 (Fall/Winter 1979): 62-76.

Hendry, Keri. "Raising Cane—A History of Big Sugar in South Florida." Florida Cracker Crumbs, June 1, 2008.

Henry Morrison Flagler Museum. "Henry Morrison Flagler Biography." https://flaglermuseum.us/history/flagler-biography.

Herbers, John. "Martin Luther Kind and 17 Others Jailed Trying to Integrate St. Augustine Restaurant." New York Times, June 12, 1964.

Herrera, Chabeli. "How the Seminole Tribe Came to Rock the Hard Rock Empire." Miami Herald, May 22, 2016.

Historic Property Associates, Inc. Historical Development of Titusville. Titusville, FL: Brevard Historical Society.

History.com. "Blackbeard Killed Off North Carolina." History.com. http://www.history.com/this-day-in-history/blackbeard-killed-off-north-carolina.

Holt, Lynne, and David Colburn. "Senior Citizens - Their Place in Florida's Past, Present, and Future." Bureau of Economic and Business Research, University of Florida College of Liberal Arts and Sciences. February 17, 2015. https://www.bebr.ufl.edu/economics/website-article/senior-citizens-—-their-place-florida's-past-present-and-future

Hooker, Robert. 100 Years St. Petersburg Times, July 25, 1884 to July 25, 1984: The Times and Its Times. St. Petersburg, FL: Times Publishing Company, 1984.

Houghton Mifflin Company. The American Heritage Dictionary of the English Language. Boston, 1976.

Huriash, Lisa, and Emily Miller. "Orlando Shooter Has History of Fistfights, Aggression in School, Records Whow." Sun Sentinel, June 16, 2016.

Hurley, Frank T. Jr. Surf, Sand, & Post Card Sunsets. St. Petersburg, FL: Great Outdoors Publishing Company, 1977.

Hussey, Scott. 2010. "Freezes, Fights, and Fancy: The Formation of Agricultural Cooperatives in the Florida Citrus Industry." Florida Historical Quarterly 89, no. 1 (Summer 2010): 81-105.

Hutcheson, Nicole. "40 Years of Seeking Justice." Tampa Bay Times, July 26, 2007.

Ingels, Margaret. Willis Haviland Carrier: Father of Air Conditioning. Garden City, NY: Country Life Press, 1952.

Jackson, Jerry, and Jack Snyder. "800,000 Acres Will Be Sold Off." Orlando Sentinel, March 2, 1999.

Jackson, Page S. History of St. Petersburg and Pinellas County, Florida [An Informal History of St. Petersburg]. St. Petersburg, FL: Great Outdoor Publishing Co., 1962.

Jacksonville Historical Society. "Liberty Ships." http://www.jaxhistory.org/liberty-ships/.

Jacksonville Historical Society. "The Day the Town Burned Down." http://www.jaxhistory.org/day-town-burned-115-years-ago-today/.

Jacksonville Historical Society. Consolidation. http://www.jaxhistory.org/consolidation-2/.

Jacksonville Historical Society. History of the St. Johns River. http://www.jaxhistory.org/resources/history-of-the-st-johns-river/.

Jacobs, Timothy M. 2"Sanibel and the Causeway 1963-2007." Santiva Chronicle, July 31, 2014.

Jahoda, Gloria. River of the Golden Ibis. NY: Holt, Rinehart and Winston, 1973.

Janjigian, Robert. 2014. "Island a Rich Territory with 29 Billionaires in Town." Palm Beach Daily News, March 3, 2014.

Jenkins, Chris. 2007. "Seminole Tribe Finalizes Hard Rock International Deal." Seminole Tribune, March 16, 2007: 1.

Jon. "Tallahassee Designated Capital of the Florida Territory." Florida Memory Blog. March 4, 2013. https://www.floridamemory.com/blog/2013/03/04/tallahassee-designated-capital-of-the-florida-territory/.

Jon. "Tamiami Trail, A.K.A. U.S. 41." Florida Memory Blog. April 24, 2012. https://www.floridamemory.com/blog/2012/04/24/tamiami-trail/.

Josh. "Land by the Gallon." Florida Memory Blog, May 29, 2015. http://www.floridamemory.com/blog/2015/05/29/land-by-the-gallon/.

Josh. "Flagler's Royal Poinciana Hotel." Florida Memory Blog. October 22, 2014. https://www.floridamemory.com/blog/2014/10/22/flaglers-royal-poinciana-hotel/.

Josh. "Old Punta Rassa." Florida Memory Blog, May 8, 2015. https://www.floridamemory.com/blog/2015/05/08/old-punta-rassa/.

Junior League of Tampa. Tampa - —A Town on Its Way. Tampa, FL: Hillsboro Printing Co., 1971.

Jupiter Inlet Lighthouse and Museum. "Lighthouse History." http://www.jupiterlighthouse.org/explore/history/lighthouse-history/.

Kane, Joseph Nathan. Famous First Facts, 3rd ed. New York: The H.W. Wilson Company, 1964.

Kaserman, James, and Sarah Kaserman. Florida Pirates From the Southern Gulf Coast to the Keys and Beyond. Charleston, SC: History Press, 2011.

Kathryn. "Save the Capitol!" Florida Memory Blog, May 27, 2014. https://www.floridamemory.com/blog/2014/05/27/save-the-capitol/.

Kay, Jennifer. "Settlement Reached in Florida Anthrax Death Case." *Insurance Journal*, November 1, 2011. http://www.insurancejournal.com/news/southeast/2011/11/01/222359.htm.

Kearney, Bill. "Angry About Florida's Ruined Waters, Fishermen Unite Against Big Sugar." *Miami New Times*, May 24, 2016.

Keller, Melissa L. "Pitching for St. Petersburg: Spring Training and Publicity in the Sunshine City, 1914-1918." *Tampa Bay History* 15/2 (Fall/Winter 1993): 35-53.

Kendrick, Baynard. *Florida Trails to Turnpikes. 1914-1964*. Gainesville, FL: University Press of Florida, 1964.

Kennedy, Margery, and Doris Waltz. *Pass-a-Grille: A Patchwork Collection of Memories*. St. Petersburg Beach, FL: Women's Fellowship of Pass-a-Grille Beach Community Church, 1981.

Kim. "The Caloosahatchee River: Its History and Future." *The Florida Living Magazine*, February 1, 2015. http://www.thefloridalivingmagazine.com/2015/02/01/caloosahatchee-future-bright/

Kirshon, John E. *Chronicle of America*. New York: DK Publishing, Inc., 1995.

Kleinberg, Ellot. "Polo Grounds Existed Briefly Near Airport." *Palm Beach Post*, May 22, 2014.

Korb, Michael. 2"The Collier Family Chronicles." *Gulfshore Life*, March 2014.

Lady Lake Historical Society. "Villages." http://www.ladylakemuseum.org/villages.html, 2015.

Lakeside Inn. "Lakeside Inn: Mount Dora's Centerpiece for 130 Years." Mount Dora, FL.

Lamb, Christopher. "Robinson Made History in Florida Before He Made History in Brooklyn." *The Huffington Post Blog*, April 14, 2013.

Langewiesche, William. "The Lessons of Value Jet 592." *The Atlantic Online*, March 1998.

Leger, Donna Leinwand. "End of Shuttle Program Slams Space Coast Economy." *USA Today*, July 5, 2011.

Linton, Calvin D. *The Bicentennial Almanac*. New York: Thomas Nelson, 1975.

Live Science Staff. "Alligator Hunter Nabs Florida's Longest Gator." LiveScience.com, November 11, 2010.

Livingstone, Seth. "Dale Earnhardt: 10 Years After Crash Killed NASCAR Star." *USA Today*, February 19, 2011.

Lovgren, Stegan. "Grim Life Cursed Real Pirates of Caribbean." *National Geographic News*, July 11, 2003.

Luckhardt, Alice L., and Greg E. Luckhardt. "Historical Vignettes: Ice Plants and the Need for Refrigeration." TCPalm.com, June 19, 2013.

Lycan, Gilbert L. *Stetson University: The First 100 Years*. Deland, FL: Stetson University Press, 1983.

Major Study Team. "Miami Report on Civil Disturbances in Miami, Florida, During the Week of August 5, 1968." Submission to the National Commission on the Causes and Prevention of Violence, Miami, 1969.

Marth, Del. *St. Petersburg: Once Upon a Time*, 2nd ed. Branford, FL: Suwannee River Press, 1996.

Marth, Del. *St. Petersburg: Once Upon a Time*. St. Petersburg, FL: City of St. Petersburg, 1976.

Martin, Sidney Walter. *Henry Flagler: Visionary of the Gilded Age*. Lake Buena Vista, FL: Tailored Tours Publications, 1998.

Mazzei, Patricia. "Jeb Bush, Hurricane Governor." *Sacramento Bee*, August 24, 2015.

McCarthy, Kevin. *Florida Lighthouses*. Gainesville, FL: University Press of Florida, 1990.

McCrary, Peyton. 2007. "The Struggle for Minority Representation in Florida, 1960-1990." *Florida Historical Quarterly* 86, no. 1 (2007): 93-111.

McGoun, Bill. "A History of Broward County." *Broward Legacy* 2, no. 3-4 (1978): 15-22.

McRobbie, Linda Rodriquez. "The Surprisingly Cool History of Ice." MentalFloss.com. http://mentalfloss.com/article/22407/surprisingly-cool-history-ice.

Mendels, Col. Walter B. *Florida Military Academy*. St. Petersburg, FL: St. Petersburg Printing Company, 1941.

MetroJacksonville.com. "Distinguish Jacksonville: The Bridges of Downtown." July 6, 2007. http://www.metrojacksonville.com/article/2007-jul-distinguish-jacksonville-the-bridges-of-downtown.

MetroJacksonville.com. "The History of Downtown Jacksonville's Riverwalks." March 5, 2013. http://www.metrojacksonville.com/article/2013-mar-the-history-of-downtown-jacksonvilles-riverwalks/page/1.

Miami Digital Archive Home. "Miami Timeline: 1800s - World War I." http://scholar.library.miami.edu/miamidigital/1880.php.

MiamiHerald.com. "About Our Company." http://www.miamiherald.com/customer-service/about-us/.

Middleton, Sallie. "Space Rush: Local Impact of Federal Aerospace Programs on Brevard and Surrounding Counties." *Florida Historical Quarterly* 87, no. 2 (2008): 258-289.

Milanich, Jerald T. *Florida Indians and the Invasion from Europe*. Gainesville, FL: University Press of Florida, 1995.

Miller, Jeff. "History of WDAE, Tampa." http://jeff560.tripod.com/wdae.html.

Minster, Christopher. "Captain Morgan, Greatest of the Privateers." ThoughtCo.com. Updated March 30, 2017. https://www.thoughtco.com/captain-morgan-greatest-of-the-privateers-2136378

Minster, Christopher. "Real-Life Pirates of the Caribbean." ThoughtCo.com. Updated April 16, 2016. https://www.thoughtco.com/real-life-pirates-of-the-caribbean-2136234.

Missall, John and Mary Lou, eds.. *Florida Seminole Wars Heritage Trail.* Tallahassee, FL: Heritage Publication, 2015.

Mohl, Raymond A. "Whitening Miami: Race, Housing, and Government Policy in Twentieth-Century Dade County." *Florida Historical Quarterly* 79, no. 3 (Winter 2001): 319-345.

Mormino, Gary. *Land of Sunshine, State of Dream: A Social History of Modern Florida.* Gainesville: University Press of Florida, 2005.

Morris, Allen, and Joan Perry Morris. *The Florida Handbook 2011-2012.* Tallahassee, FL: The Peninsular Publishing Company, 2011.

Morris, Allen, and Joan Perry Morris. *The Florida Handbook 2013-2014.* Tallahassee, FL: The Florida House of Representatives, Office of the Clerk, 2015.

Morris, Elli. "Making Ice in Mississippi." *Mississippi History Now,* May 2010. http://mshistorynow.mdah.state.ms.us/articles/343/making-ice-in-mississippi.

MyFlorida.com. "1733 Spanish Galleon Trail." Tallahassee, FL: Florida Department of State, Division of Historical Resources.

Naples-Florida.com. "Naples Florida History." http://www.naples-florida.com/hiscul.htm.

National Oceanic and Atmospheric Administration. "Hurricanes in History." http://www.nhc.noaa.gov/outreach/history/.

National Parks Service. "Everglades Jetport." https://www.nps.gov/bicy/learn/historyculture/miami-jetport.htm.

National Parks Service. "Everglades: Burmese Pythons." https://www.nps.gov/ever/learn/nature/burmesepythonsintro.htm.

National Parks Service. "Florida Shipwrecks: Brief Maritime History of Florida." https://www.nps.gov/nr/travel/flshipwrecks/maritimehistory.htm.

National Public Radio. "Timeline: How the Anthrax Terror Unfolded." February 15, 2011. http://www.npr.org/2011/02/15/93170200/timeline-how-the-anthrax-terror-unfolded.

National Recreation Trails. "Marjorie Harris Carr Cross Florida Greenway." http://www.americantrails.org/nationalrecreationtrails/trailNRT/Carr-Cross-Florida-Greenway.html.

Nemours Mansion.org website. "About Alfred I. DuPont." http://www.nemoursmansion.org/dupont/about.html.

New Encyclopaedia Britannica, 15th ed, 1997.

New Port Richey Press. "History of Pasco County: Chipco." May 30, 1963.

New York Times. "In a Break From the Past, Florida Will Let Felons Vote." April 6, 2007.

New York Times. "Kennedys Sell Family House In Palm Beach." May 23, 1995.

Niles, Robert. Theme Park History: A Short History of SeaWorld Orlando." ThemeParkInsider.com August 1, 2013. http://www.themeparkinsider.com/flume/201308/3587/.

Noll, Steven, and David Tegeder. 2010. "Lessons from the Cross Florida Barge Canal Project." FloridaTrend.com, February 1, 2010. http://www.floridatrend.com/article/4509/lessons-from-the-cross-florida-barge-canal-project.

Norton, Frank. "Florida's New Smoking Ban May Affect Some Businesses More Than Others." *Miami Today,* January 9, 2003.

OldHouseOnline.com. "8 Great Addison Mizner Buildings."http://www.oldhouseonline.com/8-great-addison-mizner-buildings/.

Olds, Arthur F. *It's No Bull! The True Story of the Taming of Northeast Pinellas Count.* New Port Richey, FL: Boot Ranch Publishing Company, 1992.

OurPhosphateRisk.com. "History of Phosphate in Florida." http://www.ourphosphaterisk.com/phosphate/history. 2008.

Pallardy, Richard. "Deepwater Horizon Oil Spill of 2010." Encyclopaedia Britannica, 2011. https://www.britannica.com/event/Deepwater-Horizon-oil-spill-of-2010.

Pallesen, Tim. "90 Years Later, Gulfstream Remains Special Polo Club." *Palm Beach Post,* February 7, 2013.

Palm Beach County. "History of Incorporating Palm Beach County." 2013. http://archive.is/lGxP (saved from: http://www.pbcgov.com/courthouse/history.htm).

Palm Beach Post. "The Long and Winding Race - —Key Events From Election 2000." December 14, 2000: 28A.

ParadiseCoast.com. "Naples: A U.S. Land Developer's Dream." http://www.paradisecoast.com/articles/collier_county_history.

Parker, Terri. "9/11 Terrorists Lived, Plotted in South Florida." *ABC WPBF News,* September 11, 2015.

Parry, Albert. *Full Steam Ahead! The Story of Peter Demens.* St. Petersburg, FL: Great Outdoors Publishing Company, 1987.

Parsons, Al. *Lightning In the Sun: A History of Florida Power Corporation 1899-1974.* St. Petersburg, FL: Florida Power Corporation, 1974.

Patton, Charlie. *Downtown Jacksonville, 1832-2009.* December 4, 2009. http://jacksonville.com/news/metro/downtown-timeline.

Paulson, Darryl, and Janet Stiff. "An Empty Victory: The St. Petersburg Sanitation Strike." *Florida Historical Quarterly* 58 (April 1979): 421-433

Paulson, Darryl, and Milly St. Julien. "Desegregating Public Schools in Manatee and Pinellas Counties, 1954-71." *Tampa Bay History* 7 (Spring/Summer 1985): 30-41.

Paulson, Darryl. "Stay Out, the Water's Fine: Desegregating Municipal Swimming Facilities in St. Petersburg, Florida." *Tampa Bay History* 4 (Fall/Winter 1982): 6-19.

Pearlstine, Elise V., and Frank J. Mazzotti. "Checklist of Birds of the Everglades Agricultural Area." University of Florida IFAS Extension. December. http://edis.ifas.ufl.edu/uw179.

Pederson, Paul. *Build It And They Will Come: The Arrival of the Tampa Bay Devil Rays.* Stuart, FL: Florida Sports Press, 1997.

Pent, R.F. *History of Tarpon Springs.* St. Petersburg, FL: Great Outdoors Publishing Company, 1964.

Perez, Elizabeth P., and Rusty Ennemoser. *Florida Cuban Heritage Trail.* Tallahassee, FL: Florida Heritage.

Perry, I. Mac. *Indian Mounds You Can Visit.* St. Petersburg, FL: Great Outdoors Publishing Company, 1993.

Peterson, Dan. "Solving the Everglades Riddle: Addressing Water Quality and Quantity to Restore a Florida Legacy." www.jamesmadison.org.

Pettengill, George S. Jr. *The Story of Florida Railroads, 1834-1903.* Boston, MA: The Railway & Locomotive Historical Society, Inc., 1952.

Pierce, Robert N. *A Sacred Trust.* Gainesville: University Press of Florida, 1993.

Pinellas County Planning Council. *Pinellas County Historical Background.* Clearwater, FL: Pinellas County Planning Council, 1986.

Piper Archaeological Research, Inc. "An Archaeological Survey of the City of St. Petersburg, Florida." Unpublished. (August 1987.

Pittman, Craig. "Oh, #Florida!" *Slate,* July 22, 2013.

Pitzer, Robert. "Florida A&M University." BlackPast.org. http://www.blackpast.org/aah/florida-m-university-1887.

Pletcher, Keneth. "Beringia Ancient Landform, Pacific Ocean." *Encyclopaedia Britannica.* Last updated June 27, 2014.

Plumb, Mary. "50 Years Ago Today - Remembering Northwest Orient Flight 705." U.S. National Park Service. February 12, 2013. https://www.nps.gov/ever/learn/news/50-years-ago-today-remembering-northwest-orient-flight-705.htm.

Poets.org. "James Weldon Johnson." http://www.poets.org/poetsorg/poet/james-weldon-johnson.

Poole, Leslie Kemp. "The Women of the Early Florida Audubon Society: Agents of History in the Fight to Save State Birds." *Florida Historical Quarterly* (Winter 2007): 297-323.

Port Everglades, Broward County Florida. *Fiscal Year 2015 Commerce Report.* Fort Lauderdale, FL: Port Everglades.

Port Everglades. 2015. *Fiscal Year 2015 Commerce Report.* Fort Lauderdale: Broward County Commission, 2015.

PortEverglades.net. "History." http://www.porteverglades.net/about-us/history/

Proctor, Helen. *Indian Rocks: A Pictorial History.* Indian Rocks: Indian Rocks Area Historical Society, 1985.

Provenzo, Eugene F. Jr. "The St. Petersburg-Tampa Airboat Line." *Florida Historical Quarterly* 58 (July 1979): 72-77.

Rajtar, Steve. *A Guide to Historic Orlando.* Charleston, SC: History Press, 2006.

Rathgeber, Bob. "Hard Lessons: Hurricane Charley, 10 Years Later." *The News-Press,* August 13, 2014.

Ratjar, Steve. *A Guide to Historic Tampa, Florida.* Charleston, SC: History Press, 2007.

Reagan, Ronald. "Remarks in Miami, Florida, to Members of the South Florida Task Force and Members of Miami Citizens Against Crime." November 17, 1982. http://www.presidency.ucsb.edu/ws/?pid=42013.

Reid, Andy. "Water District Rejects Buying Sugar Land for Everglades Restoration." *Sun Sentinel*, May 14, 2015.

Reither, Joseph. *World History: A Brief Introduction*. New York: McGraw-Hill, 1973.

Ringling.org. "History of the Ringling." https://www.ringling.org/history-ringling.

Robinson, Thomas. *The Bible Timetable*. New York: Thomas Nelson, 1992.

Robison, Jim. "A Sinkhole Chronology." *Orlando Sentinel*, December 27, 1987.

Rocco, Matthew. "Wold's Biggest Retirement Community is Getting Bigger." *Fox Business*, June 15, 2015.

RogerSimmons.com. "Florida TV History." http://rogersimmons.com/florida-television-history/.

Roland, James. "9/11: Venice Was Center of Terror Probe." *Herald Tribune*, September 8, 2011.

Rossman, Sean. 2016. "Threasher Ppoints to FSU's Eeconomic Iimpact." *Tallahassee Democrat*, August 21.

Ruane, Laura. "5 Years After BP Oil Spill, Florida Claims Continue." *Fort Myers News -Press*, April 20, 2015.

Russell, J.C. E-mail message to author, November 9, 2016.

Salisbury, Susan. "Palm Beach County Sugar Cane Growers Finish Longest-ever Harvest." *Palm Beach Post*, June 6, 2016.

Sanders, Michael L. "The Great Freeze of 1894-95 in Pinellas County." *Tampa Bay History* 2/1 (Spring/Summer 1980): 5-14.

Sarasota County, History Exhibitions. "Bertha Honoré Palmer – —The Manatee County Years." https://www.scgov.net/BerthaPalmer/Pages/About.aspx.

Schafer, Daniel L., and Frederick Gaske. *Florida British Heritage Trail*. Tallahassee, FL: Florida Association of Museums.

Schneider, Paul. *Brutal Journey: The Epic Story of the First Crossing of North America*. New York: Henry Holt and Company, 2006.

Schnur, James A. "Desegregation of Public Schools in Pinellas County, Florida." *Tampa Bay History* 13/1 (Spring/Summer 1991): 26-43.

ScienceHeroes.com. "The DDT Controversy." http://www.scienceheroes.com/index.php?option=com_content&view=article&id=309&Itemid=263.

Scott, Rick. Inaugural Address. January 4, 2011. http://www.flgov.com/2011/01/04/florida-governor-rick-scott-inaugural-address/.

Shedden, David B. "St. Petersburg Times Historical Chronology (1984-1994)." Unpublished.

Sheppard, Donald. "A Brief History of Florida's Phosphate Business." http://www.floridahistory.com/phosphate.html.

Simon & Schuster. *Webster New World Dictionary,* 2nd College Ed. New York: Simon & Schuster, 1982.

Simonds, Willard B. "The Sea Breeze: The First Newspaper on the Lower Pinellas Peninsula." *Tampa Bay History* 5/2 (Fall/Winter 1983): 75-80.

Slacum, Marcia A., John Harwood, Frank DeLoache, and Theresa White. *Blacks in St. Petersburg 1980*. St. Petersburg, FL: Times Publishing Company, 1980.

Slicker, William D. "The Building Boom in St. Petersburg: A Photographic Essay." *Tampa Bay History* 11/2 (Fall/Wint"er 1989): 22-33.

South Florida Water Management District. "Managing South Florida's Water Conservation Areas." May, 2015. http://www.swfmd.gov.

St. Petersburg Arts Commission. *St. Petersburg's Historical Suite*. St. Petersburg, FL: City of St. Petersburg, 1980.

St. Petersburg City Economic Development Administration. "Profile of Recent and Current Downtown Development Activity." City Economic Development Administration January 1999. Unpublished.

St. Petersburg College/go.spcollege.edu. "History of SPC." https://go.spcollege.edu/pages/dynamic.aspx?id=2147484171.

St. Petersburg Museum of History. *St. Petersburg Goes to War, 1941-1945*. St. Petersburg: Florida Humanities Council, 1995.

St. Petersburg Times. "FBI: Letters to NBC, N.Y. Times Sent from St. Petersburg." October 12, 2001.

St. Petersburg Yacht Club. *A Nautical Heritage - —The St. Petersburg Yacht Club Story 1909-1989*. St. Petersburg: The St. Petersburg Yacht Club, undated.

St.JohnsRiverKeeper.org. *St. Johns River Timeline*. http://www.stjohnsriverkeeper.org/the-river/history/.

Stafford, John W. "Egmont Key: Sentinel of Tampa Bay." *Tampa Bay History* 2 (Spring/Summer 1980): 15-29.

Stapleton, Christine. "Florida Marine Research Group Gets $10 Million from BP to Study Oil Spill's Effects." *Palm Beach Post,* June 15, 2010.

Starkey, Jay. *Things I Remember, 1899-1979*. Brooksville: Southwest Florida Water Management District, 1980.

Stellin, Susan. 2010. "Airport Built, It's Time to See If the Traffic Comes." *New York Times,* March 9, 2010.

Stephenson, R. Bruce. *Visions of Eden.* Columbus, OH: Ohio State University Press, 1997.

Stevens, R. Randolph. "The Railroad Depot: A Photo Essay." *Tampa Bay History* 6/1 (Spring/Summer 1984): 36-45.

Straub, William L. *History of Pinellas County, Florida.* St. Augustine, FL: The Record Company, 1929.

Sugar Cane Growers Cooperative of Florida. 2012. "50th Anniversary Edition" booklet. Belle Glade, FL: SCGC.

Sumners, Lauren. "Prohibitionists' Domain and Smugglers' Paradise: Florida's Peculiar Status During Prohibition." *Journal of The James Madison Institute* (Winter 2016).

Sun-Sentinel.com. "2005 Hurricane Wilma." October 2005.

Tampa Bay History. "Preserving for the Future: An Interview with Three Generations of the Starkey Family." *Tampa Bay History* 4/2 (Fall/Winter 1982): 58-75.

Tampa Bay History. "War and Peace on the Suncoast: A Photo Essay." *Tampa Bay History* 3/2 (Fall/Winter 2981): 40-57.

Tampa Bay Rowdies website. "History." http://www.rowdiessoccer.com/history.

Tampa Bay Times. "A Timeline of the 123-year History of the Tampa Tribune." May 3, 2016.

Tampa Hillsborough Expressway Authority. "Background." http://www.tampa-xway.com/about-the-authority/. 2016.

Tampa International Airport. *2016 Fact Sheet.* Tampa, FL: Tampa International Airport, 2016.

Tapley, Kay. "Camping and Cruising Along the Suncoast in 1899." *Tampa Bay History* 2 (Fall/Winter 1980): 61-72.

Taylor, Paul. *Discovering the Civil War in Florida.* Sarasota, FL: Pineapple Press, 2012

Taylor, Robert A. "The Great War: A Photo Essay." *Tampa Bay History* 8 (Spring/ Summer 1986): 47-61.

Tebeau, Charlton W. *A History of Florida.* Coral Gables, FL: University of Miami Press, 1971.

Tegeder, Michael David. "Economic Boom or Political Boondoggle? Florida's Atlantic Gulf Ship Canal in the 1930s." *Florida Historical Quarterly* 83, no. 1, 2004.

The305.com. "Miami's Ffirst Rradio Sstation - —WQAM 560." The 305. http://the305.com/2011/03/27/miamis-first-radio-station-wqam-560/.

Thompson, Keith H. Jr. The Weedon Island Story, 1st ed. Tallahassee: Florida Department of Natural Resources, 1992.

Times Atlas of World History. London: Times Books, 1978, 1979, 1980.

U.S. Census Bureau. "American FactFinder, 1940."

U.S. Coast Guard. "Orange Grove House of Refuge." U.S. Coast Guard History Program, U.S. Department of Homeland Security.

U.S. Department of the Interior, National Parks Service. "Epping Forest." National Register of Historic Places Inventory - —Nomination Form. Jacksonville, FL: National Parks Service, February 5, 1973.

U.S. Fish & Wildlife Service. "American Alligator." January 1, 1998. https://www.fws.gov/endangered/esa-library/pdf/alligator.pdf.

U.S. News and World Report Higher Education. "Florida A&M University." 2016. http://colleges.usnews.rankingsandreviews.com/best-colleges/famu-1480.

U.S. Newspaper Directory. "Chronicling America." Newspaper Directory, Washington, D.C.: Library of Congress, 2013.

U.S. Sugar.com. "Our History." http://www.ussugar.com/history/.

United States History. "U.S. Territorial Acquisitions." http://www.u-s-history.com/pages/h1049.html.

University of Central Florida."Research Park (1982)." http://stars.library.ucf.edu/buildings_researchpark/.

University of South Florida. "USF System Overview." http://system.usf.edu/index.asp.

USAToday30. "Castor Concedes Senate Race to Martinez." *USA Today,* November 3, 2004.

Vesperi, Maria. *City of Green Benches: Growing Old in a New Downtown.* Ithaca, NY: Cornell University Press, 1985.

Villages-News.com. "Villages Developer H. Gary Morse Praised for His Remarkable Vision." October 30, 2014.

VisitMaryland.org. "Maryland History Timeline."http://www.visitmaryland.org/info/maryland-history-timeline.

Vizcaya.org. "Timeline." http://vizcaya.org/about-timeline.asp.

Vovsi, Dr. Eman, et. al. *Florida French Heritage Trail.* Tallahassee, FL: Florida Heritage, 2014.

Walker, Craig. "The Forgotten Coast: Old Florida Mill Town Loses Stench, Gains a Remarkable Tourist Sight." *Sun Sentinel,* April 4, 2003.

Webb, Kristina. "A Look Inside Mar-a-Lago, Donald Trump's Palm Beach Estate." *Palm*

Webster, Donovan. "Pirates of the Whydah." *National Geographic,* May, 1999.

Webster, Nancy. "History: The Tale of Olde Naples Pier." *Naples Daily News*, Nov. 6, 2008.

White, Gay Blair. *The World's First Airline*. Largo, Florida: Aero Medical Consultants, Inc. 1984.

Williams, John M., and Iver W. Duedall. *Florida Hurricanes and Tropical Storms*. Gainesville, FL: University Press of Florida, 1997.

Williams, Lee. "Flight School DCirector: 9/11 Terrorists Gave 'No Red Flags'." *Bradenton Herald,* September 7, 2011.

Wilson, Jill. "Second Time Arounders: Biggest Band in Big Apple Parade." *Tampa Bay Times,* November 27, 2008.

Wilson, Jon L. "Days of Fear: A Lynching in St. Petersburg." *Tampa Bay History* 5/2 (Fall/Winter 1983): 4–26.

Winsboro, Irvin D.S., and Abel A. Bartley. "Race, Education, and Regionalism: The Long and Troubling History of School Desegregation in the Sunshine State." *Florida Historical Quarterly* 92, no. 4 (2014): 714-745.

Wolff, Mark J. "Home Rule In Florida: A Critical Appraisal." *Stetson Law Review* 19/3 (Summer 1990): 853-929.

Work Projects Administration. *Report of the State and Local Government Survey: Florida State Planning Board.*

Wright, Lynne. *Disasters and Heroic Rescues of Florida*. Augusta, GA: Morris Book Publishing, 2006.

Wynne, Lewis N., and Robert A. Taylor. *Florida in the Civil War*. Charleston, SC: Arcadia Publishing, 2001.

Wynne, Lewis N., and Robert Taylor. *Florida in the Civil War*. Charleston, SC: Arcadia Publishing, 2001.

Wynne, Nick, and Richard Moorhead. *Florida in World War II: Floating Fortress*. Charleston, SC: History Press, 2010.

Wynne, Nick, and Richard Moorhead. Florida in World War II: Floating Fortress. Charleston, SC: Arcadia Publishing, 2011.

Yanez, Luisa. "1972: Nightmare in the Everglades." *McClatchy Newspapers,* December 29, 2007.

Yanez, Luisa. "Jan. 19, 1977: The Day It Snowed in Miami." *Miami Herald,* January 19, 2007.

Young, June Hurley. *Florida's Pinellas Peninsula,* updated ed. St. Petersburg: Southern Heritage Press, 1996.

Young, June Hurley. *The Don Ce-Sar Story*. St. Petersburg: Partnership Press, 1983.

Young, June Hurley. *The Vinoy: Faded Glory Renewed*. St. Petersburg: Partnership Press, 1999.

Ziewitz, Kathryn, and June Wiaz. *Green Empire: The St. Joe Company and the Remaking of Florida's Panhandle.* Gainesville, FL: University Press of Florida, 2004.

Maps

1903. Map of Florida issued by Clyde Steamship Company. Copyright 1903: C.S. Hammond & Co., N.Y.

1910. A New Sectional Map of Florida. Florida Department of Agriculture. Copyright 1901: J.N. Mathews Co. Buffalo N.Y.

1915. Map of Florida - Southern Railway System. Copyright 1915: Poole Bros. Chicago.

1926. Grant's official Auto Route Map of Florida. Copyright 1926: H.D. Grant.

1936. Official Road Map of Florida. Florida State Road Department.

1948. Florida Highways. State Road Department of Florida.

1965-66. Florida Sunoco. Copyright: Diversified Map Corp. St. Louis.

Laws

Florida Constitution: 1861; 1865; 1868; 1885; 1968.

Ordinances of Florida Constitution Conventions.

Other

Heritage Park Museum Collections, Largo, Florida.

University of South Florida at St. Petersburg, collections at Nelson Poynter Library.

325.

Index

List of Maps